The Great Detour

SUNY series in Contemporary Continental Philosophy

Dennis J. Schmidt, editor

The Great Detour

Heidegger and the Question of the Animal

S. MONTGOMERY EWEGEN

SUNY
PRESS

EU GPSR Authorised Representative:
Logos Europe, 9 rue Nicolas Poussin, 17000, La Rochelle, France
contact@logoseurope.eu

For information, contact State University of New York Press, Albany, NY
www.sunypress.edu

Library of Congress Cataloging-in-Publication Data

Name: Ewegen, S. Montgomery, author.
Title: The great detour : Heidegger and the question of the animal /
    S. Montgomery Ewegen.
Description: Albany : State University of New York Press, [2025] | Series:
    SUNY series in contemporary continental philosophy | Includes
    bibliographical references and index.
Identifiers: LCCN 2025016912 | ISBN 9798855804669 (hardcover : alk. paper) |
    ISBN 9798855804683 (ebook) | ISBN 9798855804676 (pbk. : alk. paper)
Subjects: LCSH: Heidegger, Martin, 1889–1976. | Animals (Philosophy).
Classification: LCC B3279.H49 E94 2025 | DDC 193—dc23/eng/20250530
LC record available at https://lccn.loc.gov/2025016912

Thank you, John, for everything.

On the great detour [*Auf dem großen Umweg*] over the abyss of beyng, beings—which are still only "objects" or "beings in themselves"—first again come to be, vibrant in beyng, vibrated by it, and borne outward into the bifurcation. (*The un-neediness of life; the great detour [der große Umweg].*)

—Heidegger (GA 94:425/309)

Contents

Preface   ix

Acknowledgments   xi

Note Regarding Citations   xiii

Introduction: Necessary Detours   1

Chapter One   The Hunter   21

Chapter Two   (Trans)position of the Human(imal)   39

Chapter Three   Authentic Beasts   77

Chapter Four   Poetic Animals   99

Chapter Five   Birdsong of Being   131

Chapter Six   The Animal-Thing   159

Conclusion   Final Word   177

Notes   187

Works Cited   209

Index   219

Preface

In the garden in front of the house there stands a grand and towering gingko tree. Every year, late into the autumn, all of the leaves fall off at once on a single day, as if they all communicated with one another *en masse* the night before and decided that life was no longer worth living for gingko leaves. The tree also drops, though more sporadically and over a period of weeks, its little circular berries, at the center of which rests an oblong and occasionally jagged seed. For some reason—probably because it smells nearly indistinguishable, at least to the rather coarse and unnuanced human olfactory apparatus, from shit—dogs find the fruit completely irresistible. Or, at least, "my" dogs always have.

One day, our eleven-year-old dachshund Atticus took ill; within a couple of days he had stopped eating entirely and had grown worrisomely lethargic. Thousands of dollars and multiple X-ray and ultrasound scans later, it was discovered that he had a clotted cluster of gingko seeds stuck in his tiny, dachshund-sized intestines. We were told, much to our dismay, that our decision was as simple as it was bleak: death or surgery. Owing to our love of that sweet dog, and to an overpowering sense of responsibility for his well-being, we opted for surgery. A few thousand additional dollars and a week of in-patient care later, we brought him home.

Immediately upon bringing him to the house, I carried him out into the garden and set him carefully down on the grass that he might relieve himself, mindfully trying to avoid brushing against his sore and shaved belly where a six-inch long scar now resided. A mere *three seconds* after I had placed him on the ground, he walked over to a rotting gingko berry and tried to eat it, jagged seed and all. I can still see the confused and troubled look on his face as I yelled and ran over to him, violently pulling it out of his jowls by the stem.

Atticus was not stupid: indeed, he possessed a kind and degree of intelligence, in both body and mind, far beyond anything of which I, or any human, will ever be capable. But he simply could not *understand* that it was the gingko seed that had almost killed him and that had caused him so much physical and emotional discomfort over the preceding weeks: and *no* amount of explanation on my part—no amount of pointing and talking and yelling or even training—could ever get him to *understand* that. Such "understanding" is simply not how he lives—or, rather, lived—in the world. His way was another way: not better, not worse, but different. And in that *moment*, as I wrested the berry from his mouth, I *felt*, with a force and clarity I had never experienced before, the *distance* that lay between us. In that *intimate* moment, flesh to flesh and hand in mouth, I felt the *abyss* that stands between us.

It is with the hope of better understanding the *intimate abyss* that stands between human and animal that I have written this book.

I miss you, Atticus, still.
February 2025, Connecticut.

Acknowledgments

To Maggie Labinski—thank you for helping me clarify my thoughts regarding the contents of this book and for putting up with my peculiar mix of obsessiveness and slovenliness.

To Benjamin Berger, Ryan Drake, Jill Gordon, Robert Metcalf, Andrew Mitchell, Sonia Tanner, and Erik Vogt—thank you for reading drafts of chapters and for making valuable suggestions on how to improve this project. Time is perhaps the most precious gift one can give, and you have given me so much of yours, always graciously and without recompense.

To JGA—*danke* for the many conversations (fuel for the mind) and for the hundreds of soy lattes (fuel for the fingers) you bought me along the way. I am looking forward to many more years of both.

To Sarah Durkee and Elizabeth Turpin—thank you for helping with research, formatting, and indexing. Buy some good sunglasses, because your futures are going to be bright, indeed.

To Trinity College—thank you for the Summer Student Research Grants that made it possible for Sarah and Liz to help me to the extent they did and to buy some nice sunglasses. (See above.)

To Members of the Heidegger Circle—thank you for listening to earlier versions of chapters 1, 3, and 5, and for your helpful questions and comments, all of which helped me clarify my thinking about these issues.

Finally, to Bailey, Atticus, Loki, Roberta, Baruch, and Artemis—thank you for *being with* me while I wrote this book. Your living bodies remind me, on a daily basis, of how frivolous my work is when compared with yours. I am grateful to you beyond the reach of any λόγος for letting me share in your world—and what a rich, lovely, expansive world it is.

Note Regarding Citations

All citations are provided in endnotes. Citations of Martin Heidegger's works first list the volume number and German pagination of the *Gesamtausgabe*, followed by the pagination of the relevant English volume (for example, GA 55:14/13). If no English pagination is included, the translation is my own (for example, GA 99:25). For all other sources, the author-date system is employed (for example, Sallis 2016, 123).

Introduction

Necessary Detours

"Existence" is the term for the sort of being we ourselves each are, human *Dasein*. A cat does not exist, but it lives.

—Heidegger (GA 26:127/159)

My dog—the "Pomeranian"—has more of the "agrarian world" [*Bauerntum*] in his snout and in his bones than do these puffed up, groundless counterfeiters craving for professorial chairs.

—Heidegger (GA 96:91/72)[1]

During his 1938–1939 lecture course on Nietzsche's *Second Untimely Meditation*, Heidegger marks it as peculiar that, although Nietzsche's investigation is focused on clarifying the nature of the *human*, it nonetheless begins with a reflection on the *animal*. In the face of this apparent *detour* at play in Nietzsche's investigation, Heidegger asks the following question: "[I]n a text concerned with the calculative account of *historiology*, that is, of *human* being for life, and thus first of all [*zufor*] with *human* life—in a text where the *human being* is thus put into question [*der Mensch in Frage steht*], was it necessary or merely accidental, merely, say, an artifice of artistic composition, to begin with a reflection on the animal?"[2] Answering his own question, Heidegger states that such a beginning, far from being accidental, was in fact a necessary (*notwendig*) path for Nietzsche to follow. Regarding such necessity, he offers the following: "With the question of the human being, we move *necessarily* within the realm of the distinction between animal and human being. Here the question becomes inescapable [*unvermeidlich*]:

where does the dividing line [*Grenzscheide*] between animal and human being lie? And does such a dividing line exist at all? And if it does, how can we determine it?"[3] Most immediately, then, Heidegger is underscoring the extent to which the question of the animal reigns over the inquiry into Nietzsche in which he and his students were then engaged; and, indeed, much of the lectures on Nietzsche's *Second Untimely Meditation* are occupied, one way or another, with the question of the animal. Heidegger then adds that the questions he has just posed regarding the differences—if there are any—between the human and the animal "extend far beyond [*greifen weit hinaus über*] the limits of Nietzsche's treatise; they are also prior [*vor*] to the questions of any 'biology' or 'anthropology.' "[4] The scope of the question of the animal is thus much, much broader than Nietzsche's text alone. Indeed, Heidegger proceeds to describe the breadth of the question of the distinction between the human and the animal, a question now seen to have an almost limitless ambit of importance:

> The question of the dividing line between animal and human being is in fact not at all a question of an academic nature, and neither is it a "question" of a "worldview" or one of Christian faith. Within the realms of these—science, worldview, religious faith—such a question either cannot be raised or is always and already decided by some doctrinal statement, and thereby dismissed as unworthy of questioning. And yet the destiny of the historical Occident, of its sciences and its worldviews and the faith of its churches, is decided [*entscheidet*] by either posing the question of the dividing line between animal and human being or by avoiding it.[5]

The question regarding the difference between the human and the animal—which includes the question of whether there even *is* a difference—is not, as Heidegger has said, "of an academic nature." Rather, as the passage makes clear, it is a *foundational* question, an *existential* question, indeed, a question regarding the very foundation of existence. Moreover, this question unsettles and implicates the very foundations of the sciences, of any worldview, and of religious faith—in other words, the intellectual and spiritual tapestry of the West—and so much so that, as Heidegger puts it, *the very destiny of the West* is at stake within this question. The future of the Western world will be *decided* on the basis of the question of the relationship between the animal and the human, on whether and how it is posed, and on whether and how it is resolved.

It would hardly be an exaggeration, then, to say that for Heidegger, *everything* depends upon the question of the relationship between the human and the animal.

Concluding his explicit thoughts on the matter, Heidegger adds the following: "We will not be able to solve this question here, nor even to pose it adequately. But we have to recognize, following these initial interpretative reflections, that this question reigns [*beherrscht*] over our exercises of thinking, even when we do not explicitly talk about it, and even though we are not yet capable of fully assessing its import."[6] Thus, the scope of the question of the animal is so broad, so extensive, and so fundamental that it exercises its reign over one's thinking *even when one is unaware of it*. This means that, even when one is not explicitly thinking about the animal and its proximity or distance to the human, the question of the animal is nonetheless there in the background as the foundation or hovering above the inquiry: an *open* question whose resolution—indeed, whose very *posing*—would change everything and would shape the future to come.

The implication is as obvious as it is staggering: namely, that *all* of Heidegger's thinking—all one-hundred-plus volumes of his *Gesamtausgabe*—is in some manner guided by the question of the animal. This would mean that even when one is reading Heidegger's inquiries into formal indication or poetics or technology; even when one is following his meditations on language and the opening of world; even when—or, perhaps, *especially* when—one is following along with his questioning of the meaning of *being*, one is also already asking about the relationship between the human and the animal. The foundational existential question regarding the dividing line between the animal and the human is always in the background of Heidegger's thinking, always there at the ground of his mindful reflections. To phrase this in a manner that will become more meaningful through the following inquiry as a whole, one could say that the question of the animal has a decisive *priority* within Heidegger's thinking and that it is one of the motive forces of that thinking. As the following inquiry will show, the question of the animal is also intimately intertwined with the *most* primary question for Heidegger, namely, the question of the meaning of being. Indeed, as will eventually be seen, one simply cannot adequately pose the latter without *first* grappling with the former.

Ranging from his earliest works to his very last, Heidegger ceaselessly raised the question of the animal.[7] Sometimes—such as in *The Fundamental Concepts of Metaphysics*—such questioning is carried out in a sustained and prolonged inquiry; other times—such as in many of the other texts explored in the present volume—the question of the animal is raised only briefly or barely within the context of a broader project. But whether expansively or briefly, Heidegger's work, throughout the entirety of his career, demonstrates a preoccupation with this most foundational of questions, a question that reigns over his thinking as a whole.

That the relation between the animal and the human was always in question for Heidegger is perhaps revealed in the fact that his understanding of the animal is hardly uniform, although it is often presented by scholars as being such. Even a cursory reading of his corpus reveals a multifarious understanding of animality that undergoes radical changes throughout the course of his long career. Take, for example, the matter of *world* and the animal's relation to it. In some of his lectures on Aristotle from the early and mid-1920s, the animal, not unlike the human, *has a world*; then, in *The Fundamental Concepts of Metaphysics* from 1929, the animal is "poor" in world and can only properly be said to inhabit an *environment*. By the time Heidegger is delivering the material of *Introduction to Metaphysics* in 1935, the animal no longer even has an environment; however, in the "Letter on Humanism" from 1946, animals are again said to occupy an environment, and as late as 1952 (in the Zollikon seminars) Heidegger claims that this environment "has a certain correspondence [*Entsprechung*]" to the world of the human.[8] It would hardly be possible, then, to claim that Heidegger's understanding of the animal's relation to world was statically fixed or rigidly decided; even less would it be possible to distill that understanding, as many scholars have done, into the single phrase "poor in world."

One sees similar vacillations in Heidegger's understanding of the animal's relation to *language*. Heidegger is almost univocal across his corpus in his claims that the animal has no language, that it is outside of λόγος, although at one point he insists that the question of the animal's capacity for λόγος must remain open.[9] Yet, as the present volume will show, in his work on Nietzsche, Hölderlin, and Heraclitus from the 1930s and 1940s, Heidegger *shows* the animal as engaging in operations of *pointing* and *gathering* that at least approximate λόγος, though Heidegger never calls it that. Furthermore, in several texts with which the present study is concerned, Heidegger will speak of the animal *as speaking* and engaging in language (*Sprache*), though a careful analysis is required to properly contextualize and understand these passages.

Or, take the example of *mourning*. Heidegger claims in his 1934 lectures on Hölderlin's "Germania" that animals are incapable of mourning.[10] And yet, in his 1943 lectures on Heraclitus, Heidegger suggests that a certain animal *does* mourn, or, at the very least, that it relates to the closure and concealment of death "as in mourning."[11] Finally, and relatedly, take the example of *death*. Heidegger famously argues in *Being and Time* (1927) that the animal does not die but only perishes (*verenden*);[12] yet, in the Heraclitus lectures from 1943, he says that the animal, as a living being, "finds death" (*den Tod finde*).[13] The issue is not only a terminological one: rather, it points to a continued effort on Heidegger's part *to think* the animal Other, to understand its unique character and capacities. Such efforts, as we will see, are instrumental for Heidegger in clarifying and solidifying the nature of the human.

Heidegger's understanding of the animal and its relation to the human can thus in no way be said to be stable or consistent, though it is often presented as such. Rather, what one finds throughout Heidegger's work is a fluid and dynamic attempt *to think* the animal, a vibrant *questioning* of the animal that alters and adjusts itself in terms of how the animal shows itself. This vibrant dynamism at times leads Heidegger to make determinative claims about the nature of the animal, and at other times to insist that there is little determination that can be made, claiming instead that the essence of the animal must forever remain a puzzling mystery. Heidegger's understanding of the animal could thus not be charted on a line graph as a straight, unwavering line, but only as a series of peaks and valleys that rise and dip precipitously over time. These peaks and valleys are indicative of the continual *uncertainty* Heidegger has regarding the perpetual question of the relationship between the human and the animal and evidences his enduring attempts to engage that question honestly and openly.

Of course, the principal objection against Heidegger's questioning of the animal is that it is not in fact a questioning at all but is rather the carrying out of an unreflective metaphysical program utterly infused with a host of pernicious anthropocentric biases regarding the priority of the human. This almost ubiquitous charge has been raised by dozens of scholars, though it finds its finest and most powerful articulation in the work of Jacques Derrida.[14] Over the course of several decades and at least a half-dozen texts, Derrida alleged again and again that Heidegger's engagement with animality was thoroughly and irrevocably pervaded by certain unquestioned (or, at least, inadequately questioned) metaphysical preconceptions and biases that served to situate Heidegger within a long line of thinkers who have privileged the human over the animal.[15] All of this amounts to the charge that Heidegger's "question" of the animal is not really a question at all but that Heidegger had already decided, long before *apparently* asking about the animal, what the animal is and where it stands in relation to the human.

As a corrective to Heidegger's approach, Derrida offers an account of the animal—or, rather, of *an* animal—that seeks to displace the hierarchical understanding of animality that has beset the entire Western philosophical tradition and attempts to free the understanding of the animal from such humanistic biases.[16] In *The Animal That Therefore I Am*, Derrida describes a certain *scene* wherein a cat—a real cat, he insists—gazes at him while he is naked. The scene of the cat's gaze serves as a dramatic enactment of the careful argument Derrida gives regarding the instability of the human's various claims of authority and hierarchical priority, an argument that results in a destabilizing of the presumed priority of the human by demonstrating the extent to which the ipseity of the self and the humanness of the human follow upon, and follow after, the animal Other, all of which leads Derrida to ask: "Who am I, therefore? Who is that I am (following)? Whom should this be asked of if not the other? And perhaps of the cat itself?"[17]

Derrida's text reaches its deconstructive apogee during another animal scene, this one from the *Book of Genesis* in the Hebrew Bible. In this animal scene—a scene that, at least on its surface, seems to install a hierarchical framework in which the human exercises its God-given dominion over the animal Other—Adam is told by his god to name the animals. As Derrida shows, this moment of author(itarian)ship whereby the human confers names upon the animals *actually* shows, despite a long history of scholarly interpretation to the contrary, that the animal *comes before* the human and thus maintains a decisive priority over it. Derrida draws attention to this reversal with a series of rhetorical questions that connect back to his encounter with the cat: "For so long now, it is as if the cat had been recalling itself and recalling that, recalling me and reminding me of this awful tale of *Genesis*, without breathing a word. Who was born first, before the names? Which one saw the other come to this place, so long ago? Who will have been the first occupant, and therefore the master? Who the subject? Who has remained the despot, for so long now?"[18] What the *Genesis* story suggests, when properly understood, is that whenever the human arrives on the scene—via either a theological, metaphysical, or even evolutionary mechanism—the animal will always already have been there. In this sense, the animal (thus) comes before the human, and in such a way that the human would (then) measure itself against the animal. For Derrida, then, there is thus a decisive and incontestable *priority* to the animal Other within the context of the human/animal encounter, an *absolute apriority* that utterly disrupts the human's claims to superiority and privilege and destabilizes the metaphysical tradition, *including Heidegger*, that has undergirded those claims.

And yet: What if the animal were already found in Heidegger to have such priority? That is, what if Heidegger's thinking, from beginning to end, pointed to an *absolute apriority* that belongs to the animal Other? What if one found, throughout Heidegger's works, certain encounters with the animal—or, even, with *particular animals*—that demonstrated, again and again, this apriority? In other words, what if one already found within Heidegger's thinking the kind of encounter with the animal so crucial to Derrida's deconstructive overturning of the humanistic privileging that he claims is operative within Heidegger?

By analyzing a variety of Heidegger's texts spanning the entirety of his career, the present book argues that one indeed finds such a privileging of the animal within Heidegger's work, and one that is very similar, if not structurally identical, to that presented by Derrida. As will be shown, one finds such prioritizing on Heidegger's part even in those texts most crucial to Derrida's critique of Heidegger, such as *The Fundamental Concepts of Metaphysics*, *What Is Called Thinking?*, and the Parmenides lectures. Throughout Heidegger's corpus, one finds a recurring if overlooked prioritizing of the animal Other that resists and disrupts the scholarly claim that Heidegger deprioritized the animal in favor of the human.

Such apriority is operative within Heidegger's thought in three distinct but related senses. To begin with, one finds what could be called a *methodological* priority afforded to the animal. In the texts with which the present study deals, Heidegger attempts again and again to (re)determine the nature of the human; and whenever he does so, he *first* turns to the animal, the animal who is (therefore) always already there as that to which the human can be compared. Insofar as Heidegger's method for reaching a determination of the essence of the human necessarily entails a turn (or, as we will see, a *detour*) to the animal, there belongs to the animal a determinate priority within the methodological structure of Heidegger's thought.

However, properly understood, this methodological priority indicates a deeper, more fundamental priority that belongs to the animal for Heidegger. The methodological turn toward the animal is undertaken by Heidegger for the sake of bringing about a transformation of the essence of the human, of moving the human away from its (self-)understanding as the "human" in the metaphysical sense (as the *animal rationale*) toward an understanding (and *enacting*) of itself as *Dasein* (understood as the *there* of being's unfolding). In this way, the animal serves as the ground upon which the human undertakes a transformation of its proper essence, of its proper *Dasein* or existence. For Heidegger, the human is indeterminate, *unsettled*, undefined in its very being, and requires a confrontation with the animal in order to reach any kind of definition, any kind of settlement. In this way, the animal holds an *ontological* priority in Heidegger's thought, insofar as the animal precedes, and is constitutive of, the proper determination of human *being*. Simply put, without detouring through an encounter with the animal, the being of the human cannot come into proper clarity or determination: the very being of the human thus depends upon the animal, the animal who is always already there as the ground of such ontological determinations.

Moreover, this ontological priority, when seen in its proper light, can be understood as constituting an *ethical* priority as well. As several of the texts that the present study addresses show, the human is primarily and for the most part *not at home* in its being: the human is, for Heidegger, characterized by an enduring *homelessness* and *homesickness*. The encounter with the animal is that path that the human must travel in order to enter into its own proper essence—in order, that is, to come to *dwell* steadfastly within the site of (its own) genuine being, in order to come to be at home in it. Precisely because it is a question of *settlement*, of coming to be at *home*, it is a question of *ethos*, of *dwelling* steadfastly within the open of the truth of being. As Heidegger writes in "Letter on Humanism," the Greek word *ethos* "names the open region in which the human dwells. The open region of his abode allows what pertains to the human's essence, and what in thus arriving resides in nearness to the human, to appear. The abode of the human contains and preserves the advent of what belongs to the human in his essence."[19] The *ethos* of the human—namely, the open of being itself—preserves and contains what shows itself to the human. The thinking of being as this abode is thus, for Heidegger, the highest (or most foundational) ethical thinking in which one can engage: "If the name 'ethics,' in keeping with the basic meaning of the word *ethos*, should now say that 'ethics' ponders the abode of the human, then that thinking which thinks the truth of being as the primordial element of the human, as one who *eksists*, is in itself the original ethics."[20] To the extent that Heidegger's turn to the animal is undertaken for the sake of bringing the human into a more genuine relationship with its own primordial element, it is an ethical enterprise in a Heideggerian sense; and because the animal is that through which the human must pass in order to understand its own relation to being, the animal occupies an ethical priority to this extent.

In what follows, the animal will thus be seen to occupy a method-ological, ontological, and ethical priority within Heidegger's thinking. Such a thesis runs counter to much that has been written about Heidegger's understanding of animality. Almost all of the scholarship dealing with Heidegger's engagement with the animal focuses on the various moments throughout his work that seem to carry out a denigration of the animal Other by *deprioritizing* it in the face of the human. More often than not—and this is the Heidegger with which we are all so familiar—Heidegger presents the animal as poor in world, as lacking language (or "the word"), as impoverished with respect to its ability to stand freely within the open of being, et cetera.[21] Even at those seemingly rare moments within his corpus when he refrains from overdetermining the animal in this way, instead allowing it the space to remain mysterious,[22] Heidegger still routinely refuses the animal the ability to speak, taking it to be without language, and thus without the possibility of an open and solicitous relationship toward being, to be without history, to be incapable of laboring or mourning, and so forth.[23] Heidegger, like nearly every other thinker before and after him, seems to place animals beneath or apart from the human, that human who, for Heidegger, is itself not *truly* an animal at all.[24]

However, despite all of this, the three aforementioned priorities will be seen to be operative in Heidegger's thinking of the animal to varying extents and degrees, even in those texts where Heidegger seems to carry out the most outrageous deprioritizing of the animal. The extent and manner to which this is so will be seen in the chapters that follow, but for now it can be said that such priority is operative if for no other reason than the fact that the animal must *already be there* in order for Heidegger to categorize it, denigrate it, and submit it to a biased, metaphysically laden hierarchical thinking. For Heidegger, in nearly all of the texts with which the present study deals, the animal is the *starting point* for any rigorous determination of the human, a determination that therefore *always* follows upon a prior exposure to the animal. In this way, the animal is the detour through which the human must travel in order to enter into its ownmost essence, a detour that is therefore required in order for the human to attain to its utmost authentic being. It is therefore what one could call *a necessary detour.*[25]

The full demonstration of the above claims—claims that can only seem incredible at the outset—requires the unfolding of this book as a whole. However, by way of introduction, a brief turn to two well-known passages within Heidegger's corpus will help orient the inquiry. These passages—one from the 1942 lectures on Parmenides and the other from the 1951–1952 *What Is Called Thinking?*—were particularly important to Derrida for establishing Heidegger's alleged metaphysical humanism. Although Derrida's analysis is surely true in a certain sense, one can also see in these passages a decisive priority on the part of the animal in the human's process of coming to clarify its own essence. For example, in the Parmenides course, during an analysis of the Greek word πρᾶγμα, Heidegger writes that

> things [*die Dinge*] "act," insofar as the things present and at hand [*Vorhandenen und Zuhandenen*] dwell within the reach [*Bereich*] of the "hand." The hand reaches out for them [*langt*] and reaches them [*erlangt*]: πράττει, the reaching arrival at something (πρᾶγμα), is essentially related to the hand. [. . .] The human itself acts through the hand; for the hand is, together with the word, the essential distinction of the human. Only a being which, like the human, "has" the word (μῦθος, λόγος), can and must "have" "the hand." Through the hand occur both prayer and murder, greeting and thanks, oath and signal, and also the "work" of the hand, the "hand-work," and the tool. The handshake seals the covenant. The hand brings about the "work" of destruction. The hand exists as hand only where there is disclosure and concealment. No animal has a hand, and a hand never originated from a paw or a claw or a talon.[26]

This passage, according to Derrida, evinces an "authoritarian rhetoric" that expresses "the profoundest metaphysical humanism" by unreflectively measuring the animal in terms of the human.[27] On the surface, such a judgment is difficult to dispute. And yet, despite what seems to be a certain anthropocentricity at play here, this passage in fact—or, at the very least, *also*—gestures toward the priority of the animal Other in Heidegger's thought. To begin with, there is a methodological priority insofar as it is precisely at that moment that Heidegger wishes to articulate the essence of the human—precisely, that is, at the moment that he wishes to set the human out it its uniqueness—*that he turns to the animal*. In other words, at the very moment that he attempts to delineate the proper essence of the human (i.e., its being), he does so by *taking a detour* through the animal Other, the animal who is (therefore) already there as that in terms of which the human will be compared. We will see such comparative moves undertaken by Heidegger in nearly all of the texts with which the present study deals: indeed, it is the guiding thesis of the present study that such a detour through the animal Other is programmatic in Heidegger's lifelong attempt to delineate the nature of the human.

This methodological priority, properly understood, also indicates the ontological priority of the animal: for it is only on the basis of this move that the human will enter into a proper understanding of its own *being*. Within these pages from the Parmenides lectures, Heidegger attempts to demonstrate the essential connection between the hand and the *word*, that is, the manner in which being opens up to and for the human in language (λόγος).[28] However, in order to show this essential connection, Heidegger (in the above passage) must *first* distinguish the human from the animal, must *first* turn toward the animal as a point of comparison and measure the human against it. In this way, the animal is that without which the human cannot properly grasp its own being: it thus serves as the ground of the possibility of a determination of human being. However, and precisely for this reason, the encounter with the animal is also necessary for the human's proper reckoning of *being itself*: for it is only by coming to understand its role as *Dasein*, as the *there* of being's unfolding, that the human grasps its ownmost essence—and it can only do this by *first* turning to the animal and differentiating itself from it. Thus, although "a hand never originated from a paw or a claw or a talon" according to Heidegger, there is a very real sense in which one can say that the hand originates from the paw, claw, and talon, though certainly not in an evolutionary sense. The animal Other is that from out of which the human's self-understanding originates, and that on the basis of which an articulation of human essence becomes possible.

One can also discern an *ethical* priority allotted to the animal in this passage, at least in a Heideggerian sense, insofar as the very domain of the ethical—of "prayer and murder, greeting and thanks, oath and signal"—opens up from out of a proper understanding of the human, an understanding that is only possible on the basis of a comparison to the animal Other. For Heidegger, the possibility of properly grasping human ethical life in its various dimensions follows upon the human's clarification of its own essence, a clarification that originates from out of a comparison with the animal. (This will be shown at length in chapter 4 through an analysis of Heidegger's interpretation of Hölderlin's "Ister" poem.) In this way, an encounter with the animal grounds the very possibility of ethics, so long as we understand this term in its properly Greek sense (as dwelling). Whether or not the encounter with the animal has other ethical consequences for Heidegger's thought is a question to which we will return in chapter 6.

Thus, the passage from the Parmenides lectures, precisely as it undertakes a determination of the human, *also* betrays the prior presence of an Other, an encounter with whom is structurally constitutive of such a determination. Heidegger arguably indicates the space of such otherness through his description of the various operations of the hand. Heidegger says that the hand *reaches out* (*langt*); more literally, *langen* means to *lengthen* or *elongate*. The hand reaches out, lengthening and elongating itself toward that which it does not have, that for which it *longs*, one might say, that which, regardless, is *out in front of it*, present to it, *always already lying before it*. The hand can only reach out for that which is at-hand for it, that which is present to it, that which, therefore, has already arrived *before* it is reached for. The hand only comes in handy *because* there are always already beings manifesting themselves to the hand, spreading themselves out in advance for its advance. Indeed, every one of the examples that Heidegger gives gestures toward the independent primacy and factical apriority of an Other: prayer is made to the god who is always *already there*; murder is always and only of the Other who is *already there*; greetings are made to the Other who *shows itself*; thanks are given to those who have *already* done something; oaths and signals are made for the benefit of the Other, et cetera. These examples, while in some ways serving as indicators of a subtle (or not so subtle) humanism operative throughout the history of metaphysics,[29] nonetheless point toward the absolute priority that certain Others have within the realm of human experience. As the present book as a whole demonstrates, the animal is one of those Others, and indeed a particularly important one within the contours of Heidegger's thinking.

The apriority of the animal is also evident in the passage from *What Is Called Thinking?* that, according to Derrida, is equally infused with an unapologetic metaphysical humanism:

> The hand is a peculiar thing. In the common view, the hand is part of our bodily organism. But the hand's essence can never be determined, or explained, by its being an organ which can grasp. Apes, too, have organs that can grasp, but they do not have hands. The hand is infinitely different from all grasping organs: paws, claws, or fangs [*Fängen*]—different by an abyss of essence. Only a being who can speak, that is, think, can have hands and can be handy in achieving works of handicraft.
>
> But the craft of the hand is richer than we commonly imagine. The hand does not only grasp and catch, or push and pull. The hand reaches and extends [*empfängt*], receives and welcomes—and not just things: the hand extends itself, and receives

> its own welcome in the hands of others. The hand holds. The
> hand carries. The hand designs and signs, presumably because
> the human is a sign. Two hands fold into one, a gesture meant
> to carry the human into the great oneness.[30]

It is difficult to deny that these comments, which David Krell calls "complacent and some-times mystifying," evince and carry out a certain metaphysical humanism.[31] Indeed, for Krell, this passage, and others like it, signify an ineradicable "human exceptionalism" at work in Heidegger's thinking,[32] one that seemingly measures the animal in terms of the human.[33] And yet, there are three matters to note about this passage that gesture toward a certain priority of the animal operative in Heidegger's thought that calls into question such exceptionalism, or at least adds crucial nuance to it. To begin with, while there is no denying the way in which this passage seeks to free the hand from the paw or claw of the beast and set the human apart from the animal (and, indeed, by an "infinite" expanse), such a critique overlooks the apriority of the animal Other at play in such a methodological move. *Precisely* when Heidegger wants to know more about the hand—wants, that is, to know more about the essence of the human—he detours *away* from the human and toward the animal, the animal who was therefore already there. "The hand's essence cannot be determined," Heidegger says, "by its being an organ that can grasp": and then, in order to set the hand apart in its uniqueness, he turns toward an animal, toward, in this case, an ape: "Apes, too, have organs that can grasp, but they do not have hands." It is only through this turn to the ape that the essence of the hand will come into its proper clarity. But this demands that the animal Other, with its paw or talon or claw, *must always already be there as that to which the human can turn.* Said otherwise: the paw, the claw, or the talon is that in terms of which, and on the basis of which, the hand is to be understood; or, said more generally, the animal is the ground of the human's understanding of itself.

Second, as was the case with the passage from the Parmenides lectures, every example Heidegger adduces here points to this prior at-hand-ness of beings within the human's world. *Grasping, pushing, pulling, reaching, extending, receiving, welcoming, holding, carrying, signing, praying*: each one of these only is what it is because of its relation to some Other who is already in the world whom or which one might grasp, push, or reach for, or whom one might welcome or receive.[34] All of Heidegger's examples here point to the priority of an Other to which the human stands in relation. As this book as a whole shows, the animal is among those Others that occupy a priority in Heidegger's thinking, and is indeed exemplary among them.

Third, it is worth noting that precisely when Heidegger seeks to differentiate the human hand from other apparatuses of seizing and grasping—such as *fangs* (*Fänge*)—he does so by emphasizing the hand's ability *to receive* (*empfängt*). *Empfangen* means *to receive, to welcome,* also *to catch* and *to accept*; its root *-fangen* means *to catch, to capture, to snare* or *entrap,* and is the same root of the German *Fänge* ("fangs") and the English *fangs.* In other words, emp*fangen* means to *catch, grasp, trap,* or *seize in the manner that an animal does with its fangs.* The question, of course, would be: Which came first? Does the human understand the animal's fangs in terms of its own operations of seizing and grasping carried out by the hand? Or does the human model its grasping after the sort in which the animal, with its fangs, engages? In light of the comparative/methodological turn toward the animal delineated above, it is the thesis of the present study that, for Heidegger, the essence of the human follows upon, and is dependent upon, the presencing of the animal: it is thus the animal's *fangs* that come first and make possible a proper understanding of human *empfangen.* But even if this thesis fails to prove itself in the following pages, one can at least still ask whether it is possible to hear the word *fangen,* or for Heidegger to employ it, without also hearing *fang.* Would *catching* and *capturing* always, for Heidegger, carry a trace of the animal's mode of latching onto things with its fangs, talons, and claws? One can imagine a reading of Heidegger that would hear such a reference to the animal in his extensive use of *-fangen* as he carries out his thinking of the inception (*Anfang*), where the human, as the sole being capable of catching or trapping the inceptual throw of being, grasps onto it the way, say, a *fox* traps or grasps its prey in its fangs.[35]

Regardless of the tenability of such a reading, the two passages mentioned above hint at the sort of structural apriority that this book as a whole draws out in greater detail. Both passages occur within the broader context and project of determining the essence of the human and in bringing about a transformation of that essence. As the above passages have suggested, and as this book as a whole shows, the necessary detour through the animal is the very ground of that transformation, serving as that without which the human cannot enter into its own proper essence and (therefore) an authentic relation to being. There is, then, no doubt that Heidegger's thought, in these passages and others, evidences a certain human exceptionalism, setting the human being apart from other beings: however, such a setting-apart *depends* upon a prior Other in relation to whom the human is set apart. Etymologically, the word "exception" denotes a taking out or withdrawing, a removing of one thing from another. In seeking to determine the unique capabilities of the human, Heidegger withdraws or removes the human from the animal—the animal who is (therefore) always already there prior to such an operation of withdrawing. The very project of human exceptionalism, of taking the human as an exception from other beings, depends upon the absolute apriority of those beings.

Heidegger speaks of such prior openness in his 1926–1927 lecture course *Geschichte der Philosophie von Thomas von Aquin bid Kant* (The History of Philosophy from Thomas Aquinas to Kant). Precisely at that moment when he differentiates human existence from that of "lark and rose," Heidegger points to a priority of the human's immersion in the presencing of such things:

> However, it is not first through the sciences of nature, life, space, and history [that the human first encounters beings]; rather, prior to that [*vordem*] *Dasein* is already [*schon*] related to nature, sky is determined by day and night, seasons and weather, cult of the sun and the stars, having to do with animals, hunting, animal husbandry, house pets, animal sacrifices. *Dasein* relates itself to others, is with them in tribe and clan, ancestor worship, tradition, custom. That and everything else has to do with house and farm, animals. *Dasein* essentially relates to things like that, i.e., it belongs to the very sense of existence to be in a world in which things like that presence, happen, and occur.[36]

Thus, prior (*vordem*) to any conceptual or theoretical reflection about the world, the human is always already immersed within that world alongside other living beings. Serving as the very basis of human experience, there lies a foundational presencing and happening that constitutes the very being-in-the-world of the human: and other living beings (i.e., animals broadly construed) are among the principal entities of that foundational presencing.

That being said, one might perhaps balk at this suggestion regarding the priority of the animal Other in the face of Heidegger's examples in the above passage of how the human relates to animals: namely, in terms of "hunting, animal husbandry, house pets, animal sacrifices." Such examples testify to the exploitive, violent, and decidedly unethical manner that characterizes the human's typical attitude toward animals in the era of modern technology (and, perhaps, in every historical era heretofore). (We will return to such violence in chapter 4 during a discussion of Heidegger's reading of

Sophocles's *Antigone*.) Nevertheless, Heidegger's broader point here is that, in order for the human to relate to animals in *any* way, the animal needs to already be there: it needs to presence itself within, and as, the opening of the world. It is only on the basis of such prior presencing that the human can *then* relate to the animal violently or nonviolently, kindly or criminally, ethically or unethically. It is in this sense, at the very least, that the animal has an absolute priority that precedes the human's comportment toward it.

One lingering question, perhaps among many, is this: Is the apriority of the animal in Heidegger's thought *deliberately* indicated on Heidegger's part, or does it show itself *despite* Heidegger's attempts to set the human apart as exceptional? In other words: Does the following book, by means of a deconstructive process, attempt to undermine Heidegger's various attempts to set the human apart from the animal, or does it offer an exegesis of Heidegger's own overlooked but *intentional* privileging of the animal Other?

The answer is: *a little bit of both*. On the one hand, several texts addressed within this study suggest that Heidegger was aware, at least at times, of such apriority on the part of animals. On the other hand, certain other texts show such an apriority *despite* attempts on Heidegger's part to demote the animal and prioritize the human. At his best moments, Heidegger is aware of and emphasizes the priority of the animal for the human's project of self-understanding and transformation; at his worst, he seems to forget this priority, though it *never* leaves his thinking entirely. A chronological tour of Heidegger's various encounters with the animal, as this book carries out, permits one to conclude that *from beginning to end* the animal maintained a certain priority in Heidegger's thought, anywhere and everywhere that he considered it.

Simply put, the animal was always an open question for Heidegger. More precisely, the relationship between the human and the animal was always in question for Heidegger as he sought, time and time again, to set out and determine the essential nature of human being. Recalling the passage from Heidegger's lectures on Nietzsche's *Second Untimely Meditation* mentioned at the outset of this introduction, where Heidegger writes that "with the question of the human being, we move *necessarily* within the realm of the distinction between animal and human being," one could say that *every single time* Heidegger raises the question of the "human" or of "Dasein"—which he does in nearly every text of his *Gesamtausgabe*—he is always already thinking about the animal, to the extent that the animal is implicated—if only "negatively"—in any determination or delineation of the essence of the human. In this way, the animal is literally *everywhere* in Heidegger's thought.

In order to see the extent to which this is the case, the following book focuses on certain key texts spanning Heidegger's corpus where the priority of the animal is most visible. Chapter 1 offers an analysis of Heidegger's *Ponderings II–VI*, his so-called "Black Notebook" from 1931–1938. Within this text Heidegger articulates a succinct program outlining his approach to animality, a program that verifies, and in many ways orients, the above-articulated thesis regarding the priority of the animal within Heidegger's thought. By attending to this program and supporting passages, it will be seen that for Heidegger the human's project of determining the parameters of its own essence *necessarily* entails an encounter—or what Heidegger will call a "detour"—with other living beings (i.e., the animal broadly conceived). In short, the human's ability to answer the question "Who am I?" *follows upon*, and is in part constituted by, an encounter with the animal Other.

Chapter 2 offers a reading of Heidegger's most infamous text that addresses the question of the animal, *The Fundamental Concepts of Metaphysics* (1929–1930), a text that is utterly central to nearly all criticisms of Heidegger's understanding of animality (including Derrida's).[37] By reading this text alongside two others—namely, *Basic Questions of Aristotelian Philosophy* (1924) and *Being and Time* (1927)—this chapter argues that *The Fundamental Concepts of Metaphysics* can be understood as *enacting* the program that Heidegger described within his "Black Notebook," an enactment that demonstrates, and indeed depends upon, the apriority of the animal Other. Without entirely denying the viability of those critiques of Heidegger that see within this text a prejudicial denigrating of the animal, it is shown that the animal nonetheless occupies a pride of place for Heidegger within his project of bringing about a transformation of the human's self-understanding (and, indeed, of the human itself).

In light of the findings of the first two chapters, chapter 3 offers a close examination of Heidegger's 1937 lectures on Friedrich Nietzsche's *Thus Spoke Zarathustra*. By focusing on two sections in particular—"Zarathustra's Animals" and "The Convalescent"—this chapter analyzes a remarkable scene within this text wherein two animals serve as the model upon which Zarathustra transforms himself into his ownmost essence. It light of this scene, it is argued that the encounter with the animal is one way in which the human overcomes the superficial understanding of time and becomes aware of its authentic temporality, thereby becoming truly historical (in the fullest sense). As the chapter shows, such a transformation is only possible on the basis of a "poetic listening" that lets the animal show itself as it truly is.

Picking up on the theme of poetry, chapter 4 explores the crucial role that animals play within Heidegger's various readings of Hölderlin throughout the 1930s and 1940s. This chapter argues that all of Heidegger's major engagements with Hölderlin—namely, his lectures on "Germania," "Der Ister," and *Elucidations of Hölderlin's Poetry*—demonstrate, to varying extents, the logic of the necessary detour. In each of these texts, the animal plays a crucial role in Heidegger's understanding of *homecoming*, the process by which the human enters into its own proper essence. In short, this chapter argues that the animal is the *foreign* to which the human must turn in order to grasp, and thereby transform, its essential being.

Chapter 5 offers a reading of Heidegger's *Heraclitus* lectures from 1943 and 1944, focusing on a particular passage in the 1943 course in which a *bird* reawakens the human's inceptual understanding of being. According to Heidegger, a proper comportment toward the bird—what one might call, in light of the conclusions from chapter 3, a "poetic listening" that seeks to move beyond the strictures of metaphysical thinking—experiences the bird as heralding the opening of being understood in terms of the fourfold. Through an analysis of Heidegger's claim that the bird's singing unfolds "the tidings, the call, and the enchantment" of being itself, it is argued that an encounter with the animal Other is one of the ways, if not the principal way, in which the human can overcome the forgetfulness of being characteristic of the modern era.

Chapter 6 extends the consideration of the animal's relation to the fourfold by turning to Heidegger's Bremen lectures from 1949. Through a reading of "The Thing" and "Positionality," it is argued that the animal, properly understood, is among those *things* capable of reawakening the human to the inceptual unfolding of being. Such a reawakening, it is shown, characterizes the "original ethics" to which Heidegger alludes in "Letter on Humanism." Additional consideration is given to the ethical promise of Heidegger's understanding of the "animal-thing" by showing the ways in which the encounter with the animal pulls the human out of its immersion in the dominance of standing-reserve characteristic of the age of "enframing," thereby opening the possibility for a new relation to the earth, the human, and the animal.

The book concludes by analyzing the role that the animal Other plays in the advent of what Heidegger calls "the other inception," that is, the crisis whereby the human transitions into a new experience and understanding of being and thus of itself as the *there* of being's unfolding. By focusing mostly on *Contributions to Philosophy* (GA 65) and *On Inception* (GA 70), I show that the role of the human as the shepherd of being, brought about by the other inception, is principally inaugurated through the encounter with the animal. Such shepherding of being(s) both brings the human into its own proper essence (i.e., by ex-posing it to being) and opens a space in which a new understanding of the animal, and of the human *as* a special kind of animal, can unfold.

In the end, the present study shows that not only did the animal occupy a place of priority in Heidegger's work in the sense that Heidegger returned to the question of the animal again and again, but that within Heidegger's thinking itself the animal holds a special priority in the sense that it serves as the ground upon which the human bases its self-understanding and from out of which it carries out a transformation of its existence. To phrase this in a way that will gain meaning as this book progresses: the animal *called* to Heidegger again and again throughout his work, each time challenging him to respond and, through such challenging, demonstrated the absolute priority of the animal Other in the face of whose call the human must respond. The present study is an attempt to attend to the animal's call in Heidegger's work and to track the various ways in which Heidegger responded to this call.

Chapter One

The Hunter

Essential thoughts are to be hunted [*hindurchjagen*] ever anew through the hardest questions.

—Heidegger (GA 94:266/195)

Heidegger's so-called "Black Notebooks"—philosophical diaries that he kept between the 1930s and 1970s—were first published in German in 2014, with English translations of three of the volumes quickly following. Although much of the scholarship to date dealing with the notebooks has focused on the passages therein in which Heidegger's anti-Semitism is most visible, such passages take up very little space within the notebooks themselves: indeed, of the hundreds of pages that comprise the heretofore published notebooks, only about two-dozen paragraphs deal explicitly with Jews and Judaism, and even fewer express any overt antipathy toward Jews. (Of course, even one such passage is one too many.) The vast majority of the material within the notebooks is much less incendiary and sensational, at least on the surface, consisting instead of dense and terse philosophical entries that range from challenging to incomprehensible. Some have argued that an underlying cultural or even metaphysical anti-Semitism pervades Heidegger's notebooks—and, indeed, his thinking as a whole—and important work continues to be done in this direction.[1] Regardless of whether or not this is the case, Heidegger's notebooks contain interesting material relevant to many of the philosophical ideas he developed throughout his career, including fascinating insight into his understanding of animality.

Owing to their arcane style, it is a mistake to attempt to read any of the notebooks systematically as if they were treatises comprising, either wholly or in part, a philosophical system or program. Indeed, Heidegger himself, in an epigraph to the volume with which the present chapter is principally concerned—namely, GA 94, which spans the years 1931 to 1938—warns against such a reading:

> *The entries in the black notebooks* are at their core attempts at simple designation—not statements or even sketches for a planned system.[2]

Yet, despite this prefatory proviso, one can at times discern a certain order operative within the notebooks, insofar as certain entries relate thematically to those that come before or after. Heidegger himself cross-referenced certain entries, indicating that even he discerned a kind of subterranean order or clandestine logic operative within the notebooks. Thus, while one certainly does not find a *system* within the notebooks in any rigorous sense, one also does not find merely unrefined chaos. Rather, one finds certain *movements* of thought to which Heidegger made posted contributions over a period of years, movements in which a certain inner coherence can often be discerned. The result is a text that reads no more or less desultorily than his *Contributions to Philosophy* or *On the Event*, although the individual entries in the notebooks are typically of shorter, oftentimes even aphoristic, length.

Several major themes organize themselves through the unfolding of GA 94. One of the themes—if not the primary, overarching theme—already presents itself from the very first entry, written in 1931. The entry occurs prior to the first numbered entry, the entry numbered with the arabic number 1; and the entry itself is without a number. One could consider it, then, to be the "zero" entry, the entry that makes possible the entries that follow and in some sense serves as their ordinal ground. The entire "zero" entry is as follows:

> What should we *do*?
> Who *are* we?
> Why should we *be*?
> What are beings?
> Why does being happen?
> Philosophizing proceeds out of these questions upward into unity.[3]

Although each of these five questions asks something different, and in a different mode (i.e., "who," "what," "why"), they are all essentially related and, as Heidegger himself intimates, are oriented toward a single underlying unity (*Einheit*). Indeed, the first three question all ask, in some manner, about the same issue—namely, the *we* (*wir*)—and in this way can be seen as reducing down into the second question, a question that not only hangs above the entirety of the notebook but, arguably, the entirety of Heidegger's corpus: "Who *are* we?" (*wer* sind *wir*).

It is crucial to observe how Heidegger here, in asking "Who *are* we?" does *not* ask "Who is the *human*?" The force of Heidegger's questioning in this notebook is so radical as to leave open whether the "we" in question has the nature of the human, or if it is of some entirely other, or even entirely *alien*, nature. As the text as a whole (if such a phrase makes sense when applied to this, or any, of the "Black Notebooks") attests, the human—its status, its designation, its being, the parameters of its identity—is very much in question within the notebook, as it is indeed throughout Heidegger's vast body of work. Moreover, by placing the "are" (*sind*) in italics in the second question, Heidegger indicates that the question of the "we" is not just a question about "us"—whoever, or *whatever*, "we" are—but also a question about *being*. (This is further indicated in the three questions that immediately follow the second, whose emphasis switches to *being* in relation to the "we," and then more directly to being itself.) In other words, the question regarding the character of the "we" is always already intertwined with the question of being, with the mysterious happening of being, and in a manifold sense. In order to capture what is at stake in this question, one might pose it differently than Heidegger himself does by amplifying what is implicit within it: *Who is the "we"?* Or, even more strongly: *Who, or what, is the "we"?* Or, more strongly still: *Who, or what, is the "we" such that the question of the meaning of being itself is also raised in this question regarding the identity of the "we"?*

That the character or identity of the "we," and its relation to being, is in question within the notebooks becomes immediately evident within the first numbered entry:

What we extol as blessing depends on what afflicts us as distressing necessity [*Not*].

And on whether distressing necessity truly urges us on, i.e., urges us away from staring at the situation and talking it over.

> Greatest distressing necessity—that we must finally turn our backs on ourselves [*den Rücken kehren müssen . . . uns*] and on our "situation" and *actually* seek ourselves.
>
> Away from detours, which merely lead back to the same beaten paths; sheer evasions—remote and desultory—before the ineluctable.
>
> The human must come to itself [*Der Mensch soll zu sich selbst kommen*]![4]

In the face of the distressing necessity confronting the human—namely, the forgetfulness of being through which the human's relation to being has become tenuous[5]—the character or identity of the human becomes questionable. Thus, although the "we" is formally designated here as the human (*der Mensch*), it is so designated precisely in such a way as to indicate the human's separation from itself, its *distance* from itself, and the manner in which it still has yet to come truly to itself. In other words, although the "we" is named here as the human, the precise character of that "human" is still very much in question: or, rather, what is made clear is that the greatest distressing necessity—the most pressing matter that imposes itself upon the contemporary human—is that "we" finally (*endlich*) come to turn away from ourselves precisely in an effort to seek ourselves, to come to ourselves, to inquire after ourselves, a turn *away* that is thus essentially a turn *toward*.

As Heidegger will later write, rather than seeking to evade this distressing necessity through "a mendacious flight into now empty Christianity or through the heralding of a National Socialist 'worldview' that is *spiritually* questionable and of dubious origination,"[6] it is necessary that the human face this plight head-on by turning its back on itself, by turning around away from the human as it is understood within the contemporary epoch and toward the human to come, toward the human that "we" *shall* become, a human who is not at all a human, understood within the terms of contemporary metaphysics, but is rather *Dasein*.[7] The contemporary human is *entangled* (*versticken*) in beings, in the hustle and bustle of daily life, in machination, in calculative thinking, and in the modern abandonment of being.[8] This necessarily entails a certain entanglement in "the human," that is, in the concept or experience of the human as it has been conceived within modern philosophical and scientific thought (namely, as the *animal rationale*). What is needed is a movement away from—or, rather, *through*—this entanglement in the modern understanding of the human, a *path* or a *track* that cuts through it and opens up upon an experience of genuine *Da-sein*: "We must go back to the place where the human throws himself adrift into the essence of being. And re-find the swinging arc of the throwing; clear this track [*Bahn*] for humans."[9] The contemporary human, entangled in the forgetfulness of being, is off track. Heidegger's project within the notebook—and perhaps throughout his work as a whole—is to help the human get back on track; and this track, by way of a throwing-adrift whose character will come into greater clarity in what follows, will lead the modern human to the *there* of (its) being, to the *Da* of (its) *Sein*.

As comes to light within the notebooks, this track toward the proper essence of the human entails a movement *backward*, away from modernity, and toward the Greeks—namely, toward those Greeks whom Heidegger will call "inceptual thinkers": "How far advanced are the Greeks over us; there is accordingly no returning to them—only a catching up. But that requires the power of throwing oneself forward in a primally arisen disclosive question-ing. And that means simply to liberate the Da-sein in today's humanity."[10] Thus, although the movement is in a certain sense a movement *backward*, it is equally (or more essentially) a movement *forward*.[11] Returning to the Greeks is a futural gesture insofar as it opens up the heretofore inexhausted possibility of a futural determination of the human as the *Da* of *Sein*, a possibility that was broached, but never fully exhausted, by those inceptual thinkers thinking at the inception of Western thought. It is also, in this way, a *liberatory* movement, insofar as it frees the modern human from its entanglement in the forgetfulness of being characteristic of the modern era and the designation of the human as *animal rationale* operative therein. This liberatory movement is understood by Heidegger as a "throwing adrift" of the human that will free the human from its entanglement in the forgetfulness of being (and thus from the strictures of the "human" itself). It will also free the human from Christianity, metaphysics, representational thinking, and so forth, all of which serve as mechanisms of the errant thinking of the West that have culminated in the destitution of the current historical moment.

Regarding this futural movement backward, Heidegger asks, "*Why must we place ourselves back into the beginning?*" to which he offers the following answer: "Because we have been thrown off the *track* [*Bahn*]. The evidence of it is the absence of the affliction[. . . .] The track, however, is that of the self-throwing adrift of humans into the (essence); on this track [*Bahn*], the essence of being is opened to him. Only on this track and in the momentum of the directionality of its throwing is the question of being to be raised—perhaps as a dismantling question."[12] The modern human, owing to the abandonment of being that has carried itself out through machination, has become entangled in the forgetfulness of being, a forgetfulness that plays out in various registers (such as the flight into technology, faith, or National Socialism). It is also a forgetfulness that plays out in the human's assessment of itself *as human*, and specifically as a kind of *animal*, namely, the *animal rationale*.[13] It is this flight into such a self-understanding that needs to be avoided if the human is to bring itself before the greatest distressing necessity and get back on track toward the unfolding of the essence of being.

The pressing question thus becomes: *How*, exactly, is the human to get (back) on track? *How* is the human to throw itself adrift such that the essential will once again spring forth?[14] How is the human to come to *know* being, if such knowing is even possible?[15] And what is the precise character of the track onto which the human must set itself in order that it might come to know being in its inceptual character? How is the human to proceed toward a genuine encounter with (its) being?

Heidegger has told us, back within the very first entry, that this path must proceed "away from detours [*Umwegen*], which merely lead back to the same beaten paths; sheer evasions—remote and desultory—before the ineluctable."[16] And yet, as we soon see, it is precisely a *detour* that is needed to bring the human to itself, to bring it away from its errant self and unto its true self, to bring it away from the human understood as the rational animal and into an experience of *Dasein*.

Specifically, what is needed is a detour through the *animal*.

∿

In section 201, the question of the relationship between the human and the animal is posed explicitly within the notebook for the first time. The section begins: "*The animal and the human*."[17] In German, the parsimony of the pairing is even more evident: *Tier und Mensch*. Animal and human, bound together by the copula. It is perhaps worth noting here that, in this pairing, the animal comes *first*. Such a syntactic priority afforded here to the animal is emblematic of the priority that Heidegger will allot to the animal within the notebook—and, indeed, within his thinking—as a whole.

The section continues: "Animals do not know, provided the disclosability of beings pertains to knowledge. Because no truth, so also no need to question which 'world' of individual animal or of species is 'truer' than the others among themselves or in relation to humans."[18] In stating that animals "do not know," Heidegger aligns himself with a long line of philosophers and scientists who have denied animals the ability to cultivate knowledge, to stand in a knowing relation to being(s).[19] However, whereas most have done this owing to the animal's lack of *reason*, Heidegger attributes the animal's inability to know to its lack of exposure to the "truth," that is, to the clearing of being. Because the animal lives without the disclosure (i.e., the openness) of being, the animal is without the truth: not *untrue* or *false* in some way but standing entirely outside of the truth so as to utterly lack any relation to it.[20] Here, it seems, the animal is without *world*, at least to the extent that "world" and "truth" for Heidegger name the same:[21] the animal is without ἀλήθεια as the open expanse of the unconcealment of beings. Thus, one seemingly finds here the same sort of denigrating hierarchy that one seemingly finds expressed in *The Fundamental Concepts of Metaphysics*, Heidegger's most infamous and panned engagement with animality (to which we will turn in the next chapter).

However, it is crucial to remember that the human in the contemporary epoch is *also* without world in the fullest sense, to the extent that it has gotten off track and has become entangled in a woeful forgetfulness of being. Because the human has forgotten being, it can also be said to stand outside of the truth of being, outside of the *world* in the richest sense: for it is not the "human" who stands within the truth of being, but only *Dasein*—and "we," who have yet to even become bothered by (or even aware of) our forgetfulness of being, *are not yet Dasein*. Thus, one sees here a certain conceptual equivalence between the human of the contemporary era and the animal: both are outside of being, outside of the world, albeit in essentially different ways.

Another way to put this would be to say that the human of the contemporary epoch has become so *entangled* in beings (to the detriment of its awareness of being) as to become *almost like an animal*, whose entanglement in its environment prevents it from having a world and relating to being as such.[22] Moreover, it is precisely such entanglement that has resulted in the human's assessment of itself *as* an animal, that is, as the *animal rationale*.[23] The abandonment of being characteristic of the modern era has brought about a situation in which the human and the animal, owing to their respective entanglements, have come to occupy similarly *impoverished* positions.

Despite these similarities, Heidegger marks here what he takes to be an essential difference between the animal and the human: the former *essentially* lacks the world of which the latter is capable.[24] And yet, he continues, despite not having a world, the animal is nonetheless "sentiently related to . . ." (*sinnlich "Bezogen auf . . ."*).[25] Such "relating to" takes place, Heidegger says, at the level of the animal's entire corporeality (*Leiblichkeit*): that is, as a body, as a bodily (i.e., *living*) being, the animal is such as to enact a relation. This relational corporeality is to be understood as "a surrounding field [*Umfeld*] thus in a certain way 'open.' "[26] Thus, even though it is without world, the animal is nonetheless "open" (*offen*) in a certain way (*in gewisser Weise*), namely, in the sense that it is able to, or rather simply always does, enact or embody or carry out a relation.

But—a relation to *what*, exactly? Heidegger does not say; moreover, his use of ellipses ("*Bezogen auf . . .*") suggests a certain indecision, or even openness, on his part: by leaving the sentence open, he leaves it open to what, precisely, the animal stands in relation. That being said, he proceeds to give an example meant to clarify the character of this relation: "Scent and color, e.g., for bees." Scent and color are examples of the way in which bees, as living bodies, are in a certain way *open to . . .* and thus enact a relation. But, again—to what precisely do the bees relate? Presumably they relate to *beings* with odor and color—i.e., flowers—although one would need to place the word "beings" under erasure here: for although bees relate to the scent and color of a flower, they do not relate to the fragrant and chromatic flower *as* a being, because they, according to Heidegger, do not relate to beings *as such*. And yet—and this is worth emphasizing, given Heidegger insistences elsewhere that the animal lacks the *open*—the flower, through its color and scent, is "in a certain way open" to the animal. In some sense, then, the flower is given to the bee, the latter of which relates to the former in some manner of openness.

Heidegger proceeds to say more about the unique openness that belongs to the animal; or, rather, he says that there is not much more that can be said about this open: "But we do not know what is open here and how it is so." The manner in which the animal (as living) is open is inaccessible to us: its character remains *mysterious*. Thus, the animal, because it does not have a world (i.e., does not stand in the truth of being), cannot have knowledge; and yet, the human, *despite* standing in the truth of being and being capable of knowing, does not know anything about the animal open; knows so little of it, in fact, that even the word "open" is placed in scare quotes by Heidegger when applied to the animal here. The most, then, that one can say is that the animal has an open that is *otherwise than world*.

But—*why* don't we know? That is, why can nothing more be said about the animal and its open? As comes to light through Heidegger's notebook, the human's inability to say more about the openness of the animal is owed to the manner in which the human is *trapped* within its own world: "[W]e speak and question even here on the basis of our own world [*unserer Welt*]."[27] Worse, we do so unreflectively: "[W]e do not meditate on how unavoidably this unspoken point of departure requires a clarification and a securing."[28] When the human speaks of the animal, it does so from out of an entanglement in its unclarified experience of its own world. In other words, not only does the human not know about the animal open—it does not even know about its *own* open with sufficient clarity. The human understands the animal from the basis of its own misunderstood ground; or, rather, the human *misunderstands* the animal from the basis of its own misunderstood ground. When the human turns toward the animal in order to come to know it, it finds that it cannot do so; and this is owed to the fact that the human has yet to clarify the true character of its own world, its own open, its own truth, in which it remains unreflectively entangled.[29] (As we will see in greater and greater detail through the chapters that follow, the possibility of clarifying the character of the human depends foundationally upon such a turn toward the animal Other.)

However, despite lacking this knowledge of the animal's open, humans do have what Heidegger calls "a foundational experience [*Grunderfahrung*] of animality and life."[30] Heidegger uses the expression *Grunderfahrung* periodically throughout his corpus; and while it never becomes a rigidified technical term, it does serve a crucial role within the edifice of his thinking. A "foundational experience" is, as the name suggests, a kind of fundamental or basic exposure to beings that precedes conceptual formulation and makes the latter possible: it is an openness to beings in their everydayness that is, as he puts it in his lecture course *Basic Concepts of Aristotelian Philosophy*, "primarily not theoretical, but instead lies in the commerce [*Umgang*] of life with its world."[31] A foundational experience is thus a kind of interaction or intercourse with the world through which the concrete character (*Sachcharakter*) of things becomes accessible in the first place, and on the basis of which any further knowledge of those things can be developed and obtained. (One could say that it is the elementary exposure to beings that makes a return "to the things themselves" possible.) In his lecture course on Hölderlin's "Germania" from 1934 (to which we will return at length in chapter 4), Heidegger writes that "care" (*Sorge*) is "the fundamental experience of the essence of the historical Dasein of the human being that in the first instance demands to be named."[32] The human thus has an originary and pretheoretical exposure to animality and life, a foundational intercourse with animals in their animality: in a word, the human *cares* about them through a concern that belongs to its very ontological constitution.

And yet, this foundational experience is insufficient to give us *knowledge* of the animal. Rather, as Heidegger puts it, we are involved in "a great and profound detour [*Umweg*] to reach the animal":[33] thus, despite experiencing an originary going-into (*Umgang*) the animal that serves as the ground of our awareness of it, we are nonetheless on a profound detour (*Umweg*) to access the animal in its being. The path to the animal is a detour precisely because we are always compelled to begin from the human (and, indeed, from a misunderstanding of the essence of the human): the human intercedes itself between itself and the animal with which it is foundationally inter-connected or in fundamental intercourse. Seeking to determine the animal is thus "always a matter of *revoking or retracting* [*Zurucknehmen*] *from the human.*"[34] In seeking to understand the animal, one must revoke or retract, cancel out or negate, those elements belonging to the human (i.e., world, openness to truth, language, etc.) that would otherwise impose themselves upon the animal.[35] However, this retraction cannot be carried out in such a way that the animal would be seen *to lack* certain qualities that properly belong to the human. (Here one sees that expressions like "poor-in-world" cannot be comparative designations.) Rather, this retraction is undertaken so as to let the animal show itself, to the extent possible, on its own terms, unfiltered by the lens of human experience and (mis)understanding.

In light of this, Heidegger provides a five-step program of sorts by means of which the animal might be encountered in its own terms. How-ever, this program quickly shows itself as primarily a means by which to clarify the essence of the human *by way of* an encounter with—or a *detour* through—the animal. Moreover, what this program shows is that an engage-ment with the animal is instrumental in the process by which the human transforms itself into its own proper *Dasein*, thus taking on and bearing the greatest plight emphasized by Heidegger at the outset of the notebook. The five-step program is as follows:

1. Adequate gaze at the human—soul—body

2. From this (1), looking ahead to animal [*vorblickend auf Tier*]—life

3. The guiding wayposts of going backward, to and fro [*Hin- und Her-gehens*]

4. Therein the inversion of the throwing oneself adrift [*Sichlos-werfens*]

5. The positive element in the retrograde modes of determination[36]

The first step in this program is, as Heidegger writes, to obtain an "adequate gaze at the human—soul—body." The process begins, then, with an attempt to clarify the essence of the human: not, however, the human to come (i.e., *Dasein* in the full, futural sense) but rather the human as it is presently (i.e., entangled in the forgetfulness of being and its own designation as *animal rationale* and conceived of within the metaphysical dualism of soul and body).[37] Despite the fact that Heidegger's five-step program begins with the human, it would be a mistake to conclude that his thinking here remains (therefore) anthropocentric: for it is precisely against such anthropocentricity that Heidegger warns in his immediately preceding comment regarding the revoking of the human. It would also be a mistake to interpret Heidegger's starting point here as allotting a definitive anthropocentric *priority* to the human. This becomes clear with the second step: "From this (1), looking *ahead* to animal [*her vorblickend auf Tier*]—life." In a sense, the phrasing of "looking ahead" makes it sound as though the human comes first, only to be followed by the animal; however, the greater context of this step makes it clear that the inverse is in fact the case. Just before articulating his five steps, Heidegger writes that "although a fundamental experience [*Grunderfahrung*] of animality and life does hold good, we yet find ourselves involved in a great and profound detour to reach the animal."[38] Thus, *prior* to the initiation of this program—and thus prior to obtaining an adequate grasp of the human—we already have a foundational experience of the animal, a basic intercourse with animals that belongs to our very orientation toward the world. All of this points to a certain *priority* that is allotted to the animal here: the animal is always already there, in a certain sense, prior to us, standing on its own such that we can experience it (and misunderstand it). Looking out ahead toward the animal is thus, in a certain sense, *a looking back* through or beyond the contemporary misrepresentations of animal life. In this way, the animal—*as that to which we look ahead (vorblickend)*—stands *before* (*vor*) us, stands *in front* of us, having already come before.

After engaging in this looking-ahead that is a looking-back, the third step entails "the guiding wayposts of going backwards, to and fro."[39] Jaran interprets this "to and fro" as referring to the movement back and forth between the human and the animal, a kind of ongoing comparison between the two.[40] Although this is correct, the greater context of the notebook suggests that there is a further meaning at play here. The movement back intended by Heidegger is a movement back beyond the limitations of the contemporary understanding of animal life, human life, and their relation. Indeed, as the notebook makes clear, Heidegger's general project involves a movement back to the Greeks, back toward an inceptual understanding of being. (More precisely, the Greeks, having surpassed us in their greatness of questioning, are something to which we have yet to catch up.)[41] What is needed is a movement away from the entanglement in the contemporary forgetfulness of being and back toward a more authentic encounter with being(s); and, indeed, Heidegger even at one point claims that philosophy itself is nothing other than this movement backward.[42]

In any case, the result of this movement "to and fro" is, as the fourth step tells us, "the inversion of the throwing oneself adrift." Such throwing-adrift is to be understood as the manner in which the human is "jostled out of itself," pulled out of its entanglement in its contemporary, impoverished situation.[43] As the notebook as a whole makes clear, this ability to throw oneself adrift is unique to the human and accounts, in part, for its greatness.[44] In another section entitled "The Animal and the Human," Heidegger differentiates the human from the animal precisely in terms of this ability:

> The [human], as standing into being, has already very early prepared his throwing himself adrift—not first after a supposed conclusion of mammalian "development"—instead, this development is already a reversion of the basic form of humanity. If animals, and living beings in general, could "recognize"—they would never have a capacity to live. They would have been immobilized by beings and themselves determined as beings. Because this happened to humans, however, humans have not reached a goal or end—but instead possess a quite different task of world-formation and incorporation of the body in the (now for the first time appropriable) beings. In the throwing oneself adrift commences the projection—and in the projection as such—with it and not as a later result—commences the thrownness as manifestation of fearfulness. Thrown projection as opening up of the partitioning—empowerment of the essence.[45]

The ability to throw itself adrift onto the track toward the essence of being belongs essentially to the ontological constitution of the human, and it is only through throwing itself adrift that the human will reach the "there" of *Sein*, the "originary open spaciousness" and temporal unfolding of being.[46] Owing to this structure, the human has a world and can project itself forward from out of its factical thrownness. In other words, the human is not *determined*, but rather exists in an open, indeterminate relation to being. By contrast, the animal, being without world, can never be adrift but is instead firmly situated within itself and within the determination of its environment. Here again one *seemingly* finds a hierarchy wherein the animal is refused a capacity said to belong uniquely to the human, such as one *seemingly* finds in *The Fundamental Concepts of Metaphysics*.

However, there are two elements to this passage that disrupt any such apparent hierarchy. First, it is significant that it is the human, and not the animal, who is presented here in terms of a *deficit*. It is precisely because it *lacks* the kind of determinateness or completion characteristic of animal life that the human is able to form a world and project itself into the open of that world. "Having a world" is thus symptomatic of incompleteness and indeterminacy.[47] This is stated more explicitly by Heidegger in his lecture course *Logic as the Question concerning the Essence of Language*, where he, within a broader investigation into the temporal character of *Dasein*, claims that animals do not have a sense of time. However, according to Heidegger, "What is wonderful [*Wunderbare*] is not that animals have a sense of time, but that *without* a time-relationship they are in an entirely *immediate manner* [*unmittelbar*] tied into the general happening of nature and with this secure for themselves a certain field [*Feld*], a kind and way of being [*eine Art und Weise des Seins*] to which the human is not entitled [*nicht zusteht*]."[48] The human's experience of time, then—which is to say, its ecstatic experience of the openness of being—is understood by Heidegger as a deficiency of sorts, insofar as it is a *mediate* experience of the nature in relation to which animals are bound in immediacy.[49] The human stands outside of the sort of direct, entitled intimacy to nature to which the animal is, in its unique and wondrous way, open: and this standing-outside-of, this *ecstasis*, is nothing other than the human's experience of world. To be human is to *not* be entitled to the kind of immediate immersion in nature of which the animal is, by its very nature, capable.

Secondly, and more significantly, one recalls that the second step offered by Heidegger entails an engagement with the animal. Thus, an encounter with the animal is a preparatory step in pulling the human out of itself and casting itself adrift; and being cast adrift is a preparatory step toward the human's transition to its authentic *Dasein*. Said otherwise, although the human is uniquely capable of throwing itself adrift, it is only able to do so through *first* engaging with the animal. The animal, itself incapable of throwing itself adrift, is that without which the human would be unable to do so: in this way, the animal is the supplement without which the human could not otherwise come into its authentic relation to being. *Prior* to freeing itself from its entanglement in the contemporary forgetfulness of being (and all that entails), the human must engage with the animal. In other words, in order to get back on the track toward the essence of being, *the human must follow the animal*, the animal who (therefore) comes before.[50]

To cast all of this in somewhat different terms, one could say that the human must confront what is otherwise than human (i.e., animality) in order to break free of its entanglement in the contemporary self-understanding of humanity (i.e., as the rational animal) and thereby enter into its proper being.[51] Through this encounter, the *difference* between the human (as *Dasein*) and the animal announces itself. Moreover, and more crucially, through this difference another difference comes to light: namely, *the* difference, the ontological difference, the difference between beings and being. Through an engagement with the animal, the human's unique role as the *there* of being comes into greater clarity, thereby intensifying the human's express awareness of being itself. Thus, in order to remember being, and thus to free itself from its entanglement in its contemporary metaphysical (mis)understanding of itself, an encounter with the animal is needed: the animal comes before, and initiates, the human's commemoration of being. (The extent to which this is so will come into greater clarity in subsequent chapters.)

Thirdly, and finally, there is some suggestion that this process, in addition to clarifying the essence of the human, also clarifies the essence of the animal. This much is indicated by the fifth step of the program, which reads: "The positive element in the retrograde modes of determination."[52] The suggestion here seems to be that by moving backward away from our entanglement in our contemporary forgetfulness of being, an authentic experience of our own being *and* of animal being will be obtained. This much is clear, at least, much later in the text when Heidegger writes: "On the great detour over the abyss of beyng, beings—which are still only 'objects' or 'beings in themselves'—first again come to be, vibrant in beyng, vibrated by it."[53] The recollective movement toward authentic *Dasein* thus also entails entering into a more authentic relationship with animals as they are in their own right, freed from human (mis)understanding. In this way, the detour toward the animal, by freeing the human from its entanglement in its contemporary self-(mis)understanding, brings the human closer to its foundational experience of animality.

As we have seen, this detour with animality is a necessary step, for Heidegger, on the path toward the liberation of the human from its entanglement in the modern forgetfulness of being. In its pursuit of its own proper *Dasein*, the human must follow the animal, the animal that (therefore) comes before. At one point within the notebook, Heidegger casts this pursuit of human *Dasein* in terms of *hunting*:

> The human is to be *hunted throughout* [*hindurchjagen*] the entire foreignness and alienating character of the essence of being in all the essentiality of that essence.
>
> Need to effectuate both in one: the alienating character of the essence and the ineluctability of the essence.
>
> And this hunting up [*Aufjagen*] and never resting is simply "only" through a growing and pertinent disclosive questioning—the basic attunements in the view and the attitude, but never in words!
>
> To hunt up [*aufjagen*] into the (first) ineluctability.
>
> To hunt through [*hinddurchjagen*] the full foreignness.
>
> To hunt down [*erjagen*] the entire alone-ness of the human—and then commences the hunting [*die Jagd*] of the empowerment.[54]

The pursuit of the human's proper *Dasein* is thus cast here in terms of *jagen*, of *hunting, chasing,* or even *hounding* after something: and one cannot hear *jagen* without hearing a reference to the animal, to the hunting of and chasing after the animal Other. As we have seen, this hunting of the human's proper essence in fact entails an encounter with the animal, an engagement with the animal in its otherness in order to delimit the parameters proper to the human. In pursuing its own essence, the human *chases* after the animal as that in terms of which it will clarify its own essence. Owing to the pursuant character of the human's position vis-à-vis the animal, one sees a certain priority afforded to the animal here, in the sense that the human's proper self-determination follows after an encounter with the animal that (therefore) comes before.

As Heidegger goes on to suggest, this hunting of the human seeks precisely to leave the "human" behind, insofar as it seeks to escape the modern understanding of the human as the rational animal. What is desired is a casting-adrift of the "human" into otherness, into an unfamiliarity with itself whereby its essence once again becomes question-worthy. In a word, the human's hunting of its proper essence entails an *alienation* from itself, a movement whereby the human becomes other to itself: "In the midst of the forgottenness of beyng and the destruction of truth, it must not be expected that the leap into Da-sein would happen—and be intelligible—immediately.

On the contrary: the supreme alienation. Therefore, the task is to raise this alienation even more—but in such a way that in it at the same time bridges are slung for a taking hold of steadfastness."[55] The necessity pressing upon the human in the contemporary era is to cast itself adrift into alienation, to throw itself into a place of indeterminacy and uncertainty with respect to its own essence, and indeed so much so that the very "humanness" of the human disappears.[56] Only through such alienation can the human free itself from the strictures of the metaphysical understanding of the human as the rational animal and deliver itself over into a transformation of its *Dasein* whereby it opens itself for a genuine experience with what is *most* alien, namely, beyng itself.[57]

As we have seen, the encounter with the animal is structurally constitutive of this process of alienation whereby the human prepares itself for an entry into its own proper *Dasein*. Only through encountering the animal in its otherness—that is, in *its* foreign or alien character—can the human come to cast itself adrift into unfamiliarity, becoming alien to itself. The path toward alienation—an alienation that makes possible the journey away from the "human" and toward "Dasein," toward a steadfast standing within the truth of being—necessarily entails a confrontation with the animal Other whereby the latter is encountered in its difference. Thus, the track that the human must follow in order to get back on track is the track of the animal Other, a *detour* through the animal Other who (therefore) always comes before.

∽

Given the foundational role that animals play in the human's movement away from its entanglement in the contemporary forgetfulness of being toward the flourishing of its proper *Dasein*, it is perhaps not surprising that Heidegger's epigram to GA 94 itself gestures toward the animal. Just after offering his initials, Heidegger writes, in Greek, "Πάντα γάρ πολμητέον" (For all things must be ventured). These words are from Plato's *Theaetetus* (196d2) and are uttered by Socrates just prior to his famous proposal that memory can be understood as being analogous to an *aviary* in which wild birds are kept. Heidegger's notebook thus literally begins with a gesture toward an animal, toward a bird. In Heidegger's notebook, the animal *literally*, and *textually*, comes *first*.

With all of this in mind, we turn now to Heidegger's most notorious engagement with the question of the animal, namely, *The Fundamental*

Concepts of Metaphysics. What will be seen is that, despite the text's reputation for carrying out a certain denigration of the animal, it nonetheless gestures toward the absolute apriority of the animal Other within Heidegger's thinking.

Chapter Two

(Trans)position of the Human(imal)

"Is the animal happy?
Can the animal forget? (Can the stone die?)
The *joyful greeting* of the dog.
Its mournful malaise when left behind.
Human empathy?
Pets?
"*Eagle*"—dog.
Can the animal remain silent?
Critical question: What and how can we know about the animal?
It can communicate nothing to us.[1]
Thus: empathy—self-transposition [*Sichversetszen*].
How, on what basis, and how far?"

—Heidegger (GA 46:243/175)

When it comes to the question of the animal, *The Fundamental Concepts of Metaphysics* has been decisive. Delivered in 1929–1930, and first published in English in 1995, this lecture course remains the most frequently engaged text on Heidegger's treatment—or perceived *mis*treatment—of animality. It is also by far the most infamous. *The Fundamental Concepts of Metaphysics* remains almost universally panned and abhorred, at least when it comes to the three chapters in which Heidegger's sustained inquiry into animality is carried out, and especially when it comes to the thesis Heidegger puts forth therein that the animal, when viewed in comparison to the human, is "poor in world."[2] This thesis has been almost universally interpreted as denigrating the animal and as symbolizing a broader hierarchical structure, or rabid anthropomorphism, operative in Heidegger's understanding of animality.[3]

Although it is difficult to dispute the claim that Heidegger's position within *The Fundamental Concepts of Metaphysics* entails a withholding of the world, in the fullest sense, from the animal, scholars have largely overlooked the role that animals play for Heidegger in the constituting of the *human* world. More specifically, scant scholarly attention has been paid to the role that the animal—who is itself without world—plays in making the human's understanding of its own world possible. This role, as the present chapter shows, is structurally constitutive of the human's ability to grasp its own being and enter into its proper *Dasein* in an authentic way; moreover, such a role necessarily entails a certain (chrono)logical priority on the part of the animal Other.

Rather than offering an analysis of Heidegger's engagement with animality in *The Fundamental Concepts of Metaphysics* in its entirety—work that has been more than adequately carried out by various other scholars[4]—attention will primarily be paid to the manner in which Heidegger's inquiry into animality therein is expressly undertaken for the sake of bringing about a transformation in the human's understanding (and enactment) of its own *Dasein*.[5] More precisely, the present chapter is an attempt to read *The Fundamental Concepts of Metaphysics* as an articulation of the manner by which the human, precisely *as* human, remains fundamentally and foundationally *exposed* to the animal and how such exposure is constitutive of human existence (in the fullest, Heideggerian sense). Such exposure will be seen to bespeak a decisive sense in which the animal, within this text and within Heidegger's work as a whole, appreciates a certain *priority* over the human insofar as it serves as the ground of the latter's ability to grasp its own proper essence. Ultimately, *The Fundamental Concepts of Metaphysics* attests, in the strongest possible terms, to the *primacy* of the human's engagement with the animal and to the *priority* that the animal occupies in Heidegger's thought. In this way, one can understand *The Fundamental Concept of Metaphysics* as carrying out the five-step program articulated by Heidegger in his "Black Notebook" analyzed in the previous chapter. One can also understand it as prefiguring the same sort of encounter with animals that Derrida will describe in his *The Animal That Therefore I Am*,[6] an encounter that Derrida intended as a corrective to Heidegger's understanding of animality, and one in which the animal occupies a place of privileged priority.

In order to see how all of this is the case, it is hermeneutically useful to compare the analysis undertaken in *The Fundamental Concepts of Metaphysics* with other of Heidegger's engagements with the question of the animal from the 1920s. To this end, two texts with which *The Fundamental Concepts of Metaphysics* shares an essential affinity will first be analyzed: namely, Heidegger's 1924 lecture course *Basic Concepts of Aristotelian Philosophy* (GA 18) and his 1927 *Being and Time* (GA 2). Despite their many differences, all three of these texts demonstrate, to varying degrees, a certain ontological priority belonging to the animal within Heidegger's thought, even—or perhaps *especially*—at those moments when he seeks to set the human apart from the animal. In short, in all three texts the animal serves as that in reference to which a determination of human *Dasein* becomes possible, and in this way serves as the very ground of an adequate understanding of human being.

Basic Concepts of Aristotelian Philosophy

During the summer semester of 1924, Heidegger delivered a lecture course in Marburg primarily devoted to offering a close reading of Aristotle's work on rhetoric. What is most remarkable about this text, given the parameters of the present inquiry, is the extent to which Heidegger's investigation of animality therein seemingly differs from that carried out in *The Fundamental Concepts of Metaphysics* five years later or, indeed, from any other investigation within his corpus. As Cykowski has noted in her comprehensive and insightful book *Heidegger's Metaphysical Abyss*, unlike the Heidegger of the 1929–1930 *The Fundamental Concepts of Metaphysics*, the Heidegger of 1924 is "far more inclined in this earlier work to bring the animal into a close proximity to the human."[7] She further adds that "there is evidence in this text of a concern for life and animality that places the human and the animal more assuredly on what appears to be an ontological, not just an ontical, continuum."[8] In other words, unlike *The Fundamental Concepts of Metaphysics*, in which Heidegger speculates (as he will also do in his "Letter on Humanism" twenty-two years later) that the animal is separated from the human "by an abyss,"[9] *Basic Concepts of Aristotelian Philosophy* thinks the animal and human in intimate proximity, close to one another, as gradient forms of *life*.

Cykowski is verifiably correct in emphasizing the crucial differences between these two texts. However, despite these important differences, the two texts share a common structural feature: namely, both explicitly stage and carry out a *comparative analysis* of the animal and the human. (We will say much more about such "comparative analysis" when we turn to *The*

Fundamental Concepts of Metaphysics below.) More importantly, both texts, as will be seen through the following reading, point to, or at least rely upon, a certain structural priority that belongs to the animal. By comparing the two comparative analyses carried out by Heidegger in 1924 and 1929–1930 respectively, we will see that there is a certain temporal and logical priority granted to animals in both texts, insofar as animals are that to which the human must turn in order to set itself apart in distinction. Moreover, because such a detour toward the animal is constitutive of the human's very *being*, the animal will also be seen to have an *ontological* priority over the human.

One sees this priority in the 1924 lectures course almost immediately as Heidegger begins his analysis of animality. While seeking to clarify the meaning of οὐσία (i.e., the being of beings) for Aristotle, Heidegger offers the following:

> [Aristotle] designates the ὑποκείμενον as the first being-character. Beings like animals, plants, humans, mountains, and the sun are such that they already "lie there," "in advance" [*im vorhinein*], ὑπό. When I speak about them, express something about an animal, describe a plant; that about which I speak, the discussed, what I have there in speaking, is in such a way that it is at hand [*vorhanden*], already lying there in advance [*im vorhinein schon daliegend*]. The being of beings has the character of being-at-hand [*Vorhandenseins*].[10]

Beings like animals, plants, humans, mountains, and the sun—in other words, natural beings—are such as to always already be there *in advance*. By the time the human experiences them, these beings have already been there, waiting upon the human's engagement. With regard to human experience, then, the animal is characterized by a temporal and logical priority, an apriority that Heidegger captures here with the expression "being-at-hand" (*Vorhandenseins*).[11] Heidegger's understanding of *Vorhandensein* in this text thus differs from his employment of the term three years later in *Being and Time*, where the *vorhanden* character of beings will become secondary to, and derivative of, the manner in which beings are *zuhanden*, or "available."[12] Here, the *vorhanden* character of beings—their bare presence-at-hand—refers to their primitive self-showing within the open of being: that is, it refers to the very *beingness* of those beings in its most immediate manifestation.[13]

Heidegger then goes into greater detail regarding the "being-at-hand" character of these entities:

Ὑποκείμενον, "being-at-hand," the "at-hand-ness" of something. This being-character is connected with being in the sense of the customary meaning. It means what is there not only as being-there [*daseiend*], but it also means what is there in the sense of that upon which the estate rests, for example, land, earth, sky, nature, trees, what is at hand in the sense of the beings with which concrete life scrapes out its existence [*Dasein*].[14] Οὐσία—thus at-hand-ness [*Vorhandenheit*], without I myself needing to do anything vis-à-vis the being of these beings that are there.[15]

Animals (alongside land, plants, trees, etc.) are "at hand" in the sense of always already being there, and indeed being there as the basis or ground of the human's further dealings.[16] The possibility of apophantic discourse depends upon this prior availability of beings, an "already lying there in advance" of beings within the open of human experience. Thus, prior to any theoretical (or even practical) determination about the ontological status or structure of an animal, the animal is always already there in advance, "at hand" within the sphere of human *Dasein*.[17] To put this rather coarsely: before an animal can be used for food or labor or companionship—indeed, before it can be related to in any way whatsoever—it has to *be there, be present, be at hand* within the open of human experience.[18]

In passing, one should note the manner in which the above passage, written by Heidegger in 1924, arguably anticipates the language of the *fourfold* that he will employ decades later. Heidegger has stated that ὑπο-κείμενον for Aristotle means "what is there in the sense of that upon which the estate rests, for example, land, earth, sky, nature, trees, what is at hand in the sense of the beings with which concrete life scrapes out its existence [*worin das konkrete Leben sein Dasein fristet*]." This underlying *thereness* of beings—οὐσία in the full sense—constitutes the open of the world in which living beings eke out or support (*fristet*) their basic being-there, their basic *Dasein*.[19] Earth and sky, land and trees, nature in the broad sense: this is the open in which the life of living beings unfolds. This formulation prefigures the language of earth and sky, mortals and divinities, that Heidegger will later utilize to describe the unfolding of world. (We will return to the fourfold in subsequent chapters, and at length in chapter 6.)

In any event, the animal, as presencing within the world, is characterized principally by this bare being-at-handness. However, as a *living* being, the animal is more than simply "at hand" in this way. As Heidegger writes:

> Ζωή [i.e., life] is a *concept of being* [*Seinsbegriff*]: "life" refers to a
> *mode* of being, indeed a mode of *being-in-a-world* [*Sein-in-einer-*
> *Welt*]. A living thing is not simply at hand [*einfach vorhanden*],
> but is in a world in that it has its world [*in einer Welt, in der*
> *Weise, dass es seine Welt hat*]. An animal is not simply moving
> down the road, pushed along by some mechanism. It is in the
> world in the sense of having it [*es is in der Welt in der Weise*
> *des Sie-habens*].[20]

The animal, as living, *is* in such a way as to be in the world and *to have*
this world:[21] one notes in passing how seemingly far the Heidegger of 1924
is from the Heidegger of *The Fundamental Concepts of Metaphysics* five years
later, who will suggest that animals are "world-poor." For the Heidegger
of 1924, animals have a world—they are "being in the world"—and such
having of a world is conditioned upon the bare presence, the raw *Dasein*,
of the animal from out of which it can relate to the world.

In his 1926 Marburg lecture course *The Basic Concepts of Ancient*
Philosophy (offered a year before *Being and Time* was published), the world
of the animal finds what is perhaps its most stunning articulation, given
Heidegger's many later comments about the animal's impoverished relation
to its world:

> Understanding [*Verstehen*] belongs to the mode of Being of
> human *Dasein*, and in a certain way [*in gewissem Sinne*] it also
> belongs to the mode of being of animals. To say that some-
> thing is understood means that it is manifest in its being such
> and such [*in seinem Sosein offenbar*]; it is no longer concealed.
> In understanding, there resides something like truth, ἀλήθεια,
> which is unconcealed, not covered over, but, on the contrary,
> uncovered. Insofar as understanding belongs to a being, *insofar*
> *as it is alive at all*, that being is disclosive; with its being, as
> one characterized by understanding, other beings are uncovered
> in their Being. *Everything that is alive, to the extent that it exists,*
> *has a world*, which does not hold for what is not alive. Every
> living being is oriented to something, pursues it, avoids it, etc.
> To be sure, that may happen indeterminately. Thus, we can
> comprehend protozoa and other forms of life only indirectly,
> in analogy with ourselves. By the very fact that a living being
> discloses a world, the being of this being is also disclosed to it.

> It knows about itself, even if only in the dullest [*dumpfesten*]
> way and in the broadest sense. Along with the disclosure of the
> world, it is disclosed to itself. Indeed, this already goes essentially
> beyond Aristotle, but it is necessary for understanding him.[22]

Thus, not only does the animal (in 1926) have a world for Heidegger, but that world is characterized by *understanding*, by "something like truth," something, therefore, analogous to ἀλήθεια understood as the clearing of being—even if, he goes on to suggest, such a clearing may be duller or dimmer for some animals. At this stage in Heidegger's thinking—a thinking that, as Heidegger says, goes beyond Aristotle's understanding of the animal—the animal stands "in a certain way" in the open clearing of being, and in such a way as to relate to itself within that open.[23]

Back in the 1924 course on Aristotle, Heidegger proceeds to say more regarding this world that the living being (i.e., the animal broadly conceived) has. In order to dispel the notion that this world is somehow specific or idiosyncratic to the animal alone, Heidegger writes the following:

> It is also incorrect to speak of a "world of animals" and a "world
> of human beings." The issue is not modes of apprehending
> actuality according to definite points of view; rather the issue is
> being-in-the-world. Thus, since the world is encountered through
> a definite disposition [*Befindlichkeit*] of living things, animals and
> human beings are in their world [*in seiner Welt*]. The relatedness
> of animals to the world is precisely that which brings animals
> in their being genuinely into being-there [*Dasein*].[24]

Humans and animals, as living, are in the world, and are indeed *with one another* within that world. In other words, it is *one and the same* world that the human and the animal inhabit, although they do so in unique ways: "Life is a being-in-a-world. Animals and humans are not at hand next to one another, but are with one another."[25] The animal and human are both open to the same world, a world that they share from the standpoints of their own (dis)positions (*Befindlichkeit*), their own affectivities:[26] "All modes of living are characterized by the fact that, here, the mode of being is a matter of finding-oneself in the mode of being-in-a disposition-and-bringing-oneself-therein."[27] To put this a little differently, neither Heidegger nor Aristotle are making the world dependent upon an entity's apprehension or, even less, that entity's "subjective" experience: rather, they are both underscoring the manner in which all apprehension and experience depends upon a prior openness of (and to) the world, a (dis)position within it, a *being in it* on the basis of which things can matter to a being.[28] To say it very simply: there is only *one* world,[29] *the* world, the one and only world shared, in some manner, by all living beings from out of the specificity of their own (dis)positions within that one world. It is here, at the level of the mere life of all living beings, where human and animal *Dasein* meet at an originary site: a meeting that occurs temporally prior to the human's authentic relation to itself and is structurally constitutive of that relation.

This sharing of the world is implicit in Aristotle's discussion of the animal as already being *political* in a certain sense. As Heidegger writes:

> In this context, he [i.e., Aristotle] has recourse to the being of animals, and posits the ζῷον λόγον ἔχον *as compared with* a ζῷον that has only φωνή. He endeavors to show that life is already constituted through φωνή; that, furthermore, what is living in this way has a being that is fundamentally determined as being-with-one-another [*Miteinandersein*]; and that animals are already, in a certain way, ζῷα πολιτικά. Human beings are only μᾶλλον ζῷον πολιτικόν [i.e., are more of a political animal] than are, e.g., bees. By virtue of this demarcation from the being of animals, constituted through φωνή, the peculiar way of being that is determined by λόγος will become more precisely characterized.[30]

Living beings—including the human—are thus always already with one another in a community of φωνή, a shared world of significance; and the fact that humans are *more* with one another owing to λόγος further emphasizes the foundational connectivity (or being-with) of all living beings as such. This being-together of humans and living beings is expressly emphasized by Heidegger during his discussion of αἴσθησις which, for Aristotle, is shared by both humans and animals:

> Αἴσθησις is not to be translated as "sensation," for it simply means the "perceiving" [*Vernehmen*] of the world, the mode of having-it-there [*die Weise des Sie-Dahabens*]. The possibility of the extent to which the world matters to a being depends on this peculiar disclosedness. This disclosedness [*Erschlossenheit*] of the

life of animals (i.e., the mode of cultivation, of cultivatedness, and manifestation of this disclosedness) is, for animals, characterized through φωνή, and for human beings through λόγος. For Aristotle, the disclosedness of the being of the world has its genuine basic possibility in λόγος, in the sense that, in λόγος, what is living-in-a-world appropriates the world, has it there, and genuinely is and moves in this having-it-there.[31]

Αἴσθησις is the manner of having a world, of *being in it* in such a way as to have it disclosed to oneself, that is characteristic of *both* human and animal life. Prior, then, to the differentiation between animals and humans along the axis of φωνή and λόγος there is a world shared in αἴσθησις. *Disclosure* of this world for the animal—that is, *by* the animal and *for* the animal—takes place in φωνή, while disclosure of the world by the human—that is, *by* the human and *for* the human—takes place through λόγος. But beneath this difference lies a shared world that humans and animals inhabit together at the level of having it. Such is made clear by Heidegger with the following: "In the being of the animal [*Beim Sein der Tiere*] as being-in-the-world, we observe αἴσθησις. Animals perceive the world within definite limits; they are in the world in such a way that they have the surrounding world [*Umwelt*] there; they have a definite orientation in it. Therefore, this being-oriented in the world, this somehow-having-it explicitly-there, is not proper to human beings as such."[32] Within the parameters of the 1924 lecture course, *all* living beings *as such* are in the world, oriented within it, each from out of its own (dis)position: and having a *surrounding world* (or *environment*: *Umwelt*) is a *modification* of such being-in-the-world.[33]

For the purposes of the present study, what is most significant is the way in which such a shared world, as shown above, entails a prior presencing and availability of animals (their "at-handness") with respect to human experience. Indeed, as Krell writes, the very notion of (dis)position, of *Befindlichkeit*, seems to entail such a priority of the Other:

Yet if one considers *Befindlichkeit*, the "how we find ourselves to be" of Dasein, is it conceivable without the presence of other animals? That presence would not have to do with "knowing the world," which in any case is a "founded" mode; it would have to do with the more affective aspect of, or access to, the world. This is readily understood by any Dasein that during its adolescent years has had the privilege of being close to an animal and of having had its first and probably most successful psychoanalysis with that animal.[34]

The human always already has "access" to the other beings that arise within the world, the beings that are always already *there*.[35] Heidegger himself seems to verify as much when he, much later on in the lecture course, offers the following:

> Earlier, we pointed out that there are given in the world itself beings with which we have to do, but also human beings, in the sense that we directly experience, that this one appearing lives in a world. The being-at-hand of a living thing is a being-in-the-world of the living thing. I am myself something that appears in the world, that occupies itself with something—we can also say of an animal that it flees from a threat, and so on. Beings with the character of living are at hand in the world, and this is at the same time a way of being in-the-world.[36]

All living beings, as (dis)posed in the world, are open to and receptive of the others within that world: indeed, such receptivity, such openness to the Other, is nothing other than *life* properly understood. And even though the *kind* of living characteristic of the human will come to be further distinguished within the lecture course as *existence*,[37] it nonetheless remains primarily characterized by a foundational openness to the beings it encounters in the world, beings who are (therefore) always already there within the (same) world *prior* to the human's apprehension of them.

With all of this in mind, we now turn to Heidegger's *Being and Time*. Despite certain seismic shifts in Heidegger's approach to animality therein, we will nonetheless see a decisive sense in which the animal maintains a certain priority with respect to human experience and thus with respect to the human's understanding of its own *Dasein*.

Being and Time

Heidegger's engagement with animality in *Being and Time*, first published in 1927, is by no means as extensive as what he offered in the 1924 course on Aristotle.[38] Also paling in comparison to the elongated and sustained inquiry carried out in *The Fundamental Concepts of Metaphysics*, to which we will eventually turn, *Being and Time* mentions animals only a few scattered times, and never deals with the question of the animal thematically or in detail.

Nonetheless, animals are in the background of *Being and Time*, serving as a silent ground out of which the existential analytic of *Dasein* is carried out. Although this is arguably the case throughout the book, insofar as the entire existential analytic is to some extent an attempt to differentiate *Dasein* from a (merely) living being and from the metaphysical determination of the human as *animal rationale*, it is most visible during Heidegger's inquiry into *death*. Heidegger turns to the question of death in an effort to resolve the problem of gaining access to *Dasein* in its entirety. Because *Dasein* is always underway—that is, because a human life, so long as it is being lived, remains unfinished—the entirety of *Dasein* evades any attempt to analyze its ontological structure as a whole.[39] The event(uality) of death, in its existential sense, provides a means by which *Dasein* as a whole can be considered. It also reveals, as we will see, the extent to which animals contribute to *Dasein's* project of grasping its own genuine being.

Heidegger begins his analysis of death by considering the death of *others*. Precisely because the transition from being-there to no-longer-being-there (i.e., death) is not experienceable by any individual *Dasein* itself—since the moment one *would* experience one's own death would be the very moment that one ceased to experience anything at all—the death of others is "all the more penetrating" (*eindringlicher*) to us at an experiential level.[40] Because, unlike our own death, the death of the other is experienceable, it penetrates (*eindringlich*) us in a way that our own death cannot: it is powerful, forceful, even *haunting*.[41] It is because we are *with* others in an essential way that their deaths can affect us so; and it is *only* through the death of others that we are given an experience (*Erfahrung*) of death: for my own death, as obliterating my ability to experience *anything*, is not experienceable (for me).

Owing to all of this, it is *from* the Other that I come to know death: not my *own* death, which is ultimately unknowable (for me) as an event, nor what the death of the other was like *for* them (on the "inside," we might say), which also remains beyond the horizon of my experience,[42] but death as an *occurrence*, death in the abstract, so to speak, although it is always tied to the death of a particular being.[43] It is with the death of others that death becomes a matter of concern for me, something about which I am aware and, therefore, about which I *care*.[44] Simply put, if it were not for the death of the Other—a death that penetrates me through and through, haunting me after the fact—I would know nothing of death, having never experienced it in any way. *Only* through the death of the Other does death become an "object" for me.[45]

Crucially, it is not only the death of other *humans* that can penetrate us in this way, giving us an experience of the event of death—it is also, as Heidegger writes, the death of *any living being*: "In the dying [*Sterben*] of others, that remarkable phenomenon of being [*Seinsphänomen*] can be experienced that can be defined as the transition of a being from the kind of being of Da-sein (*or, rather, of life*) to no-longer-being-there. The *end* of the being qua Dasein is the *beginning* of this being qua something objectively present."[46] In the parentheses following the word "Dasein" in the above passage, Heidegger writes: "bzw. des Lebens" (or, rather, of life). This serves to broaden the scope of his claim to include not just the human, *but anything that was alive*. In other words, the possibility of passing to a state of no-longer-being-there belongs to being-there in general, that is, *to life as such*, to "the animal" in the broadest sense (i.e., that which is animate). It is thus not only the deaths of other humans that can penetrate and haunt us and allow us to experience death: rather, it is the death of *any* living being, any animal whatsoever, from a puppy to a grasshopper to a houseplant. To say it most directly: it is death in any of its "objective" forms (and the quotation marks are Heidegger's) that presses upon us, perturbing and disturbing us.[47]

Despite this penetrating, perturbing quality that belongs to the death of any living being, to death as an object within our experience, it is ultimately insufficient to provide Heidegger with his sought-after existential meaning of death. This is owing ultimately to the *nontransferability* of death, that is, to the manner in which each individual *Dasein* must come to stand in relation to its *own* death (and indeed in such a manner that, through such standing, that human *becomes* individualized). It is also owing to the fact that, regardless of the extent to which we are affected by the deaths of others—regardless, that is, of how heavily such a death presses upon us or haunts us—such a death is only ever seen from the *outside*: "We do not experience the dying of others in a genuine sense."[48] Those who experience the death of another, and who therefore *survive* the death of that other, necessarily remain *outside* of the death—which is to say, the *dying*—of that other. The *dying* of the Other—what their death is like for them, on the inside—is utterly foreclosed to any other *Dasein*; and while each of us may experience the death of others, none of us can experience that other's *own* experience of death. This would be equally true, it seems, for the coming-to-an-end of animals, of living beings in general, though this does not stop Heidegger from (in)famously stating in *Being and Time* that animals "do not die" but only "perish."[49] Even the (mere) perishing of the animal—or, perhaps *especially* such perishing—remains inaccessible to the *Dasein* who watches such perishing occur, surviving and outliving it.

Nonetheless, what all of this reveals is that the death of others, although insufficient to give the human insight into the character of its *own* dying, is nonetheless structurally instrumental to that end. The human's grasp of its own death *follows upon* and *comes after* its exposure to the death of other living beings. It is precisely in experiencing the death of the Other that I become aware of the inaccessibility of their dying *for me*, and subsequently become aware of the inaccessibility of my own death as an experienceable phenomenon. To put it a bit differently, one could say that, before one can come to terms with one's own death, one must *fail* to grasp the death of the Other. The inadequacy of the other's death with respect to one's project of coming to relate genuinely toward one's *own* death is a structural necessity within that very project. Said simply, the death of the Other is the *detour* through and beyond which one must move in order to grasp one's own dying properly.

But this means that one's understanding of one's own death *begins* with the death of the Other: the death of the Other (already) appreciates a certain priority within Heidegger's thinking, as it will come to have in, for example, the work of Derrida and Levinas.[50] Thus, while the death of others is *ultimately* unable to provide Heidegger with a suitable articulation of the existential character of death, there is nonetheless an undeniable *temporal* and *logical* priority that belongs to the death of others within the horizon of one's experience. It is from the Other that one, initially and for the most part, experiences death, where one becomes aware of it, where one learns of it. Prior to coming into an authentic relation to its own death, a human is exposed to the deaths of other living beings: and that human *needs* this exposure in order to make progress toward its own authentic being-toward-death. In this way, the death of the Other—which is to say, the death of other *living beings*, other *animals* in the broadest sense—is that without which the human cannot come into an authentic being-toward-death: it is the necessary detour through which the human *must* pass in order to enter into its own authentic essence. (We will see this precise structure again in chapter 4 when we analyze Heidegger's reading of Hölderlin's "Der Ister" from 1942.)

It is thus only in comparison with the deaths of those living beings that are *not* human that we come to differentiate the character of the being-toward-death peculiar to human *Dasein*. Heidegger makes this clear when he writes, "[I]t is evident that in our characterization of the transition from

Da-sein to no-longer-being-there as no-longer-being-in-the-world that the going-out-of-the-world of Da-sein in the sense of dying *must be distinguished [unterschieden werden muss]* from a going-out-of-the-world of what is only alive. The ending of what is only alive we formulate terminologically as perishing. The distinction can become visible only by distinguishing the ending characteristic of Da-sein from the ending of a living thing."[51] In other words, it is only by *comparing* the manner of ending characteristic of *Dasein* with (merely) living beings that the former will come into clarity within its proper aspect. Heidegger soon makes this expressly clear: "In order to thus be able, *by comparison [vergleichend]*, to define the *being of the not-yet of the character of Dasein*, we must reflect on beings to whose kind of being becoming [*das Werden*] belongs."[52] We thus see, in *Being and Time*, the same sort of "comparative analysis" that we saw carried out in *Basic Concepts of Aristotelian Philosophy* and that Heidegger will famously carry out in *The Fundamental Concepts of Metaphysics*. The living being—that is, the animal broadly conceived—is that to which the human must turn and compare itself in order to clarify the character of its own being (and, *a fortiori*, its own dying).

Dasein thus enters into the project of knowing its own death only on the basis of the death of other living beings. Although the death of the living being, be it animal or human, can give the human no insight into the experience of its *own* eventual death (i.e., its *internal* character, so to speak), it nonetheless serves as that in reference to which and on account of which the human can come to clarify the character of its own dying. The coming-to-an-end of animals is thus structurally constitutive of the human's own experience of its own death.

But this requires, as was seen in the 1924 lecture course, that the living being, as being-at-hand, is always already *there* as that to which the human can compare itself.[53] The living Other, the animal in the broadest sense, is always already there *before* one can grasp one's proper being-toward-death (and therefore one's genuine *Dasein*). Here too, then, there is an absolute priority allotted by Heidegger to the living being, to the animal, to whom the human must turn in order to clarify its own being.

One further element of Heidegger's analysis of death within *Being and Time* requires mention. In the above passage, Heidegger gestures to the manner in which living beings, so long as they are living, are living in the *world*. As he phrased it above, "the going-out-of-the-world [*das Aus-der-Welt-gehen*] of Da-sein in the sense of dying must be distinguished from a going-out-of-the-world [*Aus-der-Welt-gehen*] of what is only alive." But in order for the living being to depart from the world, *it must be in the world in the first place*. Heidegger makes all of this clear when he writes:

> In the broadest sense, death is a phenomenon of life. Life must be understood as a kind of being [*Seinsart*] to which there belongs a being-in-the-world [*ein In-der-Welt-sein*]. Dasein, too, can be considered as pure life [*pures Leben*]. For the biological and physiological line of questioning, it then moves into the sphere of being which we know as the world of animals and plants [*Tier- und Pflanzenwelt*]. In this field, dates and statistics about the life-span of plants, animals, and human beings can be ontically ascertained. Connections between the life-span, reproduction, and growth can be known. The "kinds" of death [*Todes*], the causes, "arrangements," and ways of occurrence can be investigated.[54]

Life is thus a way of being-in-the-world, a way to be distinguished from the sort of bare being-present that characterizes inanimate beings. To such life, *in all of its forms*, there belongs death as a going-out-of-the-world, albeit by way of a manner of departure that differs from the manner characteristic of human *Dasein*. Interestingly, in a later edition of *Being and Time*, Heidegger adds the following note after the word "life" (*Leben*) at the beginning of the second sentence above: "If we are talking about human life, otherwise not—'world.'" This annotation is meant to suggest that only if the life in question is *human* life can it be said to entail a being-in-the-world. However, despite this later attempt on Heidegger's part to restrict being-in-the-world solely to *human* life, the remainder of the paragraph makes it clear that when he prepared the text for the first edition he meant life *in general*, life *as such*, and not only human life. (Moreover, we saw above that the Heidegger of 1924 and 1926 thought of life as being-in-the-world.) For the Heidegger of 1927, *all* living beings as such are in the world in a certain fundamental sense.

As we saw in the 1924 lecture course, this world is one and the same for humans and animals: all living beings inhabit the same world, albeit from sometimes radically (or even abyssally) different (dis)positions. Regarding the manner of the *departing* that characterizes living beings, it is important to note that it is not "its" world that the living being leaves—that is, it is not some idiosyncratic animal-or-plant world, hermetically separate from the world of *Dasein*, that is left behind. Rather, it is *the* world, *die Welt*, the one and only world that all living beings occupy: both the human and (merely) living beings leave the same world when they reach their end, though they leave that world in different ways. There is thus a foundational belonging together, a primitive *Mitsein*, of the human and other living beings (i.e., the animal broadly conceived) within one and the same world, to the extent that they are all alive.

This is perhaps made clear within *Being and Time* when Heidegger talks about the way in which *Dasein*'s being-with others extends even beyond their death. Even after a human reaches its end, those remaining behind still share a world with the deceased: "In lingering together with him in mourning and commemorating, those remaining behind *are with him*, in a mode of concern that honors him."[55] Regarding the character of this being-with, Heidegger writes: "In such being-with with the dead, the deceased *himself* is no longer factically 'there.' However, being-with always means being-with-one-another in the same world [*in derselben Welt*]. The deceased has abandoned our 'world' [*unsere "Welt"*] and left it behind. It is *in terms of this world* that those remaining can still *be with him*."[56] Since death, for the Heidegger of 1927, is the transition of being-there to no-longer-being-there characteristic of living beings as such and not just humans, one assumes that this remaining *with* the dead would apply no less to the case of animals. When an animal perishes—a perishing that, for Heidegger, falls short of the sort of *dying* of which the human is capable—a human can still *be with it*, can still share a world with that animal. In short, the human can *mourn* the coming-to-an-end of an animal, even if, for Heidegger, animals themselves cannot mourn. (We will return to the question of animal mourning in chapter 4.) One sees, then, that although the extent of the being-together of animals and humans has diminished considerably from the more robust form one finds in *Basic Concepts of Aristotelian Philosophy*, there nonetheless remains in *Being and Time* a foundational being-with of humans and animals that makes up the (shared) world of which they are a part.

We have now seen the way in which both *Basic Concepts of Aristotelian Philosophy* and *Being and Time* point to a certain priority that belongs to the animal. With this in mind, we turn finally to Heidegger's 1929–1930 lecture course *The Fundamental Concepts of Metaphysics*, in which Heidegger carries out his most sustained engagement with the question of the animal. What will be seen is that, despite the many ways in which this text differs from the two already analyzed, it nonetheless continues to demonstrate a decisive apriority that belongs to the animal Other.

The Fundamental Concepts of Metaphysics

In order to grasp Heidegger's analysis of the animal within this text, and the structural priority that belongs to it, it is first necessary to grasp the broader context of the lecture course. As Cykowski has emphasized, Heidegger's inquiry into animality takes place within the larger question regarding the possibility and parameters of metaphysical inquiry. Unlike nearly all other scholars, Cykowski spends significant time focusing on the broader metaphysical, philosophical, and scientific context in which the inquiry into animality occurs, ultimately showing that Heidegger's more controversial claims—for example, "the animal is world-poor"—are part of a larger philosophical interrogation of the human and its relation to the world.

As Cykowski also rightly emphasizes, Heidegger's aim within the lecture course is "to recover the Greek understanding of the human as a kind of rupture in φύσις"[57] and, more generally, to reawaken the forms of primordial knowing that characterized ancient Greek thought.[58] In this way, *The Fundamental Concepts of Metaphysics* belongs squarely within Heidegger's larger project—most explicitly defined in his work on Hölderlin from the 1930s and 1940s, but operative throughout his career, from his lectures on Aristotle in the 1920s to his 1943 lectures on Heraclitus—of bringing Germany into a meaningful encounter, an *Auseinandersetzung*, with the ancient Greek world. Such a project is primarily concerned with bringing about a transformation of the understanding of the human and *enacting* that understanding at the level of human *Dasein*.[59]

When one reads *The Fundamental Concepts of Metaphysics*, one must be careful to note Heidegger's extreme hesitancy, trepidation, and even befuddlement as he carries out his inquiry into animality (and the "life" in terms of which it is to be thought).[60] The text is punctuated by articulations of this confusion; and, as it turns out, such trepidation is essential to Heidegger's overall engagement with the animal and the broader philosophical inquiry in which that engagement takes place. In light of the program articulated in the "Black Notebook" analyzed in the previous chapter, one can see such trepidation as characteristic of the "throwing oneself adrift" that takes place through an engagement with animality. *The Fundamental Concepts of Metaphysics* stages an encounter with the animal for the sake of casting the human out of its bondage to its contemporary understanding of itself, its relation to other beings (and to being itself), and to animals in particular.

Such a casting out is one step on the track toward a transformation of the human's understanding of its own essence.

Heidegger begins the lecture course by emphasizing the befuddlement that characterizes proper metaphysical inquiry, an inquiry that is intimately connected to the possibility of the human coming to grasp its own essence:

> [H]ow and to where can metaphysics as philosophizing, as our own human activity, withdraw from us, if we ourselves are, after all, human beings? Yet do we in fact know what we ourselves are? *What is the human?* The crown of creation or some wayward path [*ein Irrweg*], some great misunderstanding and an abyss? If we know so little about the human, how can our essence not be alien to us? How can philosophizing as a human activity fail to conceal itself from us in the obscurity of this essence?[61]

This passage bespeaks a great confusion regarding the precise character of the human, an ignorance regarding its identity. The inquiry thus begins by emphasizing the way in which the human remains far from possessing an adequate self-understanding—so far, indeed, that its very own essence remains *alien* (*fremd*) to it. One notes in passing a certain symmetry between Heidegger's questioning here—"Do we in fact now what we ourselves are? What is the human?"—and the beginning of the "Black Notebook" analyzed in the previous chapter, where Heidegger posed the fundamental (and fundamentally alienating) question, "Who are we?"

Drawing on Novalis, Heidegger then casts this fundamental confusion in terms of *homesickness* (*Heimweh*). Because the human is *not* at home everywhere—that is, because the human does not grasp all things innately—it longs to reach out and understand them in their totality: that is, it longs to come to be at home in the *world*, and the name of this longing to be at home in the world is "philosophy."[62] As the originary attunement of human being, this homesickness motivates, as Cykowski puts it, "all of our attempts to seek out or create stability for ourselves."[63] The very being of the human consists of this homesickness, a restless urge to come to be at home in being.[64] (We will return at length to this homesickness in chapter 4.)

Heidegger again underscores the disorientation of the human just before embarking on his consideration of animality. Emphasizing the underlying question of the inquiry—namely, "What is world?"—Heidegger immediately remarks upon the complexity of pursuing an answer: "Even now we tend to take this explicit question as a free-floating question asked along the way just like any other. Initially we do not know where we should look for an answer to it. Indeed, if we consider the matter more closely, we do not even know what we are asking about, or in what direction our questioning is moving."[65] In other words, although *world* is essential to the very essence of the human, initial reflection on its structure leads to a befuddlement so great as to threaten the very coherence of the inquiry. Indeed, the confusion is so extreme that, in asking the question of world, *we do not even know what we are asking about,* almost as though we are uttering not a word but only a sound without meaning, a φωνή without sense, like the quacking of a duck or the barking of a dog.[66] Such a question spins us about, as it were, dizzying us such that we do not know where to go or how to move forward—*or even who we are.*

Heidegger then proposes three possible paths (*Wege*) by means of which the inquiry might find orientation. The first would be to offer an analysis of the history and development of the *concept* "world," which, as Heidegger mentions, he himself had already carried out in his *On the Essence of Ground.* The second path would consist of a preliminary investigation into the *phenomenon* of world, a task that Heidegger had already under-taken in *Being and Time.* Rather than revisiting either of these two paths in the present lecture course, Heidegger says that he will follow a third path (*dritten Weg*), namely, that of a "comparative examination" (*vergleichenden Betrachtung*): that is, he will observe and examine, approach and inspect, certain others—namely, material things and animals—and will attempt to discern whether and to what extent the human is the same (*gleich*) as them. Regarding such a comparative examination, Heidegger writes:

> Through a comparative interpretation of this kind it must be possible to open up the essence of world and bring it sufficiently close to us to really begin to ask about *it for the first time* [*erst einmal*]. For the problem of world by no means lies simply in the need to provide a more exact and more rigorous interpretation of the essence of the world. On the contrary, the real task is to bring the worldly character of the world into view *for the first time* [*allererst*] as the possible theme of a fundamental problem of metaphysics.[67]

Everything depends on adequately understanding the track that Heidegger proposes.[68] Although this track will get clarified *in deed* as Heidegger undertakes and develops it through the lecture course, one can already say the following: this third way will entail measuring the human against other entities to which it is exposed in order to clarify—*for the first time (erst einmal)*—the essence of world and the manner in which the human "has" it. In other words, it is not that the being of the human, having already been clarified and grasped in advance, is being used as that against which to measure the being of animals and stones. Rather, precisely the opposite is the case. It is precisely in order to attain greater clarity regarding the structure of the human, and the role that *world* plays within that structure, that the comparative analysis is being undertaken.[69] In what follows, then, material things, and especially the animal, will be that against which the human measures itself and its experience of world: the animal will thus be the measure of the humanness of the human.[70] Heidegger will say this explicitly later on in the lecture course when he writes that "our earlier analysis of [. . .] animality provides, as it were, *a suitable background* [*der geeignete Hintergrund*] against which the essence of humanity can now be set off," and specifically with respect to the concept of world.[71] The animal, and the manner of being idiosyncratic to it, is the backdrop against which the inquiry into the human can be carried out, the necessary detour through which the human must travel in order to reach an adequate grasp of its own essence.

But this means that, in order to understand the true character of world and the precise manner in which it structures human existence, *a prior encounter with the animal is needed*. In other words, an adequate grasp of world will only arise from out of a differentiation of the human *from* the animal, a comparison of the human to the animal who is, therefore, *already there before*. The third way, then, entails setting-out after the animal, *following after it and tracking it*, in order to find the human. It is by setting out after the animal in this way that the human will move away from its confusion, away from its homesickness, toward a coming-to-be-at-home in the world.

One must be careful to note the temporal sequence operative within this third way. The human does *not yet* know the character of world: an adequate grasp of world is *yet* to come. As we have already seen, such a grasp first requires an excursus, an excursion, into the animal. Such an excursion is grounded in a prior exposure to the animal, the animal that is therefore already there *first*, is already *present*, in some sense, *prior* to the human. More precisely, the animal is already there prior to the human's understanding of itself and its world, prior to its coming-to-be-at-home in it. Precisely in order to obtain this understanding *for the first time*, a turn to the animal Other is needed.

Having thus gestured toward a certain temporal and logical priority that belongs to the animal, Heidegger then sets out on his third way. He begins by positing the three theses that are far and away the most widely "known" aspect of Heidegger's understanding of animality: "[1] the stone (material object) is worldless; [2] the animal is poor in world; [3] the human is world-forming."[72] There is little to be said about these three theses that has not already been said by other scholars: they are the focal point of nearly every scholarly treatment of Heidegger's understanding of animality, and in many ways they have become a kind of caricature of that understanding. For the purposes of the present study, there are only two points that require mention. First, recalling the hesitation with which Heidegger approaches the question of the animal, and also the confused homesickness with which the lecture course begins, it is important to note that Heidegger has here posited three *theses* (*Thesen*), three hypotheses or postulates, to serve as a *starting point* to the investigation. What he has manifestly *not* done is articulate a definitive or rigidified theory representing the conclusions of his investigation.[73] The scholarly fervor over these three theses has tended to obscure their tentative character and the confusion, trepidation, and befuddlement with which Heidegger carries out his inquiry; fortunately, Cykowski's exemplary work in this matter has begun to correct this tendency.

Secondly, and more importantly, these hypotheses are based on distinctions that "immediately manifest themselves."[74] In other words, it is on the basis of certain manifest distinctions, an exposure to something that shows itself (*zeigen sich*) to the human, that Heidegger is able to posit these three theses. He gestures toward this prior exposure again a few paragraphs later when he writes that "in order even to negotiate the problem we must *already have* [*schon . . . haben*] at our disposal certain essential distinctions [*wesenhafte Unterschiede*] between these three realms [i.e., stone, animal, human]."[75] Thus, *prior* to the formulation of the three theses, there is an *exposure* to certain readily manifest distinctions between the human and the animal, distinctions that, presumably, announce themselves through the course of the human's encounter with animals. Bracketing the question of whether Heidegger's depiction of the precise character of those essential distinctions is satisfactory, we wish only to note here the manner in which such distinctions manifest themselves *prior* to any conceptual formulation of the nature of animality or, indeed, the nature of the human in distinction to the animal.

Although Heidegger says nothing more regarding the provenance of these "essential distinctions," it is safe to assume that they are of the order of the "foundational experience" (*Grunderfahrung*) discussed in the previous chapter. Simply by virtue of being open to the world—simply by virtue, that is, of having *care* as its fundamental ontological structure—the human has a preconceptual, prethematic exposure to animals (and, indeed, to all beings) in their otherness, in their *difference*.[76] Within *The Fundamental Concepts of Metaphysics*, as was also the case in *Basic Concepts of Aristotelian Philosophy*, this pretheoretical exposure is cast by Heidegger in terms of the language of "being-at-hand" (*Vorhandenheit*). As being in the world, the human is receptive to the beings that appear "at hand" within the perimeter of its world of concern. As Heidegger writes, "[I]nsofar as we indeed exist factically, insofar as we *are there* [*da sind*], we are *transposed* [*versetzt*] into the midst of other beings. These things that are, after all, are at hand [*vorhanden*] for us at all times [*jederzeit*], in whatever scope and with whatever transparency."[77] Further on in the lecture course, Heidegger emphasizes this "at hand" availability of beings as being utterly central to a proper understanding of human *Dasein*:

> [T]he beings that surround us are uniformly manifest as simply something present at hand in the broadest sense [*Vorhandene im weitesten Sinne*]—the presence [*Vorkommen*] of land and sea, the mountains and forests, and within this the presence of animals and plants and the presence of human beings and the products of human work, and amongst all this the presence of ourselves as well. This character of beings as something simply present at hand [*Vorhandenen*] in the broadest sense cannot be insisted upon too strongly, because this is an essential character of beings as they spread themselves before us in our everydayness [*weil er ein wesentlicher Charakter des Seienden ist, wie es sich in unserer Alltäglichkeit breitmacht*], and we ourselves are also involved in [*einbezogen*] this widespread presence at hand.[78]

According to Heidegger, it is only owing to this essential exposure to beings in their present-at-hand availability that human existence has the "peculiar security, dependency, and almost inevitability" that it has. He also claims that this element of our everyday being is "what is most powerful in our *Dasein*."[79] In using the language of *Vorkommen* (presence) to describe this prior availability, Heidegger is emphasizing the way in which beings always come (*kommen*) before (*vor*) us, always lie before us *in advance*. Moreover, this is something, Heidegger has said, that *the beings themselves* are doing as they "spread themselves before us in our everydayness" (*es sich in unse-rer Alltäglichkeit breitmacht*). This prior prevailing on the part of beings, such that they are being-at-hand for us—that is, their bare presence, their manifestness, their οὐσία—is the very condition for the possibility of our experience. Simply put, only because beings *give themselves* to us in advance are we able to relate to those beings, inquire about them, and strive to come to be at home with them.[80]

This is not to say that the human grasps the *genuine* being of animals (or anything else) simply through this prior exposure: on the contrary, Heidegger's whole point within these pages is to emphasize the extent to which this is not the case.[81] Precisely because we encounter beings, for the most part, at the level of *everydayness*, we do *not* develop a genuine relationship with them. However—and this is crucial for the investigation underway—the possibility of developing a genuine relationship depends upon, and is made possible by, the *prior* manifesting of beings carried out by those beings themselves (i.e., the manner in which they "spread them-selves out" before us). Only because beings *show themselves* to the human, and only because the human is always already *involved* or *immersed* in this self-showing, can the human *then* inquire into those beings in such a way as to develop a genuine relationship with them. This means that, within the structure of human experience—a structure that differs fundamentally from the structure of merely "at hand" entities—the "at hand" nonetheless occupies a decisive priority, insofar as it is the "thereness" of beings in relation to which *Dasein* orients itself, comes to know itself, and comes to experience and understand the world.

Having now said that the investigation must begin with such exposure to these essential differences, Heidegger immediately proceeds to express the great difficulties involved in even initially distinguishing between the animal and the human.[82] The difficulty lies not in observing apparent or superficial differences between the two, but rather in locating the *essential* differences that hold the two apart. Such a procedure, he continues, first of all depends upon understanding the *living* character of the living being (*Lebendigkeit des Lebenden*)—that is, it requires that we have an adequate grasp of what it means *to live*, such that we can then set apart various modes (or kinds) of life.

However, this manner of proceeding immediately encounters a certain methodological circularity that seemingly threatens to arrest the progress of the investigation. On the one hand, in order to undertake a comparative analysis of the animal and the human (as Heidegger is attempting to do), one must have some at least preliminary determinations of animality (obtained from the prior exposure mentioned above); and yet, on the other hand, it is precisely the comparative analysis that is meant to make such determinations visible for the first time. This circularity would hold no less for the question of the character of living beings. (That is, in order to understand the character of living beings compared to nonliving beings, one must already be able to distinguish the two; and yet, it is precisely the systematic comparison of the living and nonliving that is meant to provide one with the conceptual means of distinguishing them.) Such circularity seems to undermine the viability of the third way that Heidegger has proposed; and yet, as he immediately clarifies, it in fact marks its very possibility:

> Thus we constantly find ourselves moving in a circle. And this is an indication that we are moving within the realm of philosophy. Everywhere a kind of circling. This circling movement of philosophy is of course abhorrent to ordinary understanding, which only ever wants to get the job at hand over and done with as quickly as possible. But going round in circles gets us nowhere. Above all, it makes us feel dizzy, and dizziness is something uncanny [*unheimlich*]. We feel as though we are suspended in the Nothing. [. . .] Yet anyone who has never been seized by dizziness in the presence of a philosophical question has never asked the question in a philosophical way, that is, has never entered the circle in the first place.[83]

The circularity in which the human finds itself as it sets out to investigate the animal—the animal who, therefore, must already be there before the human—marks the very possibility of a genuine philosophical inquiry into the animal and, by extension, an understanding of world.

There are a number of crucial elements within this passage that need to be clarified. To begin with, Heidegger's mention of dizziness (*Schwindel*) recalls his earlier discussion of the disorientation the human feels in the face of beings as a whole. As the human sets out into a comparative examination of animality and humanity, it spins around in circles, dizzyingly unsure of where to turn or how to proceed. But such dizziness, rather than indicating a failure of conceptual clarity or methodological rigor, bespeaks the profundity and essentiality of the inquiry the human has embarked upon.

It also, as Heidegger writes, brings the human before the *Nothing* (*das Nichts*). This remarkable claim of Heidegger's must be given its proper consideration, as it plays a significant (though largely overlooked) role in Heidegger's attitude toward the animal. The vertiginous question of the animal brings the human face-to-face with the Nothing: it suspends the human over an abyss of non-being. And yet, as Heidegger writes much later on in a passage that can be understood as a concise reformulation of what he accomplished in his essay "What Is Metaphysics" (from 1929), being brought before the Nothing is the manner in which the human is brought before *being* itself:

> All human comportment toward beings as such is only intrinsically possible if such comportment is capable of understanding what is not as such. What is not and nothingness can only be understood if Dasein in understanding holds itself from the outset and fundamentally toward the Nothing, is held out into the Nothing. The task is to understand the innermost power of the Nothing, precisely in order to let beings be as beings, in order to have and to be beings in all their powerfulness as beings.[84]

The question of the animal, and the exposure to the animal that makes such questioning possible, brings the human before the Nothing, and therefore before beings as a whole. Moreover, this Nothingness, according to Heidegger, is "that power which constantly thrusts us back, which alone thrusts us into being and lets us assume power over our *Dasein*."[85] In other words, the Nothing to which the encounter with animals leads the human is *instrumental* to the latter in coming to exercise control over itself, over its own existence. In this way, the encounter with the animal, which is one way in which the human is thrust before the Nothing, is structurally prior to, and constitutive of, the formation of authentic human *Dasein*.

But how, exactly, does the encounter with the animal thrust the human before the Nothing? What is occurring here as the human spins itself about in the face of the question of the animal? Based on the analysis so far, one can draw two essentially related conjectures to make sense out of this curious claim. First, insofar as the encounter with the animal leads the human to question its own identity, to question its own *being*, it can be said to cast the human into uncertainty, confusion, and *aporia* (i.e., into a place where one does not know who one is or even how to go about answering the question). Such a *lack* of a determinate characterization of one's own essence would remain pervaded by absence, by non-being, and thus by nothingness in this sense. (One imagines a certain *anxiety* at play as the human, spinning dizzily about, calls its own being into question, although Heidegger does not use the language of anxiety here.)

Secondly, and relatedly, we know from the above analysis of *Being and Time* that the death of others—*even of other animals*—can penetrate and haunt the human as it grants an experience of what would otherwise not be experienceable. The death of the animal Other belongs among the foundational experiences that the human has of living beings, a death on the basis of which the human can then proceed to distinguish its own dying. In *The Fundamental Concepts of Metaphysics*, Heidegger seems to gesture toward this originary experience when he writes that "[e]ven in our everyday experience [*Erfahrung*] we know of the birth, growth, maturing, aging, and death [*Tod*] of animals."[86] To the extent that death bespeaks the annihilation of being, the human's everyday experiences of animal death can bring it face-to-face with the Nothing.[87] This interpretation agrees with our claim from the previous section that, within *Being and Time*, it is from the death of others that *Dasein* first *begins* reckoning with its own death, with its own dying. But this entails, as was also the case in *Being and Time*, that the human undergoes an encounter with the animal *prior* to coming to terms with its own genuine *Dasein*: the encounter with the animal thus precedes *Dasein*'s proper grasping of itself.

After underscoring this dizzying situation in which the human finds itself face-to-face with the Nothing (i.e., with its own finitude), Heidegger begins his comparative examination of the human, material things, and the animal. He states that he will begin "in the middle," that is, with the animal.[88] Because of this intermediary position, "we shall also constantly be looking to two sides at once, both toward the worldlessness of the stone and toward the world-forming of the human, and from there *back* [*her*] toward the animal and its poverty in world. Initially, the position adopted in this comparative procedure decides nothing about the metaphysical order involved."[89] Heidegger has said that the investigation will proceed by way of a certain constant reorienting of perspective, a "looking to two sides at once": first toward the stone, then toward the human, and then *back* toward the animal. This looking back-and-forth recollects the third step from the five-step program set out in the "Black Notebook" (as discussed in the previous chapter), where it was said that a movement "to and fro" between the human and animal will be undertaken.[90] Within *The Fundamental Concepts of Metaphysics*, we see a concrete carrying out of the sort of program Heidegger succinctly described within his private notebook.

Moreover, and relatedly, because the human is one of the poles of this triadic structure (of stone, animal, human), this "looking to two sides at once" entails a moment of *reflection*, a moment, in other words, where the human looks away from the stone and the animal and toward *itself*. But—and this is important for the issues under consideration here—the human then looks *back* to the animal, backward away from itself and toward the animal, and all for the sake of better understanding *not* just the animal but, above all, itself. This looking back indicates the way in which an encounter with the animal *precedes* the human's determination of itself and the manner of its own having of world. Said otherwise: when the human reflects about itself, it realizes that it does not know itself, that it is confused about its own identity; it therefore turns back toward the animal in an effort to gain insight into its own identity. The turn back to the animal is ultimately undertaken for a greater self-understanding on the part of human *Dasein*.

One sees, then, that although there is no *metaphysical* ordering here according to Heidegger—that is, although there is no hierarchical ranking with respect to which entity is "higher" or "better"[91]—there is nonetheless a *temporal* ordering in the sense that the encounter with the animal occurs *prior* to the human's adequate understanding of itself (as having a world). But there is also, then, a kind of *logical* priority allotted to the animal here, in the sense that the very concept of "world" requires a comparison with animality and life in order to become clarified and set-out apart from it; and because world belongs to the very ontological structure of *Dasein*, there is an *ontological* priority to the animal as well, insofar as the very being of the human—its way of being-in-the-world—depends upon this prior encounter with the animal.

As Heidegger proceeds to carry out his comparative examination, he runs up against a question of *method*. Heidegger had already mentioned above that the exposure to the thereness of things characteristic of human experience consists of a kind of *transposition (versetzen)* of the human into the midst of beings.[92] He now explicitly poses the question of whether and to what extent it is possible for the human to transpose itself into the animal: "*Can we transpose [versetzen] ourselves into an animal at all? For we are hardly able to transpose ourselves into another being of our own kind, into another human being.*"[93] As it turns out, the viability of Heidegger's proposed third way ultimately depends upon such transposition (*Versetzheit*), for it is only through it that any genuine insight into the nature of the animal's experience of world (or lack thereof), and therefore of the *human's* experience of world, can come to light.[94]

However, to complicate matters further, even asking this question of accessibility already carries out, to a certain extent, the comparative analysis that Heidegger has proposed: "When we ask about transposing ourselves, about the possibility of the human's transposing himself into another human being, into an animal, or into a stone, we are simultaneously asking this question as well: what kind of beings [*Seinsart*] are these that they *permit* [*zulassen*], *resist* [*verhindern*], or possibly *forbid* [*abweisen*] as inappropriate any such self-transposition?"[95] The comparison of the human to the animal thus takes place, at least in part, as the very question of whether or not the human can transpose itself into the animal so as to understand its way of being—that is, it takes place as the question of whether the animal and the human are such as to permit any kind of meaningful transposition between one another. More precisely, the question is whether the *animal*, for its part, "permits, resists, or possibly forbids" transposition into itself. We will return to this matter of *resistance* below, but for the moment it suffices to mark that it is the animal here, and not the human, who is either allowing or disallowing entry into its being: it is the animal, in other words, who is granting or denying access, the way that a *master* or a gatekeeper does.

Heidegger then clarifies what precisely such transposition entails. As he does so, one sees a nod toward the apriority of the animal Other: "[S]elf-transposition does not mean the factical transference [*Hineinschaffen*] of one existing human being into the interior of another being. Nor does it mean the factical substitution [*Ersetzen*] of oneself for another being so as to take its place. On the contrary, the other being is precisely supposed to *remain* [*bleiben*] what it is and how it is."[96] The process of transposition into the animal Other would thus depend upon the animal having already been there *before* such transposition is undertaken and upon it *remaining* what it always already was. In other words, transposition of this sort *follows after* the animal, traces and tracks it. That such transposition demands that the other into whom one would transpose is already there in advance is made clear when Heidegger writes that "transposing oneself into this being [i.e., the animal] means going along with [*mitgehen*] what it is and with how it is. Such going-along-with [*Mitgehen*] means directly learning how it is with this being, experiencing [*erfahren*] what it is like to be this being with which we are going along in this way."[97] There is thus a certain apriority to the animal who, remaining what it already was, awaits the human as the latter attempts to transpose itself into it and go along with it.

As Heidegger goes on to say, the possibility of such transposition—which, on the one hand, belongs to the very essence of the human—depends also upon the manner in which the animal shows itself to the human: "It is somehow self-evident that the animal for its part bears with it a peculiar sphere of its own that makes possible a transposition into it in accordance with its own animality."[98] Such a self-evident truth is, no doubt, among those "essential distinctions" that are readily available to the human when it looks toward the animal—the animal, that is, who is always already there—and has a foundational experience of it. Regarding this foundational experience, Heidegger writes: "On the contrary, we already comport ourselves in this way. In our existence as a whole we comport ourselves toward animals [*Wir verhalten uns in unserer ganzen Existenz zum Tier*], and in a certain manner toward plants too, in such a way that we are already [*vornherein*] aware of being transposed in a certain sense—in such a way that a certain ability to go along with the beings concerned is already [*vornherein*] an unquestioned possibility for us from the start."[99] The human is thus always already transposed into animals (in the broadest sense):[100] its very ek-sistence, which is nothing other than "exposure to the disclosedness of beings as such,"[101] entails a comportment toward the animal Other. The animal Other is thus always already there, a priori (*vornherein*).

Twenty-two years later, in a letter to Menard Boss, Heidegger writes again of this originary transposition. In doing so, he marks an essential similarity between the human and the animal, even while emphasizing the abyssal inaccessibility of the latter:

> [A]n animal merely is insofar as it moves within an environment [*Umgebung*] open to it in some way and is guided by this environment which itself remains circumscribed by the nature of the animal. The animal's relationship to this environment [. . .] shows a certain correspondence [*Entsprechung*] to the human being's ek-sistent relationship toward the world. Thus, in a certain way the human being in his ek-sistent Da-sein can immediately participate in and live-with [*mit-leben*] the animal's environmental relationship without ever coming to a congruence [*decken*] between the human being's being-with [*Mitsein*] and the animal, let alone the other way around. Linguistic usage, according to which one speaks of human and animal "behavior" indiscriminately, does not take into account the unfathomable, essential difference between the relationship to a "world" [*Weltbezug*] and to an "environment" [*Umgebungsbezug*]. According to its own proper and essential relationship to the environment, the animal's situation makes it possible for us to enter into this relationship, to go along [*mit-gehen*] with it, and, as it were, to tarry [*verweilen*] with it. But it is not enough to consider

only that it remains far more essential to see that an animal (as opposed to a rock) shows itself to us only then as an animal insofar as we humans as ek-sistent have *engaged in advance in* [*im vorhinein . . . eingelassen*] the relationship to the environment proper to the animal. It does not matter thereby that the immediate apprehension of the environment proper to the animal and, thus, also the genuine apprehension of the animal's relationship to the environment remain inaccessible [*versagt*] to our knowledge. The strangeness [*befremdliche*] of the unfolding essence of animals is concealed in this inaccessibility [*Versagen*].[102]

Because of the originary correspondence (*Entsprechen*) between the ways in which the animal inhabits its environment and the human inhabits its world, the latter is able to go along with the former, living-with it in an unmediated (*unmittelbar*) intimacy. Such a going-along-with depends upon a *prior* exposure to the environment of the animal, an originary openness to it.[103] To play a bit with Heidegger's terminology here, one could say that there is an originary speaking-together (*Entsprechen*) that takes place between humans and animals, a correspondence that allows the human to go along with the animal in its environment. However, despite this originary going-along-with, the animal *refuses* (*versagt*) complete entry into its essence, an essence that thus remains, finally, mysterious, robbing the human of its ability to say (*sagen*) much more about the animal.[104] (We will return to such a loss of words in the concluding chapter of this study.) The originary transposition of the human into the animal is thus characterized by a going-along-with that encounters a refusal.

Back in *The Fundamental Concepts of Metaphysics*, Heidegger attempts to elucidate this originary transposition further by offering the example of domesticated animals (*Haustiere*). The example, which is really more of a *domestic scene*, is as follows:

Let us consider the case of domestic animals as a striking [*auffälliges*] example. We do not describe them as such simply because they are present [*verkommen*] in the house but because they belong [*gehören*] to the house, i.e., they serve the house in a certain sense. Yet they do not belong to the house in the way in which the roof belongs to the house as protection against storms. We keep domestic pets in the house with us, they "live" with us. But we do not live with them if living means: being in an animal kind of way. Yet we *are with* them nonetheless [*Gleichwohl* sind *wir* mit *ihnen*]. But this being-with [*Mitsein*] is not an *existing-with* [*Mitexistieren*], because a dog does not exist but merely lives [*nur lebt*]. Through this being with animals [*Mitsein mit den Tieren*] we enable them to move within our world [*in unserer Welt*]. We say that the dog is lying underneath the table or is running up the stairs and so on. Yet when we consider the dog itself—does it comport itself toward the table as table, toward the stairs as stairs? All the same, it does go up the stairs with us. It feeds [*frißt*] with us—and yet, we do not really "feed" [*fressen*]. It eats [*ißt*] with us—and yet, it does not really "eat" [*ißt*]. Nevertheless, it is with us [*mit uns*]! A going along with [*Mitgehen*], a transposition—and yet not.[105]

There are four points about this remarkable scene that need to be addressed. First, one notes the hesitancy, the *indecision*, with which Heidegger approaches the question of the animal here (e.g., on the one hand, the animal is *with* the human, on the other hand, it is *not*; on the one hand, the animal *eats*, on the other, it does not *really* eat, etc.). Heidegger's engagement with the animal here, which is an articulation of the kind of being-with that characterizes the human's originary transposition amid animals, is emblematic of the *dizzying confusion* that besets any inquiry into animality of which Heidegger spoke at the beginning of the lecture course, and serves to remind one of the hypothetical, inquisitive, and tentative nature of the inquiry.

Secondly, it is important to note the emphasis with which Heidegger insists, despite all of his reservations and confusions, that the human is *with* the animal. Near the middle of the passage, Heidegger writes: Gleichwohl *sind* wir *mit* ihnen—"Nonetheless, we *are with* them." In italicizing the *sind* (are), Heidegger is indicating that the being-with under consideration belongs to the way of *being* of the animal: it is not something that is merely added on to something present-at-hand when we incorporate it into our lives. This is further indicated by Heidegger at the end of the passage when he exclaims that, despite the differences manifesting themselves through the comparative examination, the animal is "nonetheless with us [*mit uns*]!" Despite the caveats and the provisos, despite the essential differences that announce themselves, there is an emphatic foundational being-with-the-animal that characterizes human *Dasein*. As argued above, this has everything to do with the at-handness, the apriority, of the animal Other within human experience.

Thirdly, and along these same lines, the passage suggests that the animal and the human share a world, even though they live in that world differently. In the language of *disposition* employed in *Basic Concepts of Aristotelian Philosophy*, we could say that, although the human lives with animals in the world, the human does not live with them *as they* live within it: the human does not occupy the animal's (dis)position in the world. (Even less does the animal, whose *poverty* of world Heidegger will soon emphasize, occupy the disposition of the human, only the latter of whom *ek-sists* in the technical sense.) Thus, despite the originary transposition by which the human is always already being-with animals, that being-with does not bridge the difference of (dis)position that characterizes the lives of each. Nonetheless, the two encounter one another, in some originary sense, within their shared world.

Finally, this example again shows the way in which the animal, as present (*verkommen*), is always already there *before* as that with which the human goes along in a certain sense. Regardless of whether or not Heidegger misunderstands the animal's way of being in this example, granting it mere "life" but not existence in a robust sense, it is clear that, for Heidegger, the human is *alongside* the animal, going along *with* the animal, the animal who is (thus) always already there *before*. Animals are among the beings to which the human, as standing in the open, is always already exposed in a pretheoretical foundational experience. Indeed, it is one of the defining characteristics of the human—namely, its *facticity*—to always already be transposed into the animal in an essential way.

In this way, Heidegger's domestic scene can be seen to *prefigure* and anticipate the scene that Derrida will come to stage years later in his lecture/essay *The Animal That Therefore I Am* when he describes his encounter with the cat. Indeed, to a great extent, one can *reduce* Derrida's objections regarding Heidegger's treatment of the animal, and Derrida's own corrective to him, as taking place *between* these two domestic scenes, as a battle over which scene more accurately accounts for the animality of the animal and, more importantly, for the effect that the animal has on the human. At stake in this battle (if, indeed, it is one) is how things stand within the place of domesticity, within the *house*, the οἶκος, the οὐσία (which Heidegger, in *Basic Concepts of Aristotelian Philosophy*, translates as "house"),[106] within the essence or the being: in both scenes the question is whether and how the animal belongs in the *House of Being*. For Heidegger—or, at least, for Derrida's Heidegger—the animal is "with" the human only in a certain, highly qualified sense, both in the house (of being) and yet somehow outside of it, while for Derrida the animal is *in* the house (of being) more originarily than the human ever is: the cat, in Derrida's scene, marks the very possibility of the human coming to know itself within its own house. Simply put, for Derrida's Heidegger, the human has priority over the animal, while for Derrida the animal is there *first*.

Derrida mentions Heidegger's scene at the very end of *The Animal That Therefore I Am* "in order to finish, very quickly," and says that he wants to discuss it because he had spoken of the cat earlier:[107] Derrida himself, then, notes the essential connection between the two scenes. However, Derrida gives only a very cursory and hurried treatment of Heidegger's scene—indeed, it is almost as though he does not quite have the time for it.[108] (Derrida's entire treatment of Heidegger within this lecture is marked by constant deferrals—indeed, one is tempted to call it a *logic* or *strategy* of deferral.)[109] What little time he does have he spends emphasizing the way in which the animal, for Heidegger, lacks a relation to beings "as such," to the "as such" *as such*.[110]

What Derrida ends up *not* having time for is Heidegger's commentary on his own example, his own *scene*, in which a number of remarkable things take place. Most remarkable, perhaps, is the way in which Heidegger's scene attests, decades before Derrida will, to the absolute apriority of the animal Other. Such becomes clear as Heidegger begins his commentary—a commentary that consists almost entirely of *questions* in the face of the animal Other:

> However, if an original transposedness on the human's part in relation to the animal is possible, this surely implies that the animal also has its world. Or is this going too far? Is it precisely this "going too far" that we constantly misunderstand? And why do we do so? Transposedness into the animal can belong to the essence of the human without this necessarily meaning that we transpose ourselves into an animal's world or that the animal in general has a world. And now our question becomes more incisive: In this transposedness into the animal, where [*wohin*] is it that we are transposed to? What is it we are going along with [*gehen wir mit*], and what does this "with" [*Mit*] mean? What sort of going is involved here [*Was ist es für eine Art des Gehens*]?[111]

For Heidegger, the entire domestic scene provokes the question of *going-along-with*, of where and with whom this originary going-along-with transpires. To make the sequence at work here clearer: Heidegger encounters the animal (i.e., the animals of the house—one imagines him looking over at his dog, "Mohrle"), and this encounter leads him into a place of questioning, indeed, into asking about the kind of *going-along-with* that characterizes his experience of animals.

The crucial question—and so much would depend upon the answer—is whether this *going-along-with* is, indeed, a *following after*? Is Heidegger, in this domestic scene, already broaching the possibility of a following-after the animal, as Derrida will do years later? That he is doing so is perhaps verified by what Heidegger does next. Immediately following the posing of his questions regarding the possibility of a transposition into the animal, Heidegger *enacts* that very transposition, imagining how this matter would look *from the point of view of the animal*: "Or, from the perspective of the animal [*vom Tier aus gesprochen*], what is it about the animal which *allows* [*zuläßt*] and *commands* [*fordert*] human transposedness into it, even while refusing [*versagt*] the human the possibility of going along with the animal? From the side of the animal [*von seiten des* Tieres], what is it that grants the possibility of transposedness and necessarily *refuses* [*Versagenmüssen*] any going along with?"[112] Heidegger thus tries to carry out the very transposition whose possibility he is calling into question as he attempts to see things "from the perspective of the animal."[113] The German here—*vom Tier aus gesprochen*—literally says, "spoken from the animal." Heidegger is speaking for the animal here, speaking *as* an animal, speaking for the animal who cannot, according to Heidegger, speak on its own. Or, stronger still: from the side (or position) of the animal there comes a speaking, a speaking that bespeaks the possibility of transposition.

What does Heidegger, speaking as if he were the animal Other, say? He speaks of an animal who *allows* (*zuläßt*) and *commands* (*fordert*) the human, and who also *refuses* (*versagt*) it. But does not such *allowing* and *commanding* on the part of the animal bespeak its decisive priority over the human? Is it not the one with the power of priority who *allows* or who, even more so, *refuses*? Is it not the *master of the house*—most of all, perhaps, the master of the House of Being—who *grants* or *refuses* entry to the Other? Moreover, is it not significant that Heidegger, when imagining himself as the animal, finds an animal who is *speaking* (ver-*sagen*)?

We thus see, in Heidegger's domestic scene, a turn to the animal Other who is always already there, who stands in a position of priority (and authority) who (therefore) maintains the right to allow, to command, and to refuse: like Montaigne's cat, Heidegger's animal can *refuse* the human.[114] One sees, then, a great proximity, if not a functional identity, between

Heidegger's domestic scene and Derrida's domestic scene, although such proximity has been largely overlooked within the scholarly reception of *The Fundamental Concepts of Metaphysics* and *The Animal That Therefore I Am.* It is truly unfortunate that Derrida did not have time for a more sustained engagement with Heidegger's domestic scene—especially since, for Derrida, such encounters and sequences as described in Heidegger's scene are the very "genesis of time."[115]

In any event, Heidegger's discourse about, and attempt at, transposition leads him to eventually conclude that the human's essential ability to transpose into the animal does not imply that the animal has a world, at least not in any strong sense; and it is in light of this claim that Heidegger will go on to argue that the animal is poor in world:

> Thus the transposability of the human into the animal, which again is not a going along with, is grounded in the essence of the animal. And it is this essence which we have attempted to capture with our thesis concerning the animal's poverty in world. To summarize: the animal intrinsically displays a sphere of transposability and does so in a way that the human (to whose Dasein a being transposed belongs) already finds itself transposed into the animal in a certain manner. The animal displays a sphere of transposability or, more precisely, the animal itself is this sphere, one which nonetheless refuses any going along with. The animal has a sphere of potential transposability and yet it does not necessarily have what we call world.[116]

The animal has, and does not have, world: it is world-poor. It is here that one might want to find traces of a denigrating metaphysical hierarchy in which the human takes pride of place. However, precisely as Heidegger suggests that the animal's experience of world differs from the human's, he points to the originary being-with that characterizes the human's encounter with the animal. As we have seen, Heidegger's entire discourse on transposition requires that the human appreciates an originary and foundational exposure to the animal Other, the animal who is (therefore) always already present before.

The notion that the animal is poor in world entails, among other things, an inability on the part of the animal to know beings *as such.*[117] However, as we have seen, the animal is that without which the human would be unable to clarify its own having of world: it is that without which the human cannot come into a genuine relation with its own world.[118] Said more strongly, because the human "primarily and for the most part does not know about world *as such* [*als solche*],"[119] it is only through the comparative examination with the animal that the human is able to grasp its own world *as such*.[120] Thus, although the animal *as such* cannot grasp the *as such*, it is that without which the human would be unable to grasp its own world *as such*.

In this way, the human, for Heidegger, is involved in an originary confrontation, an *Auseinandersetzung*, with the animal Other. It is *originary* in the sense that the very being of the human, insofar as it is always already transposed into the animal, is in part comprised of this *Auseinandersetzung*; further, and more significantly, the human's relation to itself—its *understanding* of self—is contingent upon, and subsequent to, this *Auseinandersetzung*. For Heidegger, the identity of *Dasein* must be won each time anew, and this necessarily entails that it measure itself against the other beings it finds in its world. The animal is thus the necessary detour through which the human must travel on the path toward itself.

∽

Heidegger ends the lecture course by emphasizing the transitional character of the human and the manner in which the human remains forever *on the way* toward its essence:

> The human is that inability to remain and is yet unable to leave his place. In projecting, the Da-sein in him constantly throws him into possibilities and thereby keeps him subjected to what is actual. Thus thrown in this throw, the human is a transition [*Übergang*], a transition as the fundamental essence of occurrence [*Geschehens*]. The human is history [*Geschichte*], or better, history is the human. The human is *enraptured* in this transition and therefore essentially "*absent.*" Absent in a fundamental sense—never simply at hand, but absent in his essence, in his essentially *being away*, removed into essential *having been* and *future*—essentially absencing and never at hand, yet *existent* in his essential absence. *Transposed* [*versetzt*] into the possible, he must constantly *be mistaken* concerning what is actual. And only because he is thus mistaken and transposed can he become seized by terror. And only where there is the

perilousness of being seized by terror do we find the bliss of astonishment—being torn away in that wakeful manner that is the breath of all philosophizing, and which the greats among the philosophers called ἐνθουσιασμός.[121]

To be human is to be in transition, in *transit*, on a path toward one's essence, a transit that, as such, entails a lack of determination and settlement. In this way, one can understand Heidegger's "third way"—namely, the way of the comparative examination that constitutes Heidegger's methodical approach within this text—as a formalized enactment of the conditions that belong *by nature* to the human. Such conditions necessitate a continual engagement with the other entities within the world in an effort to bring greater clarity and determination to one's existence: to be human is to be continually engaged in the process of demarcating the human, and such operations of demarcation are always carried out in relation to nonhuman others. Such engagement, for its part, entails exposure to the terror, but also the astonishment, of the *uncertainty* and *indeterminacy* of existence.

As witness to the terror and astonishment to which this path can lead, Heidegger lets Nietzsche—or, rather, Zarathustra—end the lecture course with a song. The song takes place deep within *Thus Spoke Zarathustra, after* Zarathustra has spoken with his animals and after they have taught him the lesson of the eternal recurrence of the same, the very doctrine that allows him to overcome himself and enter into his proper essence. As Karl Löwith observed, the song is a testament to Zarathustra's transformation into his proper essence: "Now he [i.e., Zarathustra] is indeed the superman, a man who has overcome himself by accepting voluntarily what cannot be otherwise, thus transforming an alien fate into his proper destiny. From now on he lives by the experience of a perfect noon-tide when 'the world is perfect' and time has flown away into the well of eternity. He is now a 'blesser and yea-sayer.' "[122] As an unqualified expression of this yea-saying, this affirmation of *life*—but, above all, as an affirmation of the transitional character of human—Zarathustra sings his "Song of Midnight," the song with which Heidegger concludes his remarkable lecture course on life.

With this in mind, we transition to Heidegger's lectures from 1937 entitled "Zarathustra's Animals," where the role of the animal in the transformation of the human into its proper *Dasein* is most conspicuous.

Chapter Three

Authentic Beasts

And you?—You have already cranked a song out of it! Yet now I lie here, so weary of this biting and expelling, still sick from my own salvation. *And you stood by watching all of it?*

—Zarathustra, speaking to his animals
(quoted from GA 6.1:399; my translation)

In 1936 and 1937—the third- and second-to-last years chronicled in the "Black Notebook" (GA 94) analyzed in chapter 1—Heidegger delivered lecture courses at the University of Freiburg devoted to the work of Friedrich Nietzsche. The lecture courses represent Heidegger's most sustained and expansive encounter with Nietzsche, with topics including the will to power, European nihilism, Nietzsche's attempt to overturn Platonism, and the eternal recurrence of the same.

In a sense, the question of the animal is nearly ubiquitous within these lecture courses, at least to the extent that Nietzsche, for Heidegger, develops and expounds what Krell has called a "metaphysics of animality." To the extent that Nietzsche thinks the human in terms of its bodily animality (as the configuration of the will to power proper to the human), he inverts the traditional metaphysical schema of the human as a *rational* animal, reducing reason to an expression of the body and thereby conceiving the human as essentially animalistic.[1] Insofar as Heidegger's lectures trace the origin and development of this reduction, the text as a whole remains oriented, at least from a certain altitude, toward the question of the relationship between the human and the animal. It is worth recalling, too, that two years later, in his

1938–1939 lecture course on Nietzsche's *Untimely Meditations*, Heidegger will claim that the question of the animal—or, rather, the question of the dividing line between the animal and the human—bears upon the entirety of his own thinking and is a question upon whose posing the very destiny of the West depends.[2] As we will see, this is certainly the case within the 1937 lecture course.

Despite carrying out a thoroughly animalistic rethinking of the nature of the human, Nietzsche's understanding of the animal—and, indeed, of the human *as* an animal—remained mired, according to Heidegger, within the conceptual strictures of the history of metaphysics, and indeed served as the culmination of that history. Heidegger's own understanding of the animal within the majority of the lectures, for its part, seemingly remains within an unreflective metaphysical framework as well, at least so far as one can glean from the few mentions of animals therein. For example, while differentiating the will from "sheer compulsion and striving," Heidegger writes that "in the case of animals the compulsion [of hunger] itself as such does not have explicitly in view what it is being compelled toward; animals do not represent food as such [*als solche*]."[3] As Heidegger argues in multiple other texts, the animal's inability to represent beings "as such" is characteristic of their lack of world, the result of which is an inability to relate to beings in their beingness. Also as in other texts, such as *The Fundamental Concepts of Metaphysics* (analyzed in the previous chapter), Heidegger here draws a distinction between the human and what he calls "mere life": "We, on the other hand, use 'life' only to designate beings that are vegetable or animal; we thereby differentiate human being from these other kinds, human being meaning something more and something other than mere 'life' [*was mehr und ein Anderes ist als bloßes 'Leben'*]."[4] The phrase "something more" seems to betray a human exceptionalism on Heidegger's part that relegates the animal to the realm of the "mere" (*bloßes*), and this is certainly how Heidegger's attitude in the Nietzsche lectures has been portrayed.[5]

However, in the 1937 course, something changes—indeed, it is hardly an exaggeration to say that *everything* changes . . . at least for a *Moment*. Within that course, which is primarily directed toward Nietzsche's understanding of the doctrine of the eternal recurrence of the same, animals come expressly to the fore—and, indeed, in such a way as to disrupt, if not polarly *invert*, any human exceptionalism that may otherwise be operative within the text. In a manner ultimately emblematic of the priority that animals have within Heidegger's thought as a whole, two animals—an eagle and a serpent—erupt onto the scene and destabilize any supposed priority or pride of place that might otherwise be thought to belong to the human. Moreover, these animals come to serve as the very ground of the possibility of Zarathustra's transformation beyond the human and into his own proper essence, thereby demonstrating a constitutive role in the ontological formation of genuine *Dasein*. It should be noted in passing that, in the analysis that follows, no attention is paid to the fidelity of Heidegger's interpretation to Nietzsche's project—in other words, no consideration is paid to whether Heidegger "gets Nietzsche right" or rather enacts unforgivable hermeneutic violence against him.[6] Rather, the following analysis attends only to Heidegger's appropriation of Nietzsche's *Thus Spoke Zarathustra* and the manner in which he places it in the service of his own philosophical project. What will be shown is that Zarathustra's animals, and "the animal" more generally, play a pivotal and foundational role for Heidegger in the forming and founding of authentic human *Dasein*.

Heidegger begins the course by analyzing Nietzsche's articulation of the eternal recurrence of the same in the concluding section of *Die fröhliche Wissenschaft*, where a certain hypothetical demon visits us "in our most solitary solitude [*einsamste Einsamkeit*]" and tells us that we shall have to live every moment of our lives—every pleasure, every pain, every thought—innumerable times over. This most solitary solitude, as the text further clarifies, is that moment (*Augenblick*) of extreme *ekstasis* in the face of one's mortality whereby one comes to stand as one's ownmost self, the moment where one makes a decision about the meaning (and, indeed, the *being*) of one's own life—a moment that Heidegger associates with Zarathustra's *down-going* (*Untergang*). (We will return to this moment of down-going below, and also in the next chapter.) In other words, this most solitary solitude is the moment of authentic resoluteness (*Entschlossenheit*): it is the burdensome and anxious moment when one becomes what one most fully *is*. One sees this posture of solitary resoluteness elucidated clearly in *The Fundamental Concepts of Metaphysics*, the text for which, as was seen in chapter 2, the animal plays such a constitutive and transformative role: "If we are to become what we are, we cannot abandon our finitude [*Endlichkeit*][. . . .] In becoming finite, there ultimately occurs an individuation [*Vereinzelung*] of the human with respect to its *Dasein*[. . . .] This individuation is [. . .] that solitude [*Einsamkeit*] in which each human being first of all enters into a nearness to what is essential in all things, a nearness to world."[7] Solitary resoluteness is thus the posture by means of which the human comes to stand cognizantly in nearness to beings and, more importantly, to being: it is how the human comes to fully grasp its situation as being in the world, as being the *there* of being, the *Da* of *Sein*. The Nietzsche lectures from 1937 offer a sustained analysis of the process by which one enters into such a posture. They also offer, as we will see, an account of the constitutive role that animals play in bringing about such a posture.

After having delineated the basic structure and function of the eternal recurrence of the same, Heidegger then carries out a focused inquiry into *Thus Spoke Zarathustra*, the text in which the principle finds its most lapidary articulation. After several pages of inquiry into Zarathustra's thinking of the eternal recurrence of the same—the "thought of thoughts" (i.e., a consideration of the being of beings)—the text undergoes what Krell calls "a massive interruption," one that Heidegger himself even announces as an interruption (*abbrechen*).[8] Quite suddenly, and seemingly out of nowhere, the inquiry turns to a meditation on Zarathustra and "his" animals, animals that, as one soon sees, do not so much belong to Zarathustra as call to him from the outside, indeed, call him *to* the outside and in such a way as to articulate for him the parameters of his inside, his essence. Within these few short pages, the animals quite literally come to take over, not just becoming a momentary focus of the lecture course but going so far as to displace Zarathustra—and, indeed, the human—from their place of presumed prominence. In other words, this interruption—one that could be called *untamed*, *feral*, or *bestial*, rather than "massive"—is an interruption not just of Heidegger's lecture on Nietzsche's doctrine of the eternal recurrence of the same but also of the notion that Heidegger privileged or prioritized the human over the animal. In this sense, Zarathustra's encounter with the animals is, in a very real way, the most crucial and structurally significant moment of the entire text, although its importance has gone largely unnoticed by scholars. Ultimately, as will be seen, the interruption of the animals brings about a rupture within the human's self-understanding, bringing it closer to the fundamental rupture of being itself (as world).

Heidegger begins his interruptive (and interrupting) account of Zarathustra's animals: "Zarathustra has in the meantime returned from his sea voyage to the solitude of the mountains—to his cave and to his animals. His animals are the eagle and the serpent. These two are *his* animals; they *belong* to him [*gehören ihm*] in his solitude. And when Zarathustra's solitude speaks, it is his animals who are speaking [*ist ein Reden dieser seiner Tiere*]."[9] Given the matter under consideration in the present study, there are three points in the above passage that require elucidation.

Firstly, the animals are said here to be Zarathustra's animals, to belong (*gehört*) to him, to be *his* (*seine*). However, everything depends upon how one understands the sense of this belonging (*gehören*), and on how one understands more generally the structure of *belonging*: for, as we soon see, it is much more the case that Zarathustra belongs *to* the animals, that he does so owing to the manner in which he listens (*hören*) to them and gives himself over to them, aligning himself with them, and that they are not "his" animals so much as he is "their" human—*if, that is, Zarathustra is a human at all.*[10] (The question of Zarathustra's humanity, of whether and to what extent he is human or something *beyond* human, is utterly central to Nietzsche's text.)[11] As one soon sees, the animals are "his" only in the sense that they preconfigure and make possible the transformation of his being that brings about his authentic identity.

Secondly, this passage suggests that, while Zarathustra himself may speak about certain things in his own (human, all-too-human) voice, when his *solitude* speaks—that is, when his most solitary solitude manifests itself in such a way as to situate Zarathustra within his own proper essence and within the open of being—it is the animals who speak: "And when Zarathustra's solitude speaks, it is his animals who are speaking [*Reden*]." Phrased otherwise, it is the animals, and not Zarathustra, who articulate Zarathustra's ownmost being, who delineate the parameters of his essence: it is the animals who *say* Zarathustra as he is, who *tell* him who he is, and who do so from out of an essential nearness to being. In other words, it is only in the face of the animal Other that Zarathustra gains entry into his own essence. (This will become even clearer in the section entitled "The Convalescent," which will be analyzed below.)

Thirdly, and relatedly, it is of course remarkable that Heidegger here speaks of these animals as *speaking*, speaking of them as if they had λόγος and were capable of articulate discourse, as if he had not already by 1937 spent significant time arguing in favor of the view that animals do not "have" or "participate" in λόγος, and as if he did not spend the rest of his career, all the way until the very end, again and again affirming the same.[12] More so even than the moment in *The Fundamental Concepts of Metaphysics* when Heidegger practices a kind of ventriloquy with the animal, transposing himself into it and speaking for it, in the Nietzsche lectures it is presented as though it is the most natural thing in the world that these animals are talking, speaking on their own in their own voices with full words and sentences, words that will penetrate to Zarathustra's deepest core and radically transform his understanding of himself.

After introducing these animals—animals which, although certainly *not* human, nevertheless possess that essential quality that, from at the very least Aristotle onward, has been presumed as being distinctive of the human (i.e., λόγος)—Heidegger proceeds to dissect the precise role of the animals within the text. He begins by noting that these particular animals, the eagle and the serpent, are *images* (*Bilder*) of Zarathustra, indeed, images of his very essence.[13] More precisely, these two animals are an image of Zarathustra's task (*Aufgabe*): namely, his task to become a teacher of eternal recurrence and thereby to bring the being of beings to language. The animals' status as image (*Bild*) seems to suggest that they copy or represent Zarathustra's essence, that they are something like metaphors or similes meant to help us understand something that is already present (though perhaps invisible) within Zarathustra. In other words, the language of imagery makes it seem as though that *first* there is Zarathustra's essence, and *then* the essence of these animals, the latter of which *images*—that is, copies or represents—the former. Such a view seems initially supported by Heidegger's claim that the eagle, in its circling, is "an image [*Sinnbild*] of eternal return" and that the serpent coiled around its neck is, for its part, "symbolic [*Sinnbild*] of the ring of eternal return."[14] All of this seems to suggest that Zarathustra's animals are nothing but allegories or metaphors that, as such, come *after* Zarathustra, representing who he (essentially) is. One is thus seemingly given a scene here where animals come *after* the human, following upon the human in the way that an image follows upon an original. Here, then, one seemingly sees emphasized the characteristic (and metaphysical) priority of the human over the animal that one seemingly finds in so many of Heidegger's works.

However, if one tracks the animals carefully through the text that follows, one sees that the situation is far more complicated and, in fact, entirely inverted: for once these animals arrive on the scene, the priority or anteriority of the human is radically called into question. This becomes clearer as Heidegger begins to trace the essential character of these two animals—not, however, what they *represent*, but rather "what they themselves *are*" (*was die Tiere selbst sind*).[15] According to Heidegger, the eagle is the proudest animal (*das stolzeste Tier*), where pride is to be understood as "the fully developed decisiveness [*Entschiedenheit*] of one who maintains himself at the level of his own essential rank."[16] One could say that the proud person is that one who *cuts* (*schieden*) himself off from all others, and in such a way as to truly know himself from out of himself without reference to others. Such a one stands apart, separated from others—as by an abyss—resolute in his authenticity. To take this even further, one could say that pride, as decisiveness, is that solitude that belongs to the one who—*like a wild animal*—holds himself utterly outside of the boundaries of the οἶκος, of the home, of the familiar, and stands wholly on his *own*, cut off from the herd, and Heidegger even at one point marks the *uncanniness* (i.e., the unfamiliarity and wildness) of these animals: "[T]he eagle and serpent are not pets [*Haustiere*]; we do not take them home with us and proceed to domesticate them."[17] These animals are the undomesticated, the unhomely, the *unhemliche* in this sense: their very presence unsettles the familiar in which the human otherwise rests.

The serpent, for its part, is the most discerning (*klügste*) animal, where discernment names the knowledge regarding the manifold ways in which beings appear. As such, discernment entails "power over the play of being and semblance" (*die Macht über das Spiel von Sein und Schein*)[18] and thus the ability to grasp beings in their being—to grasp beings, that is, *as such*. Stated most simply, discernment is the ability to withstand the openness of being so as to see beings within the light of such an open. More than being simply sly or clever, as it is traditionally presented, the serpent here is the one who has genuine insight into what *is*, the one who authentically *knows*, the one who truly knows a being *in its being*. Unlike that animal from *The Fundamental Concepts of Metaphysics* who is unable to relate to beings *as such*, who is unable *to know*,[19] here the serpent is able to comport itself toward beings in their very being.

Concomitant with this "power over the play of being and semblance" is the ability to deceive and to disguise (*verstellen*)—that is, the ability *to conceal*. Quite remarkably, the ability to deceive, and its relation to apophantic discourse (and λόγος more generally), is one of the specific abilities that Heidegger denies the animal in *The Fundamental Concepts of Metaphysics*.[20] There, the animal, as ἄλογον and thus as lacking the ability to grasp beings as such, is neither able to grasp the truth of beings nor be deceived about them, let alone deceive others about them.[21] And yet, in the Nietzsche lectures, it is exactly this ability that is said to belong to the serpent, that keenest of animals who wields power over being. The serpent here, it seems, has λόγος in its fullest dimensions, possessing both its illuminating and its concealing characters.

Taken together, these two animals—the eagle and the serpent—stand on their own in the open of being, and in such a way as to withstand that open and discern its most essential features.[22] Moreover, as discerning, the animals are able *to point* out these essential features, to articulate them, *to speak* them, to make them visible as such. (Heidegger will soon make this explicit.) In their superlative solitude, the animals stand as authentically resolute, thereby making a *decision* about being, about themselves, and thus becoming their ownmost selves: and soon they will impart this very ability, by means of λόγος, to Zarathustra.[23]

Given Heidegger's earlier mention of the imagistic character of these animals, one might be tempted to see the animals here as representing the corresponding characteristics in the human, as *metaphors* for a certain type of exceptional and resolute human. However, nothing could be further from the truth. In a remarkable moment in this text, the typical relationship between the human and the animal is inverted, and a decisive and explicit priority is afforded to these animals—for, as we immediately see, it is *from* these animals that Zarathustra is to obtain these qualities: "Zarathustra's two animals are the proudest and the most discerning of animals. They belong together and they are out on a search. That is to say, they seek someone [*sie suchen einen*] of their own kind [*Art*], one who matches their standards [*ihren Maßen*], someone who can hold out with them in solitude. They seek to learn whether Zarathustra is still living, living as one prepared for his downgoing."[24] Here, it is the animals who are seeking *one of their own kind*, someone in whom they see traces of themselves, someone for whom they are to serve as the *measure* (*Maß*). The eagle and serpent are hunting, as it were, for one like themselves, for one who exhibits pride and discernment to an extent worthy of their attention. These animals, themselves solitary in their superlative state and thus set apart (and independent) from all others, seek one who is *like themselves*, one who is set apart in the same way.[25] As the ones who are seeking another like themselves, their essence is already *decided*, it is already determined, whereas Zarathustra's essence, being sought and measured by the animals, is still open to question, is still *undecided*: "Their standing by him suggests that they are curious about him and are ever on the search for him; they want to know whether he is becoming the one he is, whether in his becoming he finds his being."[26] In short, the animals are what they are, they have found their *being*, while Zarathustra has *yet* to become who he is. As already solitary, the animals stand in nearness to being, while Zarathustra still stands at far remove.[27]

In seeking Zarathustra, the animals, as Heidegger has noted, wish to learn whether he is "still living, living as one prepared for his down-going [*Untergang*]."[28] One notes immediately the juxtaposition of *living* (*leben*)—repeated twice by Nietzsche ("*lebe, lebe . . .*")—and *down-going*, a juxtaposition that points to the *deathly* association that down-going carries within itself. Regarding the character of this down-going, Heidegger later offers the following:

"Downgoing" here means two things: first, transition as departure; second, descent as acknowledgment of the abyss. This dual characterization of downgoing must at the same time be grasped in its temporality, in terms of "eternity," correctly understood. The downgoing itself, thought with a view to eternity, is the Moment; yet not as the fleeting "now," not as mere passing. Downgoing is indeed the briefest thing, hence the most transient, but is at the same time what is most accomplished: in it the most luminous brightness of being as a whole scintillates, as the Moment in which the whole of recurrence becomes comprehensible. The apposite imagery here is the coiling serpent, the living ring. In the image of the serpent the connection between eternity and the Moment is established for Nietzsche in its unity: the living ring of the serpent, that is to say, eternal recurrence, and—the Moment [*Augenblick*][. . . .] In the end, Zarathustra hears which eternity it is that his animals are proclaiming to him, the eternity of the Moment that embraces everything in itself at once: the downgoing.[29]

The down-going is thus equated by Heidegger with the Moment (*Augenblick*), the instance of resoluteness whereby one accepts responsibility for one's self in the face of one's mortality. Regarding this Moment, Richard Polt writes that "the moment of vision [. . .] is a broad encounter with one's own temporality in its full scope. It arises as an authentic response to experiences such as anxiety that pull one out of one's fallen, everyday temporality. By facing up to one's own mortality and owning up to one's own indebted responsibility, one can become an authentic individual who resolutely accepts being-toward-death."[30] The Moment, and thus the down-going, therefore come about within the wake of one's confrontation with one's own mortality, with one's own death as an imminent, ineluctable possibility. This connection to mortality can be seen overtly in the second sense that Heidegger gives the "down-going"—namely, "decent as acknowledgment of the abyss." The down-going, as an encounter with one's mortality, is that confrontation with the abyss of the Nothing (i.e., with the nullity of death) that lets the "luminous brightness of being as a whole scintillate."[31] Phrased in terms of the analysis of anxiety within *Being and Time*, one could say that the down-going is the moment of anxiety through which one comes face-to-face with the Nothing as the obverse of being in such a way as to have one's own identity torn free from the dictatorship of the They and individuated into its proper parameters. In the Moment of down-going, one stands alertly within the shrine of the Nothing, and (thus) within the open of the truth of being.

Here, within Heidegger's lectures on Nietzsche, it is the animals who will lead Zarathustra to the Nothing, who will (therefore) lead him to being as a whole and thus into an authentic relation to himself: Zarathustra's down-going into authentic being *follows upon the animals*. All of this means, of course, that the animals manifest and exemplify that solitude (i.e., their authentic resoluteness) *prior* to Zarathustra doing so. Phrased most simply: the solitude of the animals comes *first*, it is prior, it has (chrono-)logical priority. Heidegger is quite clear on this point, stating unequivocally that "these two animals define *for the first time* [*erst*] the most solitary solitude."[32] In other words, such solitary solitude *first* arrives on the scene in and through the animals.

Moreover, as we have seen, such solitude is nothing other than that comportment characteristic of authentic existence, of authentic *Dasein*: it is the moment whereby one becomes one's *own*, thereby standing resolutely in one's individuation. Thus, it is these two animals who, *before* Zarathustra, demonstrate the highest expression of authentic resoluteness. Here, it is the animals who come first and Zarathustra who comes after: the animals are the original and Zarathustra is the image, the copy. Thus, they are not *his* animals at all: rather, he is *their* Zarathustra.

In order to achieve the most solitary solitude (i.e., the most pronounced individuation), Zarathustra must turn to the animals and must come to be like them. Above all, he must *listen* to the animals, to what the animals are saying: for, as becomes clear, the animals speak nothing other than the eternal recurrence of the same, that very idea of which Zarathustra is to become the teacher, the very idea that brings him unto his own authentic resoluteness and that leads him, as we saw at the conclusion of the previous chapter, to sing his "Song of Midnight," the song with which Heidegger chose to end *The Fundamental Concepts of Metaphysics*. In order to understand this most burdensome of ideas—in order, that is, to achieve insight into the being of beings—Zarathustra must first come to experience and endure the most solitary solitude, which he may do only by listening to, and learning from, the animals.

But what is it, precisely, that the animals tell him? The animals articulate for Zarathustra the very blueprint of his essence: "[Y]our animals know well, O Zarathustra, who you are and who you must become [*wer du bist und werden mußt*]."[33] With this foreknowledge—a knowledge of Zarathustra's *being*, a knowledge of who he *is*, a knowledge that Zarathustra himself does not *yet* have—the animals usher Zarathustra into his transformation (i.e., his down-going) into the solitary solitude that will bring him into exposure to the "luminous brightness of being as a whole" (*die hellste Helle des Seienden im Ganzen*).[34] Through this exposure, Zarathustra overcomes (his) humanity and becomes who he is: he becomes himself, he becomes his own.[35] As the following passage makes clear, this *becoming* only occurs to the extent to which Zarathustra listens to the animals, *following after* them: "Only now that the vast stillness pervades Zarathustra's spirit has he found his most solitary solitude, a solitude that has nothing more to do with a merely peripheral existence. And the animals of his solitude honor the stillness, that is to say, they perfect [*sie vollenden*] the solitude in its proper essence [. . . .] The eagle's pride and the serpent's discernment are *now* [*jetzt*] essential qualities of Zarathustra."[36] Zarathustra becomes capable of enduring the most burdensome thought (i.e., the eternal recurrence of the same) and of standing on his own under the weight of such a thought only by first becoming *like* the animals, the animals who (therefore) come before. By holding himself up against the animals, and by holding himself fast within their proximity, Zarathustra cuts himself off from all human others, thereby becoming his own resolute self. In setting himself outside of humanity, *like these animals always already are*, Zarathustra becomes more than human by entering into his proper *Dasein*: in a word, he becomes the *Übermensch*. One can thus see that, in this animal scene, a certain displacing of the traditional metaphysical priority of the human is carried out. Here, the animals take pride of place, serving as the very paradigm of authentic *Dasein*, a paradigm of which Zarathustra is a (mere) facsimile.

An obvious objection to this reading is that the eagle and the serpent are anthropomorphized images that symbolize an exceptional human. It is equally obvious, however, that this cannot be the case. As already mentioned, Heidegger is insistent that the animals are *not* images or symbols and that they *first* embody features that Zarathustra only *later* comes to possess. Moreover, it is clear that, even if the animals were representations, they cannot represent the *human*: for, within the logic of the text, the animals embody what is *beyond* the human, that toward which the human is striving and *after* which it models itself. Far from being images or symbols, the animals are existential pro-vocations in the face of which Zarathustra transforms himself beyond "the human" and into his proper *Dasein*—into, that is, the *Übermensch*. If anything, Zarathustra comes to *re*present or symbolize the eagle and serpent, animals without whom he would be unable to ascend to his ownmost essence.

Heidegger continues his focused encounter with the animals in the following section of the lecture course, titled "The Convalescent," which analyzes the chapter from *Thus Spoke Zarathustra* of the same name. Here, too, the animals speak (*sprechen*) to Zarathustra: "They speak to Zarathustra, they surround him, and remain in his solitude until a particular moment [*Augenblick*] when they leave him alone, cautiously stealing away. Their remaining suggests that they are curious about him and are ever [*immer*] on the search for him; they want to know whether he is becoming the one he is, whether in his Becoming he finds his Being."[37] The animals remain next to Zarathustra, surrounding him in solicitous concern, continually (*immer*) searching for that essence that has yet to be determined and enduringly serving as the measure of that essence. Zarathustra's search for himself—his search for his being and for the very being of beings—takes place under the gaze of, and in response to, the animal Other.

The animals remain near to Zarathustra owing to the fact that he has yet to absorb fully the thought of eternal recurrence, a thought that "lies *beside* him in bed, has not yet become one with him, is not yet incorporated in him and hence is not yet something truly thought."[38] The animals are thus there to ensure that this most difficult of thoughts is finally absorbed by Zarathustra: they are that in the face of which the thought will come to fruition. As he undertakes to incorporate this thought—a thought that is described by Zarathustra as a "sluggish worm"—the animals become afraid. However, as Heidegger writes, "they do not flee in consternation, but come nearer, while all the other animals about them scatter. Eagle and serpent alone remain."[39] Zarathustra's attempt to steep himself fully in the thought of eternal recurrence thus entails a further engagement with the eagle and serpent, the two animals who have initiated his down-going and have led him to this most transformative of thoughts. Only in nearness to these animals will his down-going be borne out.

Not long after, Zarathustra—still under the caring gaze of the animals—grasps the fundamental unity of living, suffering, and circling, and in doing so grasps the thought of eternal return. Exhausted, he collapses, and retires to bed for seven days and nights, during which time, as Nietzsche writes, "the animals do not abandon him, neither by day or night."[40] The eagle flies off at one point to obtain nourishment for Zarathustra, bringing him berries that feed his pride and further solidify his grasping of the being of beings. After seven days of convalescence, the animals wish to speak with Zarathustra about the eternal recurrence of the same. Regarding the conversation (and, indeed, *conversion*) that ensues, Heidegger writes the following: "In the dialogue between Zarathustra and his animals the thought of thoughts is now brought to language. It is not presented as a 'theory'; only in conversation does it prove itself. For here the speakers themselves must venture forth into what is spoken: conversation alone brings to light the extent to which the speakers can or cannot advance, and the extent to which their conversation is only empty talk."[41] A genuine conversation (*Gespräch*) thus comes about between Zarathustra and his animals, initiated by the animals themselves, one in which Zarathustra gives himself over to what is said, giving himself over to the being of beings. The very being of beings is brought to language through a conversation with the animal Other, a conversation that touches upon what is most essential.

The animals begin the conversation, sensing that "somehow a new insight has come to him [i.e., to Zarathustra], an insight concerning the world as a whole." This insight, of course, is the eternal recurrence of the same; and in the face of this insight "they inform Zarathustra that the world outside is like a garden that awaits him" and that the world, now seen under the light of the thought of eternal return, wishes to reach out and consummate Zarathustra's convalescence.[42] Although Zarathustra listens gladly to the animals, "he knows that they are only jabbering [*Schwätzen*]":[43] in other words, he suspects that the animals are only offering him illusions meant as anodynes to allay the grief of grasping the world (i.e., being as a whole) as it really is, speaking to him of a garden where there is only an abyss. As Heidegger writes in his 1941–1942 musings on Hölderlin's "Andenken," such jabbering (*Geschwätz*), "which always chatters in an indiscriminate manner about everything, the high and the low," threatens to corrupt the essence of genuine dialogue and disrupts one's ability to speak, and to listen, poetically.[44] It seems, then, that the animals, though they engage in λόγος here, do so only inauthentically and at the level of idle chatter, speaking to Zarathustra "in seductive words that tempt him to sheer intoxication" and that draw him away from his essential insight and thereby veil the true character of being. Such speech "dances above and beyond all things," missing the true nature of reality.

Zarathustra resists the seductive speech of the animals, not allowing the illusion obfuscating the true character of being to sway him. In the face of his resistance, the animals say: "[T]o those who think as we do, all things themselves dance." Heidegger interprets this as meaning the following: "We [i.e., the animals] do not dance above and beyond the things, they seem to say, but see the things' own dance and sway: you can trust us."[45] In other words, the animals' attitude toward beings is informed by the "dance and sway" of those beings themselves, the essential nature of those beings: the animals are attuned to the true nature of things. They then speak to Zarathustra, in an extended soliloquy, of the essential nature of the world in light of the thought of eternal recurrence:

> Everything goes, everything comes back; eternally rolls the wheel of Being.
>
> Everything dies, everything blooms again; eternally runs the year of Being.
>
> Everything sunders, everything is joined anew; eternally the identical House of Being [*Haus des Seins*] is built. Everything departs, everything greets again; eternally True to itself is the Ring of Being.
>
> In every instant Being begins; around every Here the sphere of There rolls. The center is everywhere. Curved is the path of eternity.
>
> Thus say Zarathustra's animals.[46]

This is the dance of being(s) to which the animals are attuned, the essential movement of beings that constitutes the cyclical self-identity of the House of Being.

But Zarathustra is still not convinced; indeed, he thinks that the animals are jesting and turning his hard-earned insights regarding eternal recurrence into "a mere ditty" that misses everything essential.[47] In so doing, he thinks that they are treating the matter "as humans do," that is, that they are running away from the horror of the thought of eternal return and veiling it with platitudes. Here, the animals seem to ape or parrot the inauthentic comportment toward being that flees in the face of the abyss of the Nothing. Reducing the departing, dying, and disintegration of things to some future renewal, the animals—as most human do—betray a kind of vapid optimism that expects all calamities to eventually be allayed and compensated.[48] Such an attitude, by flattening out all occurrence into indifference, robs one of the ability or inclination *to make decisions*, to stake a claim and risk oneself in action.[49] Above all, such a view flees in the face of the gravity of the Moment and represents a gross misinterpretation of it. The animals, it seems, understand the Moment as "a sort of parade passing through the gateway" on the way toward infinity, a sequence of passing now-moments that finds its resolution far off in the future in a time and place unrelated to the past and the present and to the individual living within that moment.[50] In such a view, an inauthentic understanding of time holds sway that sees the past and present as related only in terms of a pursuant sequence.[51]

By contrast, Zarathustra knows that, for the person who stands authentically in the Moment—or, rather, for the person who simply *is* herself that Moment—the past and future come together in a conflictual unity. Such a person "performs actions directed toward the future and at the same time accepts and affirms the past,"[52] "cultivating and sustaining the strife between what is assigned to him as a task and what has been given him as his endowment."[53] Said otherwise, such a person appropriates her thrownness and cognizantly projects herself forward into her future, the horizons of which are inflected by the specifics of her past. As Heidegger writes earlier in the lecture course, this moment brings about "that kind of individuation which we must grasp as authentic appropriation [*Vereigentlichung*], in which the human self comes into its own."[54] As Krell helpfully notes, such individuation, which transposes the human into the moment of being an individualized self, can be understood in terms of Heidegger's analysis in *Being and Time* of *Dasein*'s relation to its own possible death and the manner in which such a relation catalyzes *Dasein*'s formation of its ownmost self. Regarding all of this, Krell writes that "in Heidegger's subsequent view [i.e., within the Nietzsche lectures], thinking the thought of eternal recurrence is one decisive way to confront the danger [of remaining inauthentic] and to rejuvenate the task of 'authentic appropriation.' "[55]

As we have seen, it is this thought—the thought of eternal recurrence, the catalyst for authentic being—that Zarathustra gets from the animals. In order to enter into his authentic existence—in order to enter into the House of Being—Zarathustra must *first* speak with the animals, the animals who assess and measure him and who therefore have a priority over him. This can be seen in the fact that, despite having initially taken the animal's words for an idle chattering, Zarathustra's attitude toward their words undergoes an essential shift, one that coincides perfectly with his grasp of the thought of all thoughts. Although he was initially bemused by and dismissive of those who comport themselves inauthentically toward the world, Zarathustra now recognizes the *necessity* of such people: he recognizes that "if being as a whole is to be thought, the little men too wait upon their 'yes.' The recurrence of the little man too is necessary."[56] It is only once he affirms even this "dark and repulsive" side of things that Zarathustra conquers his illness and becomes a convalescent fully attuned to the being of beings.

In the face of Zarathustra's recovery, the animals speak again:

> Once more they repeat their message: the world is a garden. Again they call for Zarathustra to come out. But now they say more. They do not simply tell him to come out so that he can see and experience how all things are yearning for him. They call to him that he should learn from the songbirds how to sing: "For singing does a convalescent good." The temptation to take the thought of return merely as something obvious, to take it therefore at bottom as either contemptible mumbling or fascinating chatter, is overcome.[57]

Zarathustra now *agrees* (*übereinstimmt*) with the animals: he has as aligned himself to them, bringing himself into accord with them. Here, again, we see the animals serving as the measure of Zarathustra, as that to which he must align himself in order to enter into his authentic existence. *Überein-stimmen* literally means to attune one's voice (*Stimme*) to another's, to bring one's voice into unity (*ein*) with theirs. Zarathustra is now speaking as the animals speak, singing as they sing. It is crucial, given the broader focus of the present study, to note the sequential character of Zarathustra's agreement: *first* there is the voice, the words, of the animal, and then—and *only* then—a harmonizing on Zarathustra's part. The words of the animals *resonate* within Zarathustra; in this way, he can be understood as a kind of *echo* or *repetition* of them.

One sees, then, that the jabbering of the animals was in fact an *essential* jabbering, a jabbering that Zarathustra needed to hear and embrace in order to fully grasp the thought of all thoughts. *Only* by giving himself over to the speech and words of the animals' is he able to comport himself authentically toward his existence in the light of the being of beings: "In the words they utter they gradually come closer to Zarathustra, the more so as Zarathustra comes closer to himself and to his task."[58] The more intense this encounter between the human and the animal becomes—the more intensely that Zarathustra stands under the gaze of the animal Other—the more he is transformed into his ownmost *Dasein*. In this way, the animals bring Zarathustra to himself, leading him to his authentic being: "For your animals know well [*Wissen es wohl*], O Zarathustra, who you are and must become: behold, *you are the teacher of the eternal return—that* is now *your* destiny [*Schicksal*]!"[59] It is the animals who bring Zarathustra to his destiny, to his ownmost self: in a word, it is the animals who allow Zarathustra proper entry into the House of Being.

In light of Zarathustra's transformation, the animals announce the end of his down-going. Having now fulfilled their search for one who is like them, the animals—seeing that Zarathustra has heard "which eternity it is that his animals are proclaiming to him, the eternity of the Moment that embraces everything in itself at once"—leave him to himself: "[H]e has found what defines him, has become the one who his is."[60] Only in the face of the animal Other has Zarathustra found the loneliest loneliness, the supreme solitude: *himself.* As a parting gift, "the animals of his solitude honor the stillness, that is to say, they perfect [*vollenden*] the solitude in its proper essence in that now they too 'cautiously steal away.' "[61] Then, verifying the nonimagistic nature of the animals and the priority they have over Zarathustra, Heidegger writes: "The eagle's pride and serpent's discernment are now [*jetzt*] essential qualities of Zarathustra."[62] Only in the face of these animals has Zarathustra become who he is, become his ownmost self, become, as Heidegger says, a *hero.*

With Zarathustra's heroism—with, that is, his affirmation of the pain, destruction, and agony of life—"the tragic age commences."[63] The tragic age—the age in which the voluptuousness of being and the abyss of the Nothing are thought together in their essential unity—thus follows upon, and is made possible by, the encounter with the animal Other. One recalls, in passing, that the very *word* "tragedy" carries within itself an ineradicable reference to the animal Other.

～

According to Heidegger, the thought of eternal return is too great to be articulated, let alone understood, by humans: rather, an *other* humanity (*anderen Menschen*) is required to bring this thought to language, a humanity that has passed through humanity into a *transformed* humanity, a humanity no longer bound by the limitations and strictures that belonged to the previous humanity.[64] In short, the *Übermensch* is needed, that one who has come to stand freely and steadfastly within the open of being.[65] However, precisely because the thought of eternal return is incapable of being articulated or grasped by humans—including Nietzsche himself—Nietzsche needed to posit a *poet* (namely, Zarathustra) to bring the idea to language: "When Nietzsche creates poetically the figure of Zarathustra he creates the thinker, creates the other kind of humanity which, in opposition to humanity heretofore, initiates the tragedy by positing the tragic spirit in being itself."[66] It is this poet, in teaching the thought of eternal return (and the tragic life-affirming "yes" that this entails), who will initiate a rupture within humanity, within the "last man," and broach a crossing over to the *Übermensch*, that one capable of standing freely within the open of being. It is *poetry*, then, that initiates the overcoming of the human, an overcoming that could not otherwise occur without the creative spirit of the poet, freed as he is from the fetters of ordinary, calculative thinking.

Yet, as we have seen, this poet, this Zarathustra, is only able to accomplish this crossing-over by first listening to the animals, by giving himself over to what they say: indeed, Heidegger claims that Zarathustra first learns to speak poetically by listening *to the songs of the birds.*[67] In short, Zarathustra only overcomes humanity by first engaging with the animals, by holding himself out before them and exposing his very essence to them, by standing *naked* before them, one could say, and measuring himself against them, taking them as his measure and thus affording them priority of place. In other words, Zarathustra's encounter with the animals brings about the very rupture that Zarathustra will *then* attempt to bring about with this thought of the *Über-mensch*, that way of being *beyond* the human toward which the human must stretch itself. In the face of the animal Other, Zarathustra's own humanness is unsettled and brought into question, and he is challenged to take up himself anew and come to stand, like the animals, on his own, free of the constraints of the all-too-human world. In a word, it is in the face of the animal Other that Zarathustra is provoked into *poeticizing himself.*[68]

Moreover, as the following passage makes clear, the animals can provide *us* with such a transformative force as well, if only we learn how to listen to them correctly:

> Zarathustra's animals are all the more *implacable* inasmuch as we hear them—not expressing certain propositions or rules or admonitions—but saying from out of their essential natures what is essential [*aus ihrem Wesen das Wesentliche sagen*], and saying it with growing lucidity through the palpable presence of sensory imagery. Sense images speak only to those who possess the constructive energy [*die bildende Kraft*] to give them shape, so that they make sense. As soon as the poetic force [. . .] wanes, the emblems [i.e., the animals] turn mute [*verstummen*].[69]

In other words, if one listens poetically (i.e., with "constructive energy") to what is said poetically by the animals, the animals say what is most essential, and do so from out of their very essence. This means that, if one listens to the animals, whose very being is poetic in this way, one is called to poeticize oneself, to posit or place oneself resolutely and freely into the open of being. So long as one listens poetically in this way, the animals are much more than images: they are the unfolding of the essential itself. Such a poetic comportment toward the animals *lets* them *speak* to the human of the being of beings.

To generalize all of this a bit beyond the context of Heidegger's reading of *Thus Spoke Zarathustra,* one can say that the human is only able to become what it is through an engagement with animals, animals who, long before the human ever does, stand on their own within the open of being (though without knowing that open). Through comparing itself to the animal Other, the human becomes aware of its difference from the animal and enters into a fresh comportment to itself: in other words, *the human thereby first becomes itself.* Simply put, the human only ever enters into a grasp of its proper essence in the face of the animal Other. More-over, it is through standing before the animal Other that one first becomes authentically open to the very open of being, for this occurs only through the human's understanding of itself as the *there* of being, the *Da* of *Sein.* In this way, the animal is the origin—or, rather, *an* origin—of authentic resoluteness. Through its comparative engagement with the animal, the human overcomes its entanglement in the contemporary understanding of humanity (as *animal rationale*) and enters into its own resolute self.[70] In a word, the human only becomes *Da-sein* through moving beyond "the human," which one may only do through unsettling oneself in the face of the animal Other.[71]

One can further understand all of this in terms of Heidegger's discussion of the "Moment" (*Augenblick*) within the Nietzsche lectures. As Heidegger argues, the thought of eternal recurrence finds its highest articulation in a proper grasping of the Moment, that is, the moment of decision in the face of the collision of the past and the future. The Moment is realized within the person who grasps the conflictual unity of past and future: it is the person who resolutely takes up the past into which they were thrown and (re)configures for themselves a future. As Heidegger writes in *Logic as the Question concerning the Essence of Language,* "[T]he lore [*Kunde*] of history is given only for him who stands in resoluteness; only he can and may know the inevitability of the historical Dasein."[72] (We will have much more to say about *Kunde*, "lore," in relation to the animal in chapter 5.) Such a person experiences time authentically, becoming genuinely *historical*, insofar as they grasp (and indeed *realize*) the unified convergence of past and future within the present Moment. Authentic *history* thus begins with the appropriate appropriation of authentic time.

But animals, for Heidegger, have no history: on this point he is resolute. For example, in *Logic as the Question concerning the Essence of Language*, Heidegger argues that animals have no history owing to the fact that they do not experience a *happening* (*Geschehen*) in any genuine sense: that is, they have no *time*.[73] As essentially atemporal, animals "take over no mandate, do not submit themselves to a mission so that precisely this submitting, the undertaking, is to constitute their way of being."[74] Ultimately, for Heidegger, the animal remains outside of temporality and (therefore) outside of history because it remains outside of *language* as the opening of world.[75] Because the animal is not called by the originary Saying of being itself—because it does not stand in the truth of being[76]—it has no open relation to its past or its future, and thus cannot comport itself authentically (nor, indeed, inauthentically) to its own life as a thrown project. In other words, although it is often said that animals "live in the present moment"—a platitude that fundamentally accords with Heidegger's claim that the animal remains *entangled* in its environment—the animal is, precisely for that reason, unable to experience the Moment: it is unable to grasp the manner in which past and future, thrownness and projection, form a perfect ring whose curvature is carried out by resolute *Dasein*.

And yet, as we have seen, Zarathustra is only able to embody this resoluteness *because* of his encounter with the animals: indeed, it is *from* the animals that Zarathustra learns of eternal return and *owing* to them that he carries the thought to fruition. In a word, Zarathustra only becomes *authentically historical* in the face of the animals. Thus, although the animals themselves are not historical, they are nonetheless that in the face of which Zarathustra becomes historical: they are, in this way, the very grounding of his authentic historicity.

In light of the two previous chapters, one might understand all of this in the following way. It is only through a comparative examination with animals that the human projects itself as being fundamentally, ontologically different from them. In the face of the apparent un-language of the animal Other (i.e., the apparent way in which the animal lacks a relation to beings *as such*), the human enters into the open of its (own) language: it becomes aware of the gathering that characterizes *Sprache*/λόγος in the broad sense.

In the face of the entanglement of the animal in its environment—for example, the manner in which a dog, regardless of its intelligence, remains ineluctably entrenched in its determinate canine habits and concerns—the human becomes aware of its own *indeterminacy* and the concomitant extent to which the trajectory of its life is open to radical course corrections (or errancies). In the face of the *death* of the animal Other, as was analyzed in the previous chapter, the human first experiences death as a phenomenon, a phenomenon that penetrates the human to its core and orients it toward its own mortality (without, to be sure, giving it any insight into its own possible death). The encounter with the animal is, in this sense, a way in which the human becomes aware of the unique manner in which it stands in the clearing advent of language as the unfolding of world, a world into which it is thrown and from out of which it must project its future. In other words, the encounter with the animal is one way in which the human becomes aware of its own ecstatic temporality, thereby first encountering itself as historical in a genuine sense. In this way, authentic historicity truly *begins* with the grasping of essential uniqueness of the human, a project that can only occur from out of a comparison with the animal Other. The encounter with the animal is thus a pro-vocation into considering one's own role as the *there* of being's throw and the temporal structure that this entails.[77]

Thus, although the animal itself is not historical for Heidegger, it nonetheless serves as that in the face of which the human comes to relate authentically to its own historical *Dasein*. In this way, although the animal is outside of time for Heidegger, an encounter with the animal serves as the very *genesis* of the human's grasp of its own authentic temporality. In other words, the animal is the *outside* of human temporality, an outside in relation to which the human comes to comport authentically to its own *inside*. All of this, of course, means that the animal is always already there as that in the face of which the human understands itself: the animal thus possesses a priority over the human and is constitutive of the latter's identity.

In addition to initiating a movement toward authentic *Dasein*, such a poetic comportment also lets the human grasp the animal in a manner more faithful to its essence. Near the very end of his 1942 lecture course on Parmenides (GA 54), Heidegger references such a poetic comportment and how it would bear upon our understanding of the animal:

> Plant and animal are suspended in something outside of themselves without ever being able to "see" either the outside or the inside, i.e., to have it stand as an aspect unconcealed in the

free of being. And never would it be possible for a stone, no more than for an airplane, to elevate itself toward the sun in jubilation and to move like a lark, which nevertheless does not see the open. What the lark "sees," and how it sees, and what it is we here call "seeing" on the basis of our observation that the lark has eyes, these questions remain to be asked. *In fact, an original poetizing capacity would be needed to which more and higher things are charged, and more essential things (since they are genuinely essential), versus a mere hominization of plants and animals.*[78]

Only by leaving behind the hominizing and anthropomorphizing understanding of animals (i.e., the scientific/metaphysical understanding) can the human gain entry to what is essential about the animal; and through such entry, the human comes into a more genuine relation both to itself and to the animal Other in the face of which its self is constituted.

Crucially, however—and as we will see at greater length in the following two chapters—this poetic comportment is *given* to the human *by the animal itself.* Zarathustra learned how to sing from the animals: that is, he learned how to relate authentically toward the being of beings (i.e., the thought of eternal return) through his encounter with the eagle and the serpent. One can understand this as expressing the manner in which the human's entrenchment in its unreflective self-understanding is interrupted by the appearance of the animal Other, an appearance that provokes the human into reassessing its own identity and status among the things that are. Such an encounter *unsettles* the human—it *sickens* the human—and also sets it on the path toward setting a firmer foundation regarding its own proper *Dasein* (i.e., convalescence). Phrased otherwise, the encounter with the animal both defamiliarizes the human from itself, "casting it adrift,"[79] *and* serves as that in the face of which an erecting of genuine *Dasein* becomes possible. The uncanny animal both casts the human out of its *home* and serves as the means by which the human can attempt an authentic return. The animal is the gatekeeper—or perhaps the guard dog—of the House of Being.

With all of this in mind, we now turn to Heidegger's extensive engagement with Hölderlin, where we will encounter another eagle who plays a sustained and foundational role in bringing the human home into the *there* of (its) proper being.

Chapter Four

Poetic Animals

What withdraws from us draws us along in such withdrawal, whether or not we notice it immediately or never notice it at all. When we are drawn into the draft of the withdrawal, we are—though in a manner entirely different from that of migratory birds—caught up in the draft of what draws.

—Heidegger (GA 8:11; my translation)

Migratory birds always return to the same region.

—Heidegger (GA 46:49/39)

Thus we recognize not only the traversal of space here but also the potential to return home, *the capacity for returning home.*

—Heidegger (GA 29/30:355/243)

In his book *The Fourfold: Reading the Late Heidegger,* Andrew Mitchell has provided a singularly perspicacious analysis of Heidegger's understanding of animality as it presents itself in his "Language in the Poem," a tortuously difficult text from 1953 in which Heidegger offers a focused "elucidation" of a scattering of Georg Trakl's poems. According to Mitchell, this late text marks a rethinking of animality on Heidegger's part, one that diverges significantly—if not diametrically—from the view presented in *The Fundamental Concepts of Metaphysics.* Instead of the apparent ontological hierarchy that one seemingly finds in that text, "Language in the Poem" presents a nuanced assessment of the human/animal difference that places both within an ontological twilight of indeterminacy. Above all else, Mitchell's inquiry shows that, for the Heidegger of the early 1950s, a proper assessment of the human must necessarily take place alongside a rethinking of the animal.

Mitchell's analysis is without equal in the care with which it attends to Heidegger's nuanced understanding of animality, and, in a sense, everything that follows within the present chapter is an attempt to elaborate upon his analysis by drawing it into conversation with other of Heidegger's works. Specifically, by bringing Mitchell's text (and the text of Heidegger's it analyzes) into conversation with Heidegger's encounters with another poet—namely, with that poet whom Heidegger considered to be the very poet of poets, Friedrich Hölderlin[1]—it will be seen that Heidegger's engagement with the latter evinces an understanding of animality that is strikingly similar to what he demonstrates in his engagement with the former. One of the effects of this reading is that, despite agreeing with Mitchell on nearly all other counts, there is one claim, central to his exegesis, that will be challenged through the following inquiry: namely, that the view of animality presented in "Language in the Poem" diverges significantly from the view of animality presented in Heidegger's earlier works. By bringing Heidegger's reading of Trakl into conversation with his lectures on Hölderlin, the following chapter shows that there is a straight line, if not a proximal correspondence, between Heidegger's understanding of animality as it presents itself in his engagements with Hölderlin from the 1930s and 1940s and his engagement with Trakl in 1953. It will also show that, just as was the case in the texts from the 1920s and 1930s analyzed in previous chapters, the animal occupies a place of absolute priority within Heidegger's understanding of "the poet of poets." However, before turning to Heidegger's engagements with Hölderlin, it is necessary to summarize Mitchell's analysis. This summary will be followed by a few additional remarks on the role of animals in Trakl's poem and Heidegger's analysis of it.

Mitchell's analysis takes place within his broader exploration of Heidegger's thinking of the fourfold, that is, the gathering of earth, sky, mortals, and gods through which things open themselves within (or as) the opening of world. As a nonmetaphysical way of conceiving the relation between the human and the other beings among which it finds itself, the fourfold moves away from the modern conceptuality of the subject/object divide by seeking to grasp things in their intimate relationality to one another and to the open in (and as) which they emerge. As such, the fourfold also entails a reconsideration of animality and, therefore, a reframing of the relationship between the animal and the human. Ultimately, according to Mitchell, Heidegger's reading of Trakl shows him rethinking the animal "in terms of its exposure to world."[2] Regarding this exposure, Mitchell writes that

> [i]n the fourfold, plants and animals are on par with waters and stones; one is no less constitutive of world than the other. Otherwise put, world building is not a privilege of anyone, not even of the mortals. The mortals are participants in the gathering of the fourfold that things in the thing, that worlds in the world, just the same as the earth and its cast of waters, stones, plants, and animals. No one has privileged access to world here. The prior privilege of Dasein atop a hierarchy is undone by this thought. World is no longer restricted to Dasein, nor is it the antagonist of earth. World is the property or possession of no one. What we witness with the fourfold, then, in this simple listing of stones, waters, plants, and animals in considering the earth, is nothing less than a reconfiguration of Heidegger's conception of world, moving beyond his earlier treatments found in the period of fundamental ontology as well as in his middle works. The consequences of this should not be underestimated.[3]

The fourfold is thus, among other things, a manner of rethinking the human *alongside* animals, as engaged with them on a world-forming level. Such a rethinking entails a displacing of the human as occupying a place of privilege among (or above) other beings while also adding important nuance to Heidegger's many and various other claims that the animal is without world or world-poor.[4]

As Mitchell notes, Trakl's poem (and Heidegger's analysis of it) focuses on the movement of *wandering*.[5] Such wandering is emblematic of the indeterminacy that, for Heidegger, comes to characterize both human and animal being (in their relation to one another) as they are (re)conceived in terms of the fourfold. It also serves as the primary artery by means of which Heidegger's encounter with Trakl is connected to his encounter with Hölderlin, the latter of which is fundamentally structured in terms of (what I am calling) the logic of the necessary detour, that is, the manner in which an excursion out of one's essence is structurally necessary for the development and self-understanding of that essence. Heidegger's readings of Trakl and Hölderlin are both preoccupied with the transit of the human *from* its understanding of itself as human (or *animal rationale*) *toward* the establishing of its proper *Dasein*, a transit that, as we will see, structurally entails a necessary detour through the animal.

Heidegger begins his analysis by invoking the line from Trakl's poem, "The soul is a stranger among this earth." As such a stranger, the soul is characterized by a certain itinerant movement, a passage from one place to another. As enacting this movement of passage, the "soul"—which, as the text makes clear, is a placeholder for "the human" or, sometimes, "the poet"—stands between determinate states and is thus characterized by a certain essential unsettledness. The soul/human/poet is also associated with the figure "Elis" from another of Trakl's poems. (We will return to the importance of Elis below.)[6] In all cases, the figure of the soul/human/poet/Elis shows itself to be constituted by a restless wandering that characterizes its journey among the beings of the earth.

Drawing on the poem, Heidegger notes that the soul is "called" onto this journey. To where is it called? Into the down-going, the *Untergang*. As Mitchell explains, this *Untergang* is not to be understood in terms of "downfall" or "destruction" (as the word often expresses) but rather as a merging into the things of the world that serves to dissolve the human's understanding of itself in terms of modern subjectivity: "The soul is called to be among the things of the world, which is to say, it is called into this between."[7] Such a call results in a dissolution of self (understood as "subject") that brings the human into greater intimacy with the beings among which it finds itself. (In this way, the *downgoing* operative within Heidegger's reading of Trakl is in essential agreement with Heidegger's understanding of Zarathustra's *downgoing*, as discussed in the previous chapter.) Finding itself no longer as a subject over against objects (as their perceptual and metaphysical ground), the human enters into a kind of ontological twilight, an indeterminant relationality with other beings. This twilight of interrelationality proves to be the play-space of the fourfold, which is the very play-space of the opening of being itself.

Mitchell then casts this down-going, this passage into indeterminacy, in terms of *homelessness*: "No longer at home and not yet at its destination, the wandering soul finds itself on the way somewhere. On these paths between enclosures, it wanders exposed. The essence of this soul as a stranger means that it is never at home, not even with itself. It is not defined by being in place, but by being underway, neither here nor there. Having left the closure of the home behind, it is exposed to what comes."[8] Exposed among beings, displaced as the subjective ground of objects, the human wanders in homelessness, *not yet* at its destination, adrift in the between of the fourfold.

While wandering homelessly in such a way, the human is suddenly seen by a blue deer (*Wild*). It is here, at this moment of being seen, that we find the crux of Heidegger's rethinking of animality within this text. By presenting the deer in blueness (which, for Heidegger's Trakl, indicates a blurring of distinctions similar to the twilight),[9] the otherwise conceptually fixed definition of animality is called into question. As occurred previously with the figure of the wandering soul, the animal is here brought into a place of indeterminacy wherein the parameters of its heretofore rigidified essence are called into question. As Mitchell writes, "The animal is not some self-contained creature harboring a species-being. The animal is instead what it is on account of a relation that carries the animal out past itself to situate it in the between, to transform it into the blue deer."[10] This transformation yields a deer whose countenance is directed toward the *holy*, that is, toward the open provenance of what is to come. This results in a deer who is by no means "merely" an animal (i.e., understood as the "irrational animal" in distinction to the human), but one who can witness and *remember*—both tasks that have traditionally been reserved for the human. As Heidegger writes, "[T]he blue game is an animal, whose animality presumably does not rest in the animalistic, but rather in that watchful recollection after which the poet calls."[11] The effect of Trakl's poem is thus the dissolution of the traditional depiction of the animal as irrational (i.e., as a dumb brute) and of the metaphysically and ontologically dualistic manner of distinguishing the animal from the human.[12] Such a blurring of lines necessarily brings about a certain reconsideration of what it means to be human, insofar as it dissolves the boundaries that have traditionally separated the human from the animal. In this way, one could say that Heidegger's encounter here with Trakl's blue deer brings about a *wilding* of the human, an *undomesticating* and *defamiliarizing* of the human that renders the human strange, even *alien*, to itself.

One possible objection against all of this is that Heidegger is offering an anthropomorphized view of the deer, one that locates within it certain decisively human abilities (such as witnessing, recollecting, etc.). However, such an objection would entirely miss the force of Heidegger's analysis, the result of which is a radical rethinking both of animality and of the *anthropos*. The point of Heidegger's reading of Trakl, as Mitchell shows, is to recast both the human and the animal in terms of their shared inhabitance of the indeterminate play-space of the fourfold. And while Heidegger's true focus may be the passage of the human from its self-understanding as modern subject (and *animal rationale*) to the authentic mortality of its *Dasein*, his reading of Trakl nevertheless yields a new notion of animality, one that must necessarily remain undefined: "[T]his animality is still far off and scarcely to be sighted. The animality of the animal here intended thus vacillates in the undefined."[13]

In the wake of this rethinking of animality, *mortality* is no longer the possession of only the human, as is so often the case elsewhere in Heidegger's work. In fact, as Mitchell writes, "mortality for the human is only possible through a liberation of animality, a rethinking of the animal, our relation to animals, and the animality of ourselves. Mortality is not at all a privilege of the human, and Heidegger notes this himself, and quite strikingly: 'The name "blue deer,"' Heidegger writes, 'names the mortal.' "[14] The reconsideration of animality thus entails a reconsideration of the human and the latter's previously presumed relationship with *death*. Such a reconsideration results in Heidegger's suggestion that, contrary to what is often supposed (most vocally by Heidegger himself), the human cannot *simply* be understood as mortal: that is, the human is *not yet* mortal, having not yet moved out of its entanglement in the modern understanding of subjectivity and into the open indeterminacy of the fourfold.[15] In other words, mortality is not something that the human being simply possesses as a static and defining ontological trait, but rather something toward which it must journey, something it must work to obtain. As Mitchell further notes, this reconsideration of mortality and who possesses it undermines the many scholarly indictments against Heidegger's supposed privileging of the human.[16]

As mentioned above, Mitchell's analysis is exemplary in its attentiveness to Heidegger's nuanced understanding of animality within this text. However, there are a few additional points that need to be raised that bear upon the present inquiry, points that Mitchell either overlooked or simply did not include given the broader focus of his book. Returning now to the beginning of Heidegger's "Language in the Poem," we recall that the stranger (i.e., the soul/the human) is *called* to go-under, called to sojourn among beings in an ontological twilight. As we have seen, this amounts to a call toward a confrontation with one's own mortality, the result of which is the arrival at a thoughtful reckoning of one's own relational essence, a coming-to-be-at-home within the open fourfold of being. Simply put, this is the call away from a thoughtless immersion in the contemporary understanding (and enactment) of the human (as "subject") and toward a thoughtful acknowledgment of one's own *Da-sein*.

What is remarkable, though it goes unmentioned by Mitchell, is that this call is issued forth within Trakl's poem by an *animal*:

> O how still is a walk down the blue river's bank
> To ponder forgotten things, when in leafy boughs
> The thrush [*Die Drossel*] called [*rief*] to a strange thing to go
> under.

It is a *thrush* who calls the soul (i.e., "a strange thing") to go-under, to enter into the twilight of ontological indeterminacy. It is thus an animal who calls to the human to enter into its own essence by pulling it away from its immersion in the contemporary forgetfulness of being and moving it toward a more attentive awareness of the open fourfold of being. The movement of the human from homelessness toward the home, which is the very movement characteristic of human existence as such, is thus initiated here *by an animal*.

Later on in Heidegger's analysis, we encounter another moment where a call is made to the human, and here again the call is sounded forth by an animal:

> The poet sees the soul, "something strange," destined to follow a path that leads not to decay, but on the contrary to a going-under. This going-under yields and submits to the mighty death in which he who died early leads the way. The brother, singing, follows him in death. Following the stranger, the dying friend passes through the ghostly night of the years of apartness. His singing is the "Song of a Captured Blackbird," a poem dedicated to L. v. Ficker. The blackbird is the bird that called [*rief*] Elis to go under. It is the birdvoice [*Vogelstimme*] of the deathlike one. The bird is captured in the solitude of the golden footfalls that correspond to the ride of the golden boat on which Elis' heart crosses the blue night's starry pond, and thus shows to the soul the course of its essential being.[17]

The blackbird calls Elis into his down-going, into his being-toward-death, into a confrontation with his essential being. More precisely, it is the *bird-voice* (*Vogelstimme*) that calls Elis here: it is an animal that calls the human into its movement toward home. This is even clearer in Trakl's "An Den

Knaben Elis," where Trakl writes: "Elis, wenn die Amsel im schwarzen Wald ruft, dieses ist dein Untergang" (Elis, *when* the blackbird calls in the dark woods, this is your down-going).[18] In both the case of the thrush and that of the blackbird, an animal—that which Heidegger ceaselessly insists is without λόγος, without the world-opening activity of language—beckons the human, *calls* to it, *attuning* (*stimmend*) it toward the course of its essence. Wordlessly and without speech, the animal calls to the human, drawing it onto the track of its own mortality, its own *death*. Without a grasp of either being or nothingness, the animal nonetheless calls the human toward an encounter with both.

In light of this, one recalls the analysis of the role of the animal in Heidegger's discourse on death in *Being and Time* offered in chapter 2. Indeed, one might be further tempted to understand this call (*Ruf*) in terms of another call so critical to Heidegger's understanding of death in *Being and Time*: namely, the call of *conscience* that calls the human back from its entanglement in the They toward a more authentic configuration of its being. Within *Being and Time*, this call is voiced by *Dasein* itself, from itself to itself, in a kind of immediate autoaffection. And yet, the call does not simply come from *Dasein*, but rather seemingly from *over* and *outside* of it: a foreign (*fremd*) voice, an *uncanny* (*unheimliche*) voice, that calls the human to its proper *Dasein*.[19] Within "Language in the Poem," this uncanny call ushers forth not from *Dasein* but from an *animal*, from the thrush and the blackbird, both of whom call to the human from the outside. Far from an autoaffective call from itself to itself (i.e., from its authentic possibility to its inauthentic everydayness), this call enters into the human from a legitimate outside, calling it to travel outside of itself and into a reconfiguration of its *Dasein*.

One might be even further tempted to imagine how this animal call affects the individualized character that belongs to death in Heidegger's analysis from *Being and Time*. There, death is a very solitary affair, in that it is only through one's relationship to one's *own* possible death—a death that cannot be gleaned from anywhere else or taken from anyone else—that one initiates a movement toward one's authentic being. Yet, in Heidegger's reading of Trakl, the call toward death, toward the Nothing and thus toward an authentic reckoning of one's own *Dasein*, enters into the human from the outside through the call of the animal Other. Being-toward-death is thus presented here as something that comes about as a result of an encounter with an-Other: a tandem affair. We will soon see a similar case where the human's confrontation with its own death is provoked by the animal Other when we turn to Heidegger's analysis of the first choral ode from Sophocles's *Antigone* from his 1942 lectures on "Der Ister."

In any case, it is clear that the animal plays a constitutive and foundational role within Trakl's poems in provoking the human to confront its own essence. What this means, however, is that it is only *after* an encounter with an animal, and *following* upon it, that the human comes to stand steadfastly within its own proper *Dasein*. The movement away from the human's self-understanding as rational subject toward the authentic appropriation of its ownmost being is, within this text, initiated through an encounter with the animal. In this way, this text operates in accordance with what is here being called the logic of the necessary detour, insofar as the animal plays a necessary structural role in the human's movement toward its own proper essence.

Finally, we note in passing a certain structural similarity between Derrida's encounter with his cat (from *The Animal That Therefore I Am*) and Heidegger's analysis of the role of the blue deer in Trakl's poem. For Derrida, finding himself suddenly beneath the gaze of the cat challenges his presumed sovereignty and calls him to question his own identity: "What am I, therefore? Who is it that I am (following)?"[20] Likewise, Trakl's wanderer, upon *being seen* by the blue deer, is cast into the ontological twilight discussed above (and elucidated by Mitchell). In both cases, the encounter with an animal—and specifically finding oneself under the gaze of an animal—brings about a crisis in one's self-understanding and forces a reconsideration of one's humanity.

One important difference to note is that, unlike with Derrida's encounter with his cat, there is no mention made by Heidegger of the blue deer seeing the wanderer's *sex*: in other words, there is no mention of *nudity* within Heidegger's text. However, although there is no mention of physical nudity, can one not infer a certain *ontological nudity* implicit in the *exposure* of which Mitchell speaks? In *The Animal That Therefore I Am*, Derrida offers the following definition of nudity: "[It] is nothing other than that passivity, the involuntary exhibition of the self."[21] Derrida is seen by his cat before he sees himself *being seen* by his cat; he sees the cat, therefore, before he sees himself. But is this not precisely what happens to the stranger in the face of (i.e., under the gaze of) the blue deer—an involuntary exposure that calls into question the very parameters of the self, one that, moreover, entails a certain *melancholy* to match Derrida's malaise?[22]

Having now analyzed and supplemented Mitchell's work on Heidegger's encounter with Trakl's deer, we turn to Heidegger's readings of Hölderlin from the 1930s and 1940s, namely, his lectures on "Germania," his lectures on "Der Ister," and his *Elucidations of Hölderlin's Poetry*, each in turn. What will be seen is that animal encounters are no less crucial within these texts, and no less constitutive of the human's journey toward its own proper essence. Above all, it will be shown that Heidegger's encounter with Hölderlin is thoroughly characterized by the logic of the necessary detour, although the specifics vary in each case.

"Germania"

In 1934–1935 at the University of Freiberg, Heidegger delivered his first lecture course on Hölderlin, which focused on the two poems "Germania" and "The Rhine." The lectures on "Germania," which constitute roughly the first half of GA 39, offer a rich analysis of the structure and world-forming function of poetizing, as well as a meditation on the ur-phenomenon of founding attunements (*Grundstimmungen*). Early in the lecture course, Heidegger states that Hölderlin "speaks from out of an attunement [*Stimmung*], an attunement that determines and attunes [*be-stimmt*] the ground and soil and that permeates [*durchstimmt*] the space upon which and within which the poetic telling founds a way of being. This attunement we name the founding attunement [*Grundstimmung*] of the poetizing."[23] Conceived most broadly, a founding attunement is the manner in which beings as a whole (and being as such) emerge into the open and reveal themselves at a particular historical or epochal moment. (Drawing on the root word *stimme*, one might say the founding attunement "voices" or "articulates" beings into the open of their being.) Offering a concise definition of such founding attunements, Heidegger writes that "by founding attunement, we do not mean some vague emotional state that merely attends the [poetic] telling. Rather, the founding attunement opens up the world that in the poetic telling receives the stamp of beyng."[24] Founding attunements thus open up and sustain a world: they open up and define the horizon of meaning in which (and how) beings show themselves. The founding attunement specific to Hölderlin's "Germania," and to the age to which it gives voice, is what Heidegger calls "holy mourning." Such holy mourning is the state of an attentive readiness, born out of the flight of the old gods (i.e., the abandonment of being), that awaits (and in such waiting, prepares) the arrival of the other inception. In giving expression to this holy mourning, Hölderlin's "Germania" founds the attunement characteristic of the contemporary world, setting the ground for the locale (or site) of human *Dasein* and preparing that site for its transformation.[25]

In order to distinguish such a grounding attunement from a mere sensibility or emotion, Heidegger offers the following clarification: "With regard to this and every founding attunement, however, it must be said from the outset that what is at issue here is not some weak resignation that submerges itself in so-called feelings, a kind of sentimentality that merely 'broods over' the state of one's own soul."[26] He then adds the following, which serves to connect the ur-phenomenon of founding attunements with the problematic of animals being explored in the present study:

> Founding attunements—to use a customary distinction here—do not concern the soul, but the spirit. Pain and suffering in general are only by virtue of our enduring a conflict. Animals too can indeed endure pain and suffering, but their suffering and being in pain [*dieses Leiden und Schmerzenhaben*] is not sorrow [*Leid*], just as stomach pains are not in themselves sorrow, nor the kind of pain that mourning is. Nor are these merely a "higher" kind of feelings, but rather something essentially different [*wesentlich anderes*].[27]

In other words, although animals can experience pain, such experience does not attain to the level of sorrow (*Leid*), to the level of mourning (*Trauerarbeit*), and certainly not to the level of mourning understood as a founding attunement. Thus, animals, for Heidegger, cannot mourn, at least not in the rich, meaningful, and disclosive sense in which human beings can be said to do so. If there is any animal mourning, one would suspect, given Heidegger's typical comments regarding the animal, then it is an *impoverished* mourning specific to the parameters of the animal's *Umwelt* but abyssally different from the human's mourning within the open of the truth of being. (We will return to the question of animal mourning in the next chapter.)

In passing, one notes that here, in defining founding attunements, Heidegger demonstrates a certain methodological priority of the animal within his thinking. As we have now seen numerous times, just as Heidegger attempts to delineate the proper parameters of the human—in this case in terms of founding attunements—he *turns toward the animal* as that over against which the human is to be understood. In so turning, Heidegger marks the priority of the animal as that in terms of which, or on the basis of which, a proper understanding of human *Dasein* is possible. It is only by comparing the human to the animal that the former will come into its proper aspect.

In any case, for Heidegger, it is ultimately owing to the manner in which the animal stands outside of language that it lacks the ability to mourn, and thus the ability to enter into holy mourning:

> By virtue of language, the human being is the witness of beyng. He testifies on its behalf, stands up to it, and falls victim to it. Where there is no language, as in the case of animals and plants, there, despite all life, is no manifestness of beyng and, for this reason, there is no non-being either and none of the emptiness belonging to the Nothing. Plant and animal stand on this side of such things; here there reign only blind pursuit and opaque flight. Only where there is language does world prevail.[28]

Because the animal lacks language, it lacks world; and because it lacks world, the animal is unable to be exposed to the founding attunement of that world, through whose coloring beings take on their specific meanings. Wordless and worldless, the animal is closed off from the open.

Heidegger elsewhere in the lecture course expands on this exclusion of the animal from the open of language, from the world, noting that such exclusion cuts the animal off both from exposure to being and from the Nothing:

> Why does the animal not speak? Because it does not need to speak. Why does it not need to speak? Because it does not have to speak. It does not have to, because it is not compelled to. It is not compelled to do so, because it is closed off with respect to beyng as such. Neither being nor non-being, nor the nothing nor emptiness are accessible to it. Why is being closed off from the animal? Because it is not within language. So, the animal does not speak because it is not within language.[29]

Heidegger goes on to say that such exclusion is owed to the animal's "essential otherness." Such otherness does not prevent the animal from dealing with beings in its own way, though it does, given the above, ensure that whatever manner such dealings take they will be outside of the open of language.[30]

Later, Heidegger again gestures to the essential otherness of the animal:

We do indeed directly experience stone, plant, and animal as being. Yet who, when asked, would presume to say how things stand concerning the beyng of such beings? Does the boulder "have" its beyng, just as it "has" its extension, heaviness, hardness, and color? And where, then, does such beyng "reside"? And correspondingly in the case of the rose and the eagle: We can say one thing only, and that only on the basis of a very difficult argument: stone, plant, and animal are—but their "own" beyng remains closed off to them as such beyng, and indeed in a different way each time for each of these beings. It is even precipitous to say that they have their "own" beyng.[31]

Thus, although Heidegger exhibits a certain hesitancy here regarding the determination of animal being, and even marks that such hesitancy may be necessary, he nonetheless states that animals lack an openness to their own being, although he does so "only on the basis of a very difficult argument." Thus, the animal, outside of language, outside of *world,* is unable to mourn, and is equally unable to occupy the founding attunement by which the contemporary site is prepared for the coming of the other beginning. One seemingly finds Heidegger's hierarchical privileging of the human over the animal at its highest pitch within these pages.

However, despite refusing animals the ability to speak here, Heidegger proceeds, quite remarkably, to speak of an animal *who speaks.* As Heidegger notes, line 66 and following of Hölderlin's "Germania" presents an *eagle* calling out to the young girl, to Germania, a call that comprises the entire latter half of the poem. This eagle, whom Heidegger identifies as a messenger (*Bote*) of the god, brings tidings (*Kunde*) to the poet.[32] (We will have much more to say about such tidings in chapter 5.) The poet must stay with the eagle and attend to its message in order to be able to carry out a founding act of poetic naming. Regarding this act, Heidegger writes:

What is to be named—to be once more opened up in an originarily founding saying and knowing—is, on the one hand, the Mother, the Earth herself. But in this naming, as poetic, there resonates the "divinity of old" (line 100) together with that which is to come: History arises. Only from out of these two does Dasein attain the "middle of time" (line 103)—the true counter-turning. The latter is not what lies nearest, the mere present day and contemporaneous that we always come upon; rather, the middle of time is that which comes last, that which is only insofar as it comes to be in founding and grounding. It is that historical Dasein within which and as which the essence of this land finds and completes itself.[33]

It is thus *following* upon the eagle's call that the poet names—that is, *founds*—an epoch's historical *Dasein*. Only as a *response* to the eagle's speech can the poet initiate such a founding.

As discussed above, such a founding, within the contemporary moment, is carried out through (and within) the attunement of holy mourning, that attunement which, in the wake of the absence of the old gods, awaits the arrival of what is to come (i.e., the "last god"). Thus, the eagle—although it is an animal who, as being outside of the open of language, cannot mourn—is nonetheless that which calls the poet into its attunement of holy mourning, provoking and rendering possible the poet's act of poetic founding. Itself outside of world, the eagle is nonetheless instrumental in the poet's opening up *of* the world; itself outside of mourning, the eagle is nonetheless that by means of which the poet is brought to its place of holy mourning.

Elsewhere, Heidegger writes of this founding attunement in terms of *language*. Focusing on lines 33 and following, Heidegger notes a shift in narrative voice within the poem. Although the poem begins in the first person, it soon shifts to the language of "us," and then to the language of "the man." About this man, Heidegger asks: "Who is this man? He looks into the Orient, and from there is met by many transformations: Indus, Parnassus, Italy, the Alps. 'The man' who looks and awaits has taken our place."[34] Heidegger then observes that the man (i.e., "we" and "I") hears the eagle call out to him, speaking (*spricht*) to him, and speaking specifically of language. The eagle calls out to him, and calls out to Germania, *to speak, to name*, and *to found* the site of historical *Dasein*:

> The poem is language. Yet who properly speaks in the poem? The author, the "I," we, the man, the eagle. They speak of language that is to name (speak) and yet in naming to leave unspoken. If we have followed even vaguely the pointers just given, without conceptually "comprehending" the proper coherence of what has been indicated, then it becomes clear how far we have now

> come from reporting the content of something said here. For this saying is manifold. That which is saying transforms itself into something said and vice versa: The latter transforms itself into the former, a saying of the saying. Everything turns around, so that "no one knows what is happening to him" (line 27).[35]

One is tempted to read this confusion as indicative of the sort of ontological indeterminacy discussed by Mitchell in his analysis of Heidegger's engagement with Trakl (as discussed at the beginning of this chapter). In the wake of the poetic saying—which is nothing other than the unfolding of language itself—the identity of the speaker, of he who lets language unfold, is called into question. Indeed, the very boundaries between the *self*, the *we*, and the *eagle* all dissolve, leaving them all in a place of ontological indeterminacy and calling into question the supposed linguistic privilege of the human: indeed, one could say that there is a certain *wilding* of the human taking place here as it is brought into proximity with the animal Other.

More germane to the present inquiry, what one sees here is that the speaking of the eagle plays an integral part in the process by which historical *Dasein* forms its fundamental attunement toward beings (and thus toward being). The animal, excluded by Heidegger from standing within the open of this (or any) founding attunement, is nonetheless that without which the poet is unable to carry out its founding. *Prior* to such a poetic founding, there is an encounter with the animal, a *listening* to its call.[36]

One finds a nearly identical scene involving an eagle in the unfinished "Western Conversation" (in GA 75), written in the latter half of the 1940s, in which Heidegger presents a dialogue wherein an eagle plays a foundational role in bringing about a transformation of human *Dasein*. In this dialogue, two characters—the Younger Man and the Older Man—discuss the transformative importance of Hölderlin's poetry, and especially of his "Der Ister." The ultimate purpose of the conversation, as one of the characters says, is "to bring poetry [and Hölderlin's poetry in particular] into an essentially transformed relation to the human,"[37] a transformation that cannot be willed about through the machinations of humans but must rather come about through the dispensation (*Geschick*) of being itself. As Charles Bambach observes, this transformed relation to poetry is part of a larger transformation of German identity, an interrogating of the Germans regarding "whether [they] are ready to confront the dispensation (*Schickung*) sent to them from out of beyng—that is, whether they are fatefully attuned enough to respond to the call that emerges from Hölderlin's Ister hymn, the one calling them to the festal table to celebrate the return of the gods."[38] As one soon sees, it is an *eagle* through whom being will send its call and who will thus make such a transformation possible. Not long into the conversation, the Older Man quotes the passage from Hölderlin's "Germania" in which the eagle is said to soar (*überschwingt*) above the Alps and draws special attention to the eagle's soaring (*Schwingen*).[39] The Young Man responds by quoting a passage from Hölderlin's "Der Ister":

> Not without soaring [*Schwingen*] may
> someone grasp at what is nearest
> straightaway
> and come to the other side.[40]

The Young Man then interpolates the line "not without soaring" (*nicht ohne Schwingen*) from the above passage to mean "not without the eagle" (*nicht ohne den Adler*), to which the Old Man adds decisively that there is no passage "to the other side [*die andere Seite*]" (i.e., to Germania) without the eagle. The eagle, in other words, is that without which such a passage to Germania could not occur: one cannot make such passage without the soaring (or, perhaps, the *wings*) of the eagle.[41]

Such soaring is thematic to the conversation from its very beginning and proves in many ways to constitute the indispensable core of the text:[42] for it is such soaring that will be needed in order to bring about the transformation of the human, to prepare it for the other inception and the coming of the new gods, a transformation that is cast within the poem in terms of passage "to the other side" (i.e., of the river).[43] Regarding such passage to the other side, Bambach writes: "This is what the poetic song promises [. . .]: the poetic possibility of another way of beyng's resonating through the word. But [. . .] hearing this word and belonging to its oscillations and reverberations [i.e., its 'soaring'] can only happen with the help and sustenance of the mediating power whose force helps us to move across and between two separate realms. Within 'The Western Conversation,' the Young Man names this force 'the eagle.' "[44] The eagle is thus the motive force that will make a transformation of human *Dasein* possible. At one point, the Young Man says this directly: "[W]ithout the eagle, one may not come to the streams of Germania and to the still unnamed stream at which those who have arrived wish to build."[45] Then, a few lines later: "*Only* [*nur*] the eagle can help us to hear the word and to learn the saying in the recitation of the word."[46] The possibility of preparing the human for the other side—that is, for the other inception—depends upon a poetic reception and understanding of Hölderlin's poetry, and specifically of "Der Ister"; and the very possibility of understanding his poetry and the "soaring" named within it depends upon the eagle. Moreover, it is *only* (*nur*) the eagle who can help us understand the word and the saying operative within it: "It seem as if the eagle is now circling high above the Ister song, as if we could barely think the first stanza, let alone the whole song, without the sweep of the eagle's swaying wafting far away through our essence, in the wafting of which we hear the melodies of the song."[47] The eagle is thus presented by Heidegger within this dialogue as that without which a thoughtful reception of a new dispensation of being cannot occur. Said otherwise, an encounter with the eagle is *prior* to the unfolding of the new inception and is constitutive of it. (We will return to the role of the animal in the new inception in the book's conclusion.)

As Bambach notes, the eagle within this text—and, indeed, within Hölderlin's poetry more broadly—can be understood as a representative of the gods, "emissary to human beings [. . .] who comes from the Indus river, flies over mount Parnassus and traverses the Alps in order to deliver this message to the Germans: it is your time now. You have been chosen to take up the mission of Western responsibility bequeathed to you from father Zeus."[48] In other words, the eagle is the messenger who calls Germany—and the human more generally—into a transformation of its essence, that which calls the human *home* into its proper being,[49] a call that is heard by the poet in joyful mourning.[50]

Within the broader framework of the analysis being undertaken here, one can perhaps understand all of this as indicating the manner in which any such poetic transformation of human *Dasein* requires calling into question the traditional conceptual frameworks in terms of which the human has understood itself and set itself apart from other beings. Such a project of calling into question entails an encounter with the animal Other, an encounter in the wake of which the human sets out on the task of founding its identity. Simply put, before any new beginning can be initiated, an assessment of one's position *vis-à-vis* the living Other is required, an Other that is therefore always already there, *prior* to the coalescing of one's own identity. To put this in terms that will soon become more relevant: one's ability to grasp what is properly one's own depends upon, and follows upon, a journey into the *foreign*.

With all of this in mind, we turn now to Heidegger's lectures on Hölderlin's poem "Der Ister." As will be shown, within these lectures the animal plays a similarly central and foundational role in the process through which the human comes to understand itself and comes to be at home with (and in) itself.

"Der Ister"

The focal point of Heidegger's 1942 lecture course on Hölderlin is the latter's unpublished poem "Der Ister"; additionally, in an effort to elucidate that poem further, Heidegger offers a sustained engagement with the first choral ode from Sophocles's *Antigone*. As with nearly all of Heidegger's engagements with Hölderlin, the lectures on "Der Ister" address themselves to the question of the proper essence of the human in general, and of Germany in particular. Specifically, Heidegger's treatment of Hölderlin's poem focuses on the movement of *homecoming* that constitutes the proper being of the human, a being that is therefore initially and for the most part characterized by *not* being at home, by an unsettledness or homelessness that constitutes its essential being.[51] Such homecoming, as discussed below, can be broadly conceived as the movement by which the human, having sojourned into what is unlike itself (i.e., the "foreign" [*fremd*]), comes into a thoughtful acknowledgement of its own proper essence. For Heidegger, human being essentially consists of the journey from out of homelessness toward home, from out of unsettlement toward settlement. In the simplest terms, this can be understood as the existential project of seeking to bring determination and fixity to one's life, a project that is continuous and ongoing so long as one is alive. In a word, it is the very structure of *existence* itself in the full Heideggerian sense. In can also be understood as the *ethical* project (in Heidegger's sense) of coming to dwell properly within one's existence.

At one point in the lecture course, this structure is framed by Heidegger in terms of *translation*. According to Heidegger, being human is a matter of translating oneself into oneself, a *transposition* that necessarily entails a passage through the Other. In the case of Heidegger's/Hölderlin's Germany, this movement of translation/transposition entails a passage through ancient Greece, the land of the "heavenly fire"; and it is only through such passage that Germany can come into a thoughtful grasp of its own proper essence. In the case of the human as such, this movement entails a passage into (or through) the *Nothing*, that is, the nothingness of death, although this point will not get fully developed until the second part of the lecture course where Heidegger deals with Sophocles's *Antigone*. Only through coming face-to-face with its own death (i.e., the annihilation of its being) can the human grasp its (ownmost) being in its proper parameters.

Within the lecture course, Heidegger does not deal with the question of animality in any sustained or comprehensive manner; indeed, animals are mentioned only a few times and, even then, only tangentially. On the surface, then, animals do not play a pivotal role in the development of the lecture course or in the understanding of homecoming that is developed therein. However, despite not occupying an explicit place within the text, animals nonetheless play an essential role within the logic of Heidegger's analysis and the poems on which they are based. As we will see, animals occupy a certain pride of place both in Hölderlin's "Der Ister" and in the choral ode from Sophocles's *Antigone* and serve a foundational role in the operation of situating the human within its proper abode. As the following analysis shows, animals prove to be instrumental in bringing the human into a confrontation with the Nothing, and thereby in bringing the human into proper relation to itself. In other words, as was the case in "Germania" and "Language in the Poem," the lectures on "Der Ister" reveal a certain logic of the necessary detour to be operative within Heidegger's analysis.

To begin to see how this is the case, we turn to Heidegger's discussion of rivers within the lecture course. Heidegger interprets rivers, both here and elsewhere, as expressive of the movement of coming-to-be-at home (from out of homelessness) that characterizes human being.[52] The Ister in particular, with its at times seemingly backward-flowing current, captures the vacillatory movement between homelessness and being-at-home that belongs to the essence of the human. To relate this to Mitchell's analysis of Heidegger's reading of Trakl, one can say that rivers capture the indeterminate *between* character of human existence, that is, the manner in which the human remains perpetually on its way from unsettlement toward settlement (and thus perpetually remains *unsettled*).

But rivers also, for Heidegger, play a foundational role within the project of human settlement, and in more ways than one. Heidegger initially locates this foundational role of rivers within the following lines from Hölderlin's poem:

> For rivers make arable
> the land. Whenever [*Wenn*] plants grow
> and there in summer
> the animals go to drink,
> so [*so*] humans go there too [*auch*].[53]

Rivers thus serve a foundational role in the cultivation of places: that is, they serve a foundational role in the very process of founding. But they do much more than this. In serving such a founding role, rivers open up a site of human being, and therefore of being itself:

> The river "is" the locality that pervades the abode of human beings upon the earth, determines them to where they belong and where they are homely [*heimisch*]. The river thus brings human beings into their own and maintains them in what is their own. Whatever is their own is that to which human beings belong and must belong if they are to fulfill whatever is destined to them, and whatever is fitting, as their specific way of being. One's own is least of all something that produces itself of its own accord. One's own must come to be appropriate. And in turn, whatever has become appropriate needs to be appropriated.[54]

Rivers bring human beings into that which is properly their own, that from which, therefore, humans remain initially at a distance.

Rivers are also, for Heidegger, expressive of the poets, those who open up and found historical *Dasein*. Like literal rivers, poets make a locale "arable" (*urbar*), although in the essential sense of an original cultivating or settling whereby a site is prepared for human *Dasein*.[55] Simply put, the poet opens a horizon in which beings come to have their specific possibilities and meanings.[56] Thus, the poets give expression to, and are structurally instrumental to, the quintessential human project of journeying from homelessness toward the home. To pair this with what was said above in the analysis of Heidegger's lectures on Hölderlin's "Germania," the poet, in bringing a founding mood into articulation, founds a site wherein human beings can relate to beings, to *being*, and to themselves as the site of being's unfolding (i.e., as *Da-sein*). Thus, like the rivers, the poets set the foundation for the movement of coming-to-be-at-home in a site—that is, they set the ground for human dwelling. In the case of rivers, this occurs in a specific geographical location and surrounding a particular topography; in the case of poets, this occurs at the level of human existence in the full Heideggerian sense of the term. Crucial to the above is the manner in which the human consists of a *movement*, of a *coming-to-be*, of an *appropriation* of what up to that point has not been possessed. To be human is to move from homelessness toward home, from inappropriate toward appropriate, from inauthentic toward authentic, from unsettlement toward settlement, un-dwelling toward (ethical) dwelling. Rivers, and the Ister in particular, are expressive of this movement.

Although Heidegger himself does not do so, we must note a certain sequence operative within the passage from Hölderlin mentioned above:

> For rivers make arable
> the land. Whenever [*Wenn*] plants grow
> and there in summer
> the animals go to drink,
> so [*so*] humans go there too [*auch*].

Wenn—"when," or "provided that"—plants grow along the river and animals go there to drink, *then* (or thus [*so*]) the human will *also* [*auch*] go there to build. In other words, it is *because* plants have grown along the river and animals go there to drink that the human will (then) go there, too, following after the animal in this manner. The *so* (thus) and *auch* (also, too) indicate that the human's arrival at the site is both subsequent to, and on account of, the prior presence of other living beings, of plants and animals.[57]

Given this sequence, and given also that the river is emblematic of the human's journey from homelessness to being-at-home, one might well wonder what role animals play, if any, in this latter process. Within the lecture course, Heidegger in no way speaks directly to this issue. And yet, as we will see when we turn to Heidegger's analysis of the first choral ode from Sophocles's *Antigone*—the so-called "Ode to Man"—animals do indeed play a crucial and constitutive role in the human's passage from homelessness to coming-to-be-at-home, albeit one of which Heidegger himself makes no overt mention. For now, it is sufficient to note that the human's coming-to-be-at-home at the site of the river is subsequent to, and follows upon, the arrival of animals. To say it more strongly, the animal's settling along the river is temporally prior to, and logically constitutive of, the human's settlement at the site.

As Heidegger later argues, the "site" is not to be understood as any particular geographic location, or even as a specific nation (such as Germany), but rather as the opening of being itself: "What is characteristic of human abode is grounded in the fact that being in general has opened itself to humans and is this very open. As such an open, it received human beings for itself, and so determines them to be in a site. We here speak of the open with regard to what is said in the word and concept ἀλήθεια, unconcealment of beings, when correctly understood. As unconcealed, beings are in the open."[58] The site founded and opened by the river, and by the poets, is thus nothing other than the site of the opening of the truth of being—that is, the site of the unfolding of human *Dasein* itself. Rivers/poets open the horizon of meaning for humans operative within a particular historical epoch.

It is precisely here, in regard to the open of the truth of being, that Heidegger finally mentions animals explicitly. As is often the case, Heidegger here draws a distinction between the human and the animal in terms of the ability to experience the open: "To 'see' the open [i.e., the site], thus understood, is the distinction of human beings. The animal is animal precisely on account of its not seeing the open, as understood in this way, which is also why it is unable to say the 'is' of being, that is, is altogether unable to say. The animal is ἄλογον—without the word."[59] Thus, animals, although they are *at* the site, do not *inhabit* the site: they do not "see" the site, nor do they grasp the open of being in any explicit or thematic way; and this is owing, according to Heidegger, to the fact that they stand outside of language, outside of the very opening of being.

However, although animals are here excluded from standing thoughtfully within the site of the opening of being, we have seen that, within the logic of the poem, they nonetheless *precede* the human's arrival at this open: that is, they precede and make possible the human's coming-to-stand within the truth (i.e., the open) of being. Nothing is explicitly said by Heidegger regarding the role of animals in this process. However, the role of animals finds further elucidation in Heidegger's engagement with the first choral ode in Sophocles's *Antigone*, the primary function of which is to distinguish the human from the other beings with whom it stands in relation.

In turning to this ode, Heidegger initially addresses the question of the necessity of engaging the "foreign" in order to (re)turn to one's home (i.e., in order to come into one's own): "For only where the foreign is known and acknowledged in its essential oppositional character does there exist the possibility of a genuine relationship, that is, of a uniting that is not a confused mixing but a conjoining in distinction."[60] Such a sojourn into the foreign is undertaken not for the sake of pure, touristic engagement with the foreign, but rather for the sake of an exposure to one's own theretofore concealed essence: "The essence of one's own is so mysterious [*geheimnisvoll*] that it unfolds its ownmost essential wealth only from out of a supremely thoughtful acknowledgment of the foreign."[61] It is only owing to such exposure to the foreign that one is able to grasp one's own essence in its proper parameters. As Julian Young writes regarding such exposure, "[O]nly if there is a 'genuine,' respectful, and appreciative relationship to the otherness of the other, a relationship which, at the same time, never attempts a merging of one's own identity into it, is there the possibility of that education in and through the foreign which, according to Hölderlin's 'law,' is necessary to becoming properly at home in the *Heimat*."[62] Simply put, and as Young further notes, coming to grasp one's own distinctive identity depends upon a Hegelian-like—or, one might hazard, a *Derridean*-like—encounter with the Other, from out of which encounter one's own identity coalesces.[63]

Although Heidegger's argument within the lecture course is directed specifically toward the relationship between Hölderlin (i.e., Germany) and Sophocles (i.e., Greece), it applies no less—and, indeed, perhaps even more so—to the relationship between the human and the animal. What will be seen as Heidegger's analysis of the choral ode unfolds is that, for the human, an encounter with the animal Other is first needed in order for the former to come into its own proper essence and to stand thoughtfully within the truth of being.

To begin to understand this, we turn to Heidegger's discussion of the opening lines of the choral ode, which Heidegger calls the "essential ground" of the tragedy, and, indeed, of Sophocles's work as a whole: "Manifold is the uncanny: yet nothing more uncanny looms or stirs beyond the human being."[64] For Heidegger, the ode voices, with poetic profundity, the uncanny character of the human, where "uncanny" (*Unheimliche*) refers polyvalently both to the terrible violence of which the human is capable but also, and more essentially, to the manner by which the human remains outside of its home (*Heim*), that is, the way in which it stands in the open of being amid beings while remaining largely unaware of being itself. The ode accomplishes this by underscoring the dominion and mastery that the human extends over *animals*:

> And the flock of birds that rise into the air
> he ensnares, and pursues
> the animals of the wilderness
> and of the ocean's surging waves,
> most ingenious man.
> He overpowers with cunning the animal
> that roams the mountains at night,
> the wild-maned neck of the steed,
> and the never-tamed bull,
> fitting them with wood,
> he forces under the yoke.[65]

All manner of animals—birds, fish, wild animals such as horses and bulls—are brought under the mastery of the human, forced under the yoke of the human's own machinations and desires. And yet—and this is the true focus of Heidegger's analysis of the ode—precisely through these efforts at mastery, the human comes up against something it *cannot* master:

> Everywhere venturing forth underway, experienceless without
>   any way out
> he comes to nothing.
> The singular onslaught of death he can
> by no flight ever prevent,
> even if in the face of dire infirmity he achieves
> most skillful avoidance.[66]

Thus, despite demonstrating its superiority through mastering the animals of land, sky, and sea, the human is unable to master (i.e., prevent or evade) its own death. This can be understood as the failure of the human, in mastering *beings*, to master (its own) *being*. Heidegger casts this failure in terms of the project of homecoming, where we can see the human's efforts at mastery as an attempt to come-to-be-at-home with *beings* that leads ultimately to its failure to come-to-be-at-home in *being*. Especially uncanny is the way in which the human, who is essentially and uniquely "in" being in a manner that distinguishes it from all other beings, remains "outside" of being in the sense of not-being-at-home in it, despite (or, in fact, largely *because*) of its various attempts to find its home in beings.

It is crucial to note the temporal sequence operative within these lines from the choral ode, a sequence that matches that seen in Hölderlin's poem analyzed above. *First*, the human ventures out into the world, subduing and subjugating the myriad animals it meets, bringing those beings under its mastery. *Then*, subsequent to this venturing-forth, the human comes to nothing: that is, it comes to *the Nothing*, to death, coming up against its own mortality as an ineluctable and unsurpassable factum of its existence. Said otherwise, as the human is busying about subduing the beings of nature, it comes upon something that it cannot subdue, namely, its own death: and the more ardently and expansively the human brings the things of nature under its yoke, the more glaringly and stubbornly does its own death evade and escape that yoke.

This sequence, properly understood, is not only temporal: it is also *causal*. It is precisely *because* of the attempt to master all things, to enslave the animals, that the human becomes aware of its own mortality, its own finitude: for through its attempts at otherwise unmitigated mastery, the human becomes more and more aware that there is something it *cannot* master, namely, its own death (and, by extension, its own *life*, its own *being*). In other words, precisely through bringing death to the beings of nature, to the *animals*, the human confronts the inescapability of its *own* death. In this way, one can say that the human's engagement with the animals (i.e., its project of mastering them) delineates the boundaries of human finitude; or, to phrase it more broadly, one could say that, in mastering *beings*, the human realizes the futility of attempting to master (its own) *being*. The attempt at dominating the animals brings the human face-to-face with the reality of its own mortal being, thus individuating the human in the face of its own death. Thus, the human's uncanniness announces itself through, and *subsequent* to, an engagement with the animal.

To look at this a bit more abstractly, one could say that the human's realization of its own (uncanny) essence necessarily entails an encounter with, and a reference to, what is other than itself. (Heidegger is explicit that the human's uncanniness is "nothing human beings themselves make but rather the converse: something that makes them into what they are and who they can be.")[67] More precisely, it is through an ontological comparison with otherness (i.e., "foreignness") that the unique (uncanny) character of the human announces itself in its proper light. Phrased in terms of the essential existential project of homecoming, one could say that the human can only come to be at home in its proper essence by first venturing out and encountering the animal Other, an encounter that impels the human forward toward a confrontation with its own death, with the Nothing, and therefore with (its) being. Thus, although the animal itself, for Heidegger, cannot come to be at home in being (owing to the manner in which it essentially stands outside of being), it is nonetheless that without which the human, for its part, cannot come to be so at home.[68]

This process—which is nothing other than the process of the necessary detour—utterly disrupts the understanding of the *individualized* character of death offered in *Being and Time*. As we saw in "Language in the Poem," the lectures on "Der Ister" describe a scene where the human's relationship to its own death results not from an immediate autoaffection but is rather mediated through a confrontation with the animal Other. Specifically, it is by confronting *death* in the animal Other—that is, by bringing death to it—that the human comes up against its own finitude, its own mortality. In this way, the human's death is *given to it as a possibility* by the animal.

Thus, while the animal itself, for Heidegger, cannot die, it is that without which the human would not relate to its own death as its ownmost possibility of being. This agrees with the interpretation offered in chapter 2 regarding the primacy of the death of the (animal) Other in Heidegger's thinking, even if that death is *ultimately* insufficient to grant insight into the character of one's own dying.

To reconnect this with Heidegger's earlier comments about translation, one recalls Heidegger's argument that an encounter with a foreign language (and the *ethos* embedded within that language) is necessary in order to occupy one's *own* language.[69] The German speaker, for example, only comes into a reflective and thoughtful relation with the German language through a sojourn into the Greek language.[70] Although Heidegger does not raise the following question, it must nonetheless be posed given the results of the investigation so far: Would this process of translation, operative between *particular* languages, apply also to language *as such*? That is, would the human—the only one, for Heidegger, who "has" language, who dwells within the opening of λόγος—need to encounter that which does *not* have the word, that which is without language, that which is ἄλογον, in order to understand itself as the being "with" or "in" language? Would the project of coming into an adequate assaying of the human essence necessarily entail a journey out toward, and an encounter with, what is *not* human? In other words, would the human, in order to grasp the proper parameters of (its own) being, need first to take a great detour through the animal Other?

It is perhaps this need that is underscored within the first choral ode's account of the human's uncanniness. Heidegger himself almost intimates as much when he writes that, although the choral ode speaks exclusively of human beings, it also speaks of "the sea and the earth, of the animals of the wild and of storms, of infirmity and death, of understanding and of the word, of the gods and of ordinances, for all these things human beings stand in relation, and all these each in their own way bear the pull and the traits of the fearful, powerful, and inhabitual."[71] It is in *relation* to these elements—and *only* in relation to them—that the human comes to grasp the character of its uncanny essence, an uncanniness that exceeds that of all other entities.[72] In encountering the uncanny nature of other beings, the human comes to see itself as the *most* uncanny, as uncanny in an essentially superlative way. (Indeed, the very sense of the superlative indicates decisively that the human's uncanniness is only to be understood in comparison with other beings.) This passage underscores the relational character of human *Dasein* and the manner in which it is attendant upon other beings, following after them.

It should also be noted that the relationality of which Heidegger speaks here resonates with his understanding of the fourfold, although Heidegger does not employ such language in the "Ister" lectures. Sea and earth, animals and storms, language and gods: these are the poles of being with which the mortal human stands in relation. It is only *because* of venturing out into this open play-space that the human can come to grasp its own being in its proper distinction.

Heidegger perhaps gestures toward the causal character of this process later on in the lecture course when he writes the following:

> Yet this is no mere homeless wandering around that merely seeks a location in order then to abandon it and take its pleasure and satisfaction in a mere traveling around. The human being here is not the adventurer who remains homeless on account of his lack of rootedness. Rather, the sea and the land and the wilderness are those realms that human beings transform with all their skillfulness, use and make their own, *so that they may find their own vicinity through such realms.* The homely is sought after and striven for in the violent activity of passing through that which is inhabitual with respect to sea and earth, and yet in such passage the homely is precisely not attained.[73]

The human uses the animal *as a means*, as an *instrument* or a *supplement*, by which to come to be at home. First, and essentially, the human being is not-at-home; *then*, by way of an excursion into the otherness of animality (and nature more broadly), the human strives to find its own place, its own locale, its own home. We sees the sequential character of this process even more clearly a few pages later when Heidegger speaks of beings *refusing* themselves to the human during this process: "[B]eings even refuse to humans that which humans hope from them, namely, that with beings and among them they [i.e., humans] might come to something."[74] He then adds: "In those beings they [i.e., humans] come to, and in which they think themselves at home, they [i.e., humans] come to nothing."[75] Thus, *first*, the human, as not-at-home, longs to be at home, and seeks such a home in and among beings; *then*, beings *refuse* to let humans be at home within them. (Such *refusal* should remind us of the animal's refusal of the human's attempt at full transposition, discussed in chapter 2.)[76] The human comes to beings, journeys to them, in pursuit of home, but instead comes to (the) nothing. Thus, an engagement with beings, and with animals in particular (within the logic of the choral ode), is structurally prior to the human's encounter with the Nothing.[77] Said more strongly: prior to our encounter with (our own) finite being, and constitutive of that being, there is the encounter with the animal.

All of this structurally corresponds to Hölderlin's "Der Ister" as analyzed by Heidegger in part 1 of the lecture course. There, the animal's arrival at the site (i.e., the river) precedes the human's coming-to-be-at-home along the river. Here, in Sophocles's choral ode, the encounter with the animal precedes (and makes possible) an attentive encounter with being itself (in the guise of Nothingness). In both cases, an encounter with the animal is structurally prior to the human's exposure to being itself, and in fact makes that exposure possible. In the case of the choral ode, such exposure makes possible the human's reckoning of its own mortality: that is, it brings the human into a posture of *being-toward-death*. Within the logic of the choral ode, the human's posture of being-toward its death is the culmination of a series of encounters with others, and with animals in particular. Thus, the animal may not die, in the rich sense with which Heidegger imbues the term; but the human *also* does not die—that is, it does not grasp its death as its ownmost possibility—*until* it encounters the deaths of the animals it masters and subdues. The animal, itself incapable of death, is that without which the human could not come to stand in an authentic relationship to its own death. The animal is the detour through which the human must journey on the way toward is authentic existence.

We turn now to Heidegger's *Elucidations of Hölderlin's Poetry*, a collection of essays spanning the decades from 1930 to 1970. As we will see, this collection, no less than the "Germania" and "Der Ister" lectures, operates by way of a logic of the necessary detour, showing animals to be at the very core of the human's passage toward its own proper essence.

Elucidations of Hölderlin's Poetry

From its very first line, Heidegger's *Elucidations of Hölderlin's Poetry* is concerned with the process of homecoming. In terms of the logic of its analysis, it is nearly identical to the lectures on "Der Ister," insofar as its underlying focus is the movement into otherness that structurally proceeds an authentic appropriation of one's own essence. As in the lectures on "Der Ister," such appropriation is only possible for those who have journeyed out into the foreign: "Only he can return home who previously, and perhaps for a long time, has wandered as a traveler and borne upon himself the burden of the journey upon his shoulders, and has crossed over into the origin, so that there he might experience what that is which was to be sought, in order then, as the seeker, to come back more experienced."[78] Also as in the "Der Ister" lectures, the "foreign" for Germany (and for Hölderlin) is here presented as Greece, that land of the heavenly fire.[79] Such fire is to be understood as the holy to which the poet, and Germany more broadly, must expose themselves in order to open themselves for what is to come (i.e., the other inception). Such exposure takes place as a wandering away from the home and into the unfamiliar, all undertaken for the sake of a thoughtful appropriation of one's own essence.

During his engagement with Hölderlin's "Andenken," Heidegger comes to cast the wanderers as the mariners mentioned in the poem, those who sail off to foreign lands. These mariners are then identified by Heidegger as the poets, those who will travel out to encounter the heavenly fire in order to come home and give voice to the holy in a founding articulation.[80]

Remarkably, although Heidegger makes nothing of it, it is an *animal* who, in Hölderlin's poem, calls to the wanderers: "And the bird's song [*Vogels Gesang*] invites the wanderer."[81] It is thus on the invitation, the beckoning, of an animal that the poet travels out into the foreign for the sake of a transformative, appropriative return home. In other words, the encounter with the animal (i.e., the reception of its call) occurs *prior* to, and is causal of, a journey out into the foreign, and is thus prior to a thoughtful transformation of the human's ownmost essence. The logic operative here is precisely the same as was seen in Heidegger's elucidations of "Germania" and "Der Ister."

Interestingly, later on in the text, it is the birds themselves who are called: "The northeast wind calls the migratory birds home from foreign lands, so that in the homeland they can cast their wide-open eyes on what is their own and tend to it."[82] An identification is thus drawn by Heidegger between the mariners and the birds, and thus between the birds and the poets. The poets themselves are like migratory birds who, once out in faraway lands, are called back to the home, to the source, so that they can cultivate their essence and found the site of their historical *Dasein*. (Heidegger also identifies the poets, and "we" ourselves, with the starlings blown by the northeasterly wind in his lectures on "Andenken" from 1934–1935, although he does so rather surreptitiously and without further comment.)[83]

This identification between poets and birds finds its strongest articulation in a passage from Bettina von Arnim regarding Hölderlin's poetry, which Heidegger quotes precisely in order to clarify the nature of the latter's poetic activity. Drawing a distinction between a technically proficient but spiritually barren poet and an invigorated and inspired one, von Arnim writes: "Poets who study established forms can only repeat the once given spirit, for they place themselves *like birds on a branch* of the tree of language and rock themselves gently on it, according to the primordial rhythm which lies in its roots; but such a one cannot *soar like a spirited eagle* hatched by the living spirit of language."[84] Hölderlin, then, would not be like those birds rocking idly on the tree of language, but rather like that *eagle* who, soaring off into the land of the heavenly fire, returns home in order to prepare the site for the new beginning. This fire, and the heaven of its provenance, ring out to the poet as a destinal voice calling him to his vocation, one to which he is drawn by his very essence.

Remarkably—though, again, Heidegger makes nothing of it—such ringing out sounds, according to Hölderlin, "like a blackbird's song":

> For amid the [eyes'] blue school,
> from afar, amid the uproar of heaven,
> rings out, like the blackbird's song,
> the clouds' serene mood, well
> tempered by the existence of God, by the thunderstorm.

Heidegger then underscores that it is the *heaven* that rings out here—that is, the clouds, the lightning, the thunder, the storm, and the rain.[85] These elements are, Heidegger writes, the concealed appearance of the god. It is thus the concealed appearance of the god—an appearing that is sheltered and shows forth from *the holy*[86]—that rings forth "like a blackbird's song."

The holy is to be thought in its essential relation to nature, understood as φύσις: or, rather, the holy just "is the essence of nature" understood, in the Greek sense, as "the emerging into the open, the clearing of that clearing in which anything whatsoever appears at all."[87] As Mitchell interpolates it, "the holy is nature [i.e., *physis*] as this names the emergence of the clearing wherein something each time appears."[88] It is thus the clearing of being itself to which the heavenly points, a heaven that rings out "like a birdsong"[89] and to which the poet exposes himself (in holy mourning) in order to prepare the founding of historical *Dasein*.

As Heidegger goes on to say, it is not only the heavenly (i.e., the holy) that rings out—it is also the *earth*: "Heaven rings out. It is one of the voices of destiny [*Stimmen des Geschicks*]. The earth is another voice. It also rings out."[90] Both earth and heaven, in their essential connectedness,[91] call out to the poet. The immortal, too—the "divinity sheltered in the holy"[92]—calls out to the poet, as does the figure of the human. As Heidegger writes, "There are four voices that ring out: heaven, earth, human, and god. Destiny gathers the whole infinite relation in these four voices."[93] These four voices ring out to the poet. In their interconnection, these four constitute the unfolding of destiny—that is, they comprise the unfolding of the advent (*Ereignis*) of being itself as it gives itself to, and thereby constitutes, historical human existence.[94] It is precisely by attending to these four interconnected voices—voices that ring out like a birdsong—that the poet is able to found the site of historical *Dasein*.

It is with this in mind that we turn to Heidegger's 1943 and 1944 lectures on Heraclitus, where Heidegger will also speak of a birdsong—one that, we will see, similarly heralds the opening of being as the fourfold clearing of φύσις.

Chapter Five

Birdsong of Being

Alack! The lonely eagles mourn.

—Georg Trakl, "Klage" (in Trakl 1969, 163; my translation)

In his lecture course on Heraclitus titled "The Inception of Occidental Thinking," given at the University of Freiburg in the summer semester of 1943, Heidegger imagines a world without being: "Let us imagine [. . .] what would become of the human if it came about that every possibility of saying and understanding the words 'is' and 'being' were revoked. No catastrophe [*Katastrophe*] that could befall the planet can be compared with this seemingly most trivial of events in which the human's relation to 'is' is suddenly suspended."[1] This would not so much be a world without being as a world where being had been forgotten, a world where the human—the only one who, for Heidegger, can *see* and *say* being[2]—had come to a place of forgetfulness, a forgetfulness so radical as to bring about even a forgetting of such forgetting.[3] Such a situation, as Heidegger says here in 1943 as the Second World War continues to rage on in his own backyard, would be the worst conceivable catastrophe—or, literally in Greek, *down-going*—to befall the planet.

Heidegger then makes it clear that he is not *imagining* this situation at all but is rather *describing* it: "But this catastrophe has long since arrived, only no one has noticed it in its essence. The human, in its history, has reached the point where he has forgotten the 'is' and 'being,' insofar as he renounces any consideration of what is named by this word. Indifference to 'being' has besieged the planet. The human being allows himself to be

131

washed over by the flood of this forgetfulness of being."[4] Heidegger's lectures are thus given from out of a place and time of destitution, where and when being has been forgotten and "the planet is in flames."[5] The human—that being whose essence, in distinction to all other beings, is characterized by an awareness of, and concern with, being—has come to a point within its history where it has renounced being. This point in history is an inevitable consequence of the *essential* manner in which the human—whom Heidegger, in the lectures on "Der Ister," calls "the sole catastrophe"[6]—uncannily turns away from its own essence. Thus, the catastrophe besieging the planet—a catastrophe worse than any atom bomb, any war, or even any widespread and systematic liquidation of human life—is the catastrophe *of* the human, the catastrophe of its very essence as it turns away from itself as the open where being unfolds. The history of the West, in its unfolding, is the human's catastrophic errancy from being, and thus from its proper *Da*, its proper *site*, its proper *home*.

The lectures themselves, through their engagement with Heraclitus—one of ancient Greece's three inceptual thinkers (alongside Parmenides and Anaximander)—is an attempt to remind the modern human of its proper essence and (therefore) of the inceptual meaning of being: it is, in a word, an attempt to bring the human *home*. This mnemonic, nostalgic endeavor takes place through an elucidation of various of Heraclitus's fragments, all of which relate in one way or another to Heraclitus's underlying and inceptual experience of φύσις. In distinction to the modern, calculative, and mechanical understanding of nature, φύσις, for inceptual thinking, is to be understood as "the pure emerging in whose prevalence any appearing thing appears and thus 'is.'"[7] This pure emerging—which is nothing other than being itself, understood as the clearing[8]—is to be thought of as the manner by which that which appears does so from out of itself in an emergent way.[9] Simply put, the Greek word φύσις, thought inceptually, means "emerging from out of itself into the open,"[10] and is that opening itself.[11]

It is this open, then—the open clearing of being—that the modern human has forgotten and of which Heidegger, through his engagement with Heraclitus, seeks to remind the human. But how, specifically, does such remembrance occur? That is, within the lecture course, what is it that serves to remind the modern human of the open clearing of being? Although such remembrance takes place largely through Heidegger's focused analyses of a cluster of terms that arise in certain of Heraclitus's fragments—terms such as τὸ δῦνον (submerging), φύσις (emerging), ἁρμονία (the jointure), and Λόγος (language/gathering)—the most remarkable moment of remembrance takes place through an encounter with an *animal*. Despite remaining structurally similar in many respects to Heidegger's many other engagements with the question of animality, in the sense that it seemingly reaffirms a certain hierarchical demoting of the animal, the lecture course contains a passage that offers a radically different view of the animal, one in which the animal plays a foundational (and, indeed, inceptual) role in the human being's awareness of being. In short, this passage demonstrates that a certain encounter with animality is constitutively primary of the human being's *authentic* experience of being, and that such an encounter is needed to awaken the modern human from its catastrophic forgetfulness of being.

In short, the lectures demonstrate a logic of the necessary detour to be at the very core of Heidegger's 1943 reading of Heraclitus, and in a manner akin to what has already been discerned in preceding chapters, and especially in Heidegger's various lectures on Hölderlin discussed in chapter 4.[12] Within the context of the Heraclitus lectures, Heraclitus's thinking is the foreign to which the Germans must expose themselves in order to be freed from their entanglement in modern metaphysics and to open themselves to a transformation of their essence:[13] and, as was the case with Heidegger's engagement with Hölderlin, this exposure and the transformation it brings about is catalyzed through a confrontation with an animal.

Before focusing on the particular passage in which Heidegger stages his encounter with the animal, it is necessary to attend to a prefatory matter. Although—or, indeed, *because*—the focal point of the lectures is Heraclitus's experience of φύσις, the entire 1943 lecture course turns out to be oriented toward animals from the very outset. Heidegger begins the lecture course with a meditation on two stories from antiquity regarding Heraclitus. The first is the well-known story about the Ephesian as he warms himself at his stove, a story that Heidegger relays in order to demonstrate the essential role that fire plays within Heraclitus's thought. The second story recounts Heraclitus's withdrawal into the temple of Artemis in order to play a game of knucklebones with a group of children. It is with this second story, and specifically with the invocation of the goddess Artemis, that Heidegger's text orients itself toward an encounter with animality.

As Heidegger argues, Heraclitus's thinking, as both stories ultimately indicate, remains essentially connected to the goddess Artemis; indeed, Heidegger eventually claims that "Artemis is the goddess of the thinker Heraclitus [. . .] because she is the goddess of what the thinker has to think."[14] In other words, whatever it is that Heraclitus thinks about within the fragments that have been passed down to us—which, as we soon see, is first and foremost the inceptual character of φύσις—he does so within nearness to, and under the protection of, the goddess Artemis.[15] To think along with Heraclitus, as the lectures strive to do, is thus to tarry along with Artemis; and as Heidegger will soon make clear, the goddess Artemis is indissolubly oriented toward animals.[16]

Moving in this direction, Heidegger asks simply: "Who is Artemis?" In answering this question, Heidegger notes the insufficiency of relying upon mythology, which would merely treat Artemis as a historical curiosity belonging to time past. Instead, as Heidegger writes, "the only possible and, indeed, necessary response [*Antwort*] takes the form of a responsibility [*Verantwortung*] that entails the historical decision regarding whether or not we choose to safeguard the 'essence' of this goddess and the Greek realm of gods as something having-been."[17] For the contemporary German to relate to Artemis as something "having-been," as opposed to something that has merely past, is to fulfill their historical responsibility by making a decision regarding their belongingness to the ancient Greeks and the extent to which their history originates from them: it is, in other words, to respond appropriately to their essential indebtedness to the Greeks. It is also, as Heidegger immediately makes clear, to make a decision about their *present* and their *future*: "It is an entirely different question, however, whether the concealed essence of the history to which we belong is compelled, from out of an essential need, into a dialogue with what was, to the Greeks, their θεοί. The proper answer to the questions 'Who is Artemis?' and 'Who is Zeus?' conceals itself still in our history to come, insofar as it alone responds to the having-been."[18] In other words, the modern human is compelled from out of an essential need (*Not*) to ask the question regarding the character of Artemis and the thinking over which she presides; and the answer to this question, which has yet to be offered, amounts to a decision regarding the human's relation to the inceptual. (We will soon see that this relation to the inceptual, and the effect it has on our modern understanding of nature, has everything to do with an encounter with the animal.)

Who, then, is Artemis? After marking her affinity to her brother Apollo, Heidegger offers the following description of the goddess:

> The Greeks know Artemis as the huntress and as the "goddess of the hunt."[19] Naturally, we believe we know approximately what the concept "hunt" means and apply this notion in an unreflective way to the goddess of the hunt. Hunting and animals belong in "nature"—i.e., φύσις. Artemis is the goddess of

φύσις. Her playmates, the Nymphs, play the game of φύσις. This word names the self-opening coming-forth and emerging "up" and upwards into an unconcealed standing-there [*Dastehen*] and rising (πέλειν). The goddess of φύσις is the rising one.[20]

It is because of her intimate connection to φύσις—that is, her *presiding* over φύσις such that any discussion of the latter would *a fortiori* concern her—that she is depicted in antiquity as holding torches in her hands. With these torches she brings the light that allows beings to appear, thus letting "the concealed come forth from out of concealment."[21] Such unconcealment is to be understood in terms of the clearing (*die Lichtung*), "the illuminating and opening sheltering" of beings.[22] Artemis, as the goddess of φύσις, is thus "the goddess of emergence, of light, and of play."[23] In a word, she is the goddess of the clearing of being who presides over what emerges into the open as well as the event of emergence itself.

And yet, as Heidegger goes on to show, she is also the goddess of *death*—that is, of submergence and darkness:

> The goddess of emergence, play, and light is also the goddess of death [*Tod*], just as if light, play, and emerging were the same as death. Rather, emerging, self-illuminating, and play mark the essence of ζωή, "life," and of ζῷον, "the living." Our word "life" is already so burdened by Christian and modern-day thinking that it cannot designate what the Greeks understood by ζωή and ζῷον. Even if our word "life" remains only an imprecise and confused translation of the Greek word ζωή, it nevertheless allows us to think that "life" is the opposite of death. How, then, can the goddess of the self-illuminating, of emerging, and of play be, at the same time, the goddess of death, i.e., of the dark, of submergence, and of the rigid? Life and death turn against one another. Certainly. However, what turns against one another turns, at the moment of its most extreme opposition, intimately toward one another. Where such turning prevails, there is strife, ἔρις. For Heraclitus, who thinks strife as the essence of being, Artemis, the goddess with bow and lyre, is the nearest.[24]

Heidegger will devote considerable time to analyzing this strife and the extent to which it characterizes the structure of φύσις, and in particular to the way in which the "opposites" *emergence* and *submergence, Aufgehen* and

Untergehen, belong together in a unified counter-turning movement (akin or identical to the relationship between concealment and unconcealment). For the purposes of the present inquiry it suffices to note that, insofar as ζωή is to be understood as conceptually equivalent to φύσις (as Heidegger mentions in passing here but clarifies later on in a passage to which we shall return), Artemis is the goddess of *life* as well as the goddess of φύσις: or, rather, she is the goddess of life and the *living*—that is, of the *animal*—precisely *because* she is the goddess of φύσις. But, also for this very reason, she is the goddess of *death*. Heraclitus's thinking—but also our *own* thinking that is to come, if we can (re)awaken ourselves to the power of the inceptual—is a thinking of life and death, as well as a thinking of what lives and dies. In other words, Heraclitus's inceptual thinking—a thinking after which we are striving—is a thinking of the living, of life in its connection to death, a thinking, therefore, of the animal broadly conceived.

To phrase all of this a bit differently, the goddess of life, of animals, is *also* (therefore) the goddess of death: the goddess of emergence into the clearing (i.e., the irruption of being) is also the goddess of the submergence characteristic of death (i.e., the closure of the Nothing). Heraclitus's goddess, who presides over what is to be thought by him—namely, the inceptual character of being[25]—is a goddess of living beings, of animals, and *therefore* a goddess of death: she is the goddess who presides over being in its relation to nothingness, a relation that exists only within (or for) living beings.

The essential interweaving of life and death, of emergence and submergence (i.e., unconcealment and concealment), is to be found principally in Artemis's role as a huntress (*Jägerin*): for it is with her bow that Artemis brings death to the living animal.[26] As Heidegger writes:

The bow sends forth the death bringing [*todbringenden*] arrows. The Huntress, who tracks the living so that it may find death [*Tod*], bears the signs of play and death—lyre and bow. Her other sign, "the torch," is, as the fallen and extinguished torch, the sign of death. The Light-Bringer is the Death-Bringer [*Todbringerin*]. Life and death, like light and night, correspond to one another, in that they at the same time "contradict" one another. Artemis the elevated one, through her appearing, lets this "contra-diction" peer into beings as a whole. She is the appearance of the oppositional, and nowhere and never is she disposed to balance the oppositional or give up the oppositional entirely in favor of one side. The Light Bringer is, as the Death-Bringer, the appearance of the oppositional. She is this because she originally lets the

unfamiliarity of strife peer into the familiar. Artemis is a bringer
of the essential strife, ἔρις. This strife is not only unresolved;
rather, it belongs to the essence of strife to strive against each
resolution and every attempt at such.[27]

Artemis the Huntress *follows after* the track (*ihrer Spur nachzugehen*) of
the living animal, bringing death—the "consummation [*Vollendung*] of its
life"—upon it.[28] Remarkably, Heidegger writes here that the animal, as the
living being, *finds death* (*den Tod finde*). In contrast to the many passages
throughout his corpus where Heidegger denies the animal precisely this
ability, here the animal *dies*, and is brought unto death by the very goddess
of life: because it is living, the animal will die. Presumably, what death
means for the animal is something different than what it means for the
human, and it is important to note that Heidegger uses the word *Tod* and
not *sterben* here to speak of the dying animal; and yet, interestingly, there
is no trace here of Heidegger's famous distinction from *Being and Time* and
elsewhere that the animal only perishes (*verenden*).[29] Death is simply the
necessity that belongs to the living being as such, the "constant possibility
of so-called life."[30]

The entire consideration of φύσις to follow, which takes up the
remainder of the lecture course, is therefore essentially oriented toward the
question of the animal, the question of the living being.[31] Or, to say this
more strongly: the entire inquiry into φύσις that follows *chases after the
animal*, tracking it along its course. But this means that the inquiry *follows*
the animal, it comes *after* the animal that therefore comes before. Like the
Huntress who tracks the animal through nature, following and shooting after
it, Heraclitus's thinking of nature was in pursuit of the animal who had
always already come before; and Heidegger's thinking, insofar as it seeks to
awaken Heraclitus's experience of the inceptual understanding of φύσις—an
understanding that stands under the protection of Artemis—follows after
the animal no less.

With this in mind, we now turn to Heidegger's express engagement
with animality—or, rather, with *an* animal—within the lecture course.

~

In the fourth section of the lecture course, Heidegger offers an extended
meditation on the character of ζωή (life), which he considers to be one
of the foundational words of inceptual thinking. Having already pondered
at length the character of another such foundational word—namely,

φύσις—Heidegger comes to interpret ζωή very much in terms of the former, ultimately stating that ζωή "means the emerging itself, the self-opening into the open."[32] Both ζωή and φύσις, insofar as they indicate an emerging into the open, are essentially connected,[33] and both serve as functional synonyms for what Heidegger calls "the perpetually emerging" (*Das immerdar Aufgehen*).[34] Ultimately, such perpetual emergence, in its insoluble connection to submergence, is understood by Heidegger to be nothing other than *being*, if we take this latter in the inceptual sense of ἀλήθεια (unconcealment).[35]

It is during this inquiry into the character of ζωή, in its connection to φύσις, that Heidegger offers an account of the inceptual understanding of animality. According to Heidegger, "τὸ ζῷον is not 'the animal' nor 'the living being' in any casually conceived or indeterminate sense; rather, ζωή means the being [*Wesen*] that emerges from out of itself and into emerging."[36] The animal is thus to be understood precisely in terms of the emerging characteristic of ζωή and φύσις or, what amounts to the same, of being. It is with this understanding of animality in mind that Heidegger offers an account of a specific animal—namely, a bird—in a remarkable passage that utterly destabilizes the common interpretation of Heidegger's understanding of animality:

> Animality, thought in a Greek way, determines itself from out of the ζῷον, from what emerges and then rests properly in itself by not expressing itself. For example, we need only to take a few steps away from the vague and indeterminate modern conception of the bird in order to experience and recognize the bird as the Greeks did: namely, as the animal through whose swaying and hovering the free dimension of the open unfolds, and through whose singing the tidings, the call, and the enchantment unfold [*anwest*], so that its bird-essence whiles away and disperses [*zubringt*] in the open. To all of this also necessarily belong closure and the protecting of what is closed, for example, as in mourning [*der Trauer*]. The bird, flying, singing, connects to and points to the open [*bindet und weist ins Offene*]: it is entangled [*verstrickt*] in this. In Greek, σειρά means tether. The Sirens are, 'in Greek,' the captivating ones [*die Bestrickenden*] in a manifold sense of the word."[37]

There are several elements at play within this passage that require careful consideration. To begin with, a certain *turn* takes place within this passage—or, more precisely, a *re-turn*. As Heidegger writes, "[W]e need only to take a few steps away from the vague and indeterminate modern conception of the bird in order to experience and recognize the bird as the Greeks did." In other words, Heidegger is here taking a step *away* from modernity, away from its overly scientific, metaphysical, and Christian understanding of the bird and is stepping *back* toward the ancient Greek understanding, the *inceptual* understanding. Such retrogressive steps toward the Greek experience of the bird are needed in order to experience something of life, and thus of being, inceptually understood. For now, it suffices to mark that this retrograde movement has both a temporal and a structural aspect to it, insofar as it is an *earlier* understanding, but also an *inceptual* one, to which Heidegger is seeking to (re)turn.

After taking these steps away from the modern metaphysical understanding of animality, the bird is encountered as "the animal through whose swaying and hovering the free dimension of the open unfolds." What precisely is this open in which the bird whiles away? Heidegger is clear within the lectures that the open is the open of being, the *clearing* of being, the manner in which beings emerge into the open so as to stand freely on their own in appearance.[38] It is thus the opening of being that is unfolding (*anwesen*) here and, remarkably, it is unfolding *through* the bird, through its very swaying and hovering. Said otherwise, it is *by means* of or *by way* of the bird that the opening of being unfolds or essences. The open opens through the bird's flight, but also through its very *life*: "ζῆν means the emerging itself, the self-opening into the open."[39]

It is also said by Heidegger that, through the bird's *singing*, "the tidings [*Kunde*], the call [*Ruf*], and the enchantment [*das Zauber*] unfold, so that its bird-essence whiles away and disperses in the open." This particular claim demands a more focused analysis, as it contains three rich and essentially related terms—*Kunde*, *Ruf*, and *Zauber*—that relate to Heidegger's broader philosophical project and bear upon his understanding of animality. As will be seen, each of these terms, listed by Heidegger here as ushering forth from the birdsong, points to a fundamental feature of the unfolding of the opening of being itself.

⌒

One would be hard-pressed to say that *Kunde* occupies an extensive or prominent place within Heidegger's thought; however, it does play a certain crucial role in Heidegger's understanding of *Ereignis* (appropriating event), language, and their essential interconnection. In its most basic sense, *Kunde* refers to the substance of a saying, to what is manifest (and therefore knowable) within a saying, a sense that could adequately be captured with the English word "tidings" or "lore."[40] More fundamentally, *Kunde*, for Heidegger, refers to a happening or occurrence that manifests itself and is therefore knowable and reportable: it is what happens and is therefore sayable through a saying.[41] Ultimately, because *being*—as manifestation or phenomenality itself—is what is most manifest, it, for Heidegger, is taken to be the essential content of any *Kunde*: "Being as a whole, as it rules through and rules around us, the ruling wholeness of this whole, is the world. World is not an idea of theoretical reason, but world announces [*kündet*] itself in the lore [*Kunde*] of historical being, and this lore is the manifestness of the being of beings in the mystery. In lore, and through it, world rules."[42] In other words, being's unfolding is the worlding of the world, and this worlding unfolds as *Kunde*, as the "tidings" that being gives. Heidegger goes on to say that being, understood as this originary lore, occurs as the unfolding of language itself (which he will elsewhere designate as *Kundschaft*),[43] where we understand this latter as the opening of the open play-space in which beings come to presence: it is the unfolding of *Ereignis* through (or as) language understood as the primal opening of being.[44] In this way, language is the originary lore—the *Ur-Kunde*—of the open expanse of being.[45]

It is this connection between *Kunde*, language, and being that will lead Heidegger to speak of the poet (i.e., Hölderlin) as the *Künder*: that is, as the *proclaimer*, *announcer*, or *harbinger* of the lore of being.[46] The poet, as we saw at length in chapter 4, is the one whose poem brings the message of being to humans, opening them to it and thereby grounding human *Dasein* in its historical destiny. One recalls that in Heidegger's lectures on "Germania," the *eagle* was a *Künder* who calls to Germania, and to the German people, to prepare them for what is to come. In the Heraclitus lectures, the bird likewise plays the part of such a *Künder*, announcing and singing the originary happening of being as world, bringing its tidings to humans.

And yet Heidegger, in his 1934 lecture course *Logic as the Question concerning the Essence of Language*, is adamant that the animal has no *Kunde*—no lore or tidings—proper to itself:

A hundred-year-old forest not only has no records and reports, but it has in general no lore of its dying. The ants, which undertake raids, do not preserve them, they leave their past, as it were, behind themselves: they cannot even forget it, they

> have no lore of that which takes place with them. (This is to be established not empirically, but metaphysically.) On the other hand, in the deliberate and knowing happening [*Geschehen*] of the human being, some lore [*Kunde*] always develops at the same time, in which it is attainable and always announces [*ankündigt*] itself again. History is only possible on the basis of such lore.[47]

The animal does not have any lore: there is no *Kunde* that is proper to the animal, owing to the fact that there is no *happening* proper to the animal, and this owing to the fact that there is no *open* accessible to the animal: the animal, without a happening and therefore without a history, has nothing to report—or, as Heidegger will say elsewhere, the animal does not speak because it has nothing to say.[48] And yet, within GA 55, the animal *sings* the *Kunde*, sings the lore that belongs to that being who *does* have a happening proper to it, namely, the human. Itself without lore, the animal sings the lore to the human, thereby bringing word to the human of the happening proper to it. The animal brings the human the tidings that be-long to the latter, singing such tidings and gesturing toward them with its very *life*.

But, according to Heidegger, lore, as the articulation of being's unfolding, is the very ground of history: it is the ground of the historical essence of the human. Only because the human receives this lore and is open to it can its existence be properly founded, thereby rendering it historical in the fundamental sense of being open to the happening of being. The animal, for Heidegger, is without history, precisely because it is without lore (and this precisely because it is without language as the unfolding of being): but the human, for its part, only has a history because it is *given* a lore.[49] Within the Heraclitus lectures, it is the bird who gives the lore to the human, thus making the unfolding of its historical essence possible. Phrased more strongly: although the animal has no history, the human has no history without the animal. In this way, the detour through the animal is the beginning of authentic human history.[50]

To phrase this in more general terms, the human becomes authentically historical only on the basis of its receptivity to being—its open relationship to the open—and to the beings that appear within that open. But this, for its part, only comes about through the human's understanding of itself as the *there*, the *Da*, of being—an understanding that, as we have seen in previous chapters, only arises through the human's engagement with what is other than itself, and most especially with other living beings (i.e., the animal broadly conceived). It is only by *differentiating* itself from animals that the human opens itself to the difference that most determines its essence: namely, the ontological difference, the difference between beings and being. The articulation of this difference is the most fundamental *Kunde* that the human can receive.[51] Only by coming to compare itself to the animal does the human grasp its own essential role as the *there* of being's unfolding. We recall, in passing, that it is the eagle who brings tidings to the poet in Heidegger's lectures on Hölderlin's "Germania," tidings that enable the poet to found the site of historical *Dasein*.

In addition to bringing the tidings of being, Heidegger says in the above passage that the bird's singing lets "the call" (*Der Ruf*) unfold and come to presence.[52] *Ruf* occupies a much more extensive role within Heidegger's thinking than *Kunde*, most famously in his discussion of the call of conscience (*Ruf des Gewissens*) in *Being and Time*, a call that beckons the human out of its immersion in everydayness and awakens it to its ownmost potentiality for being. Beyond *Being and Time*, *Ruf* and related terms feature within Heidegger's engagement with Hölderlin's understanding of poetry and, especially, of the vocation (*Beruf*) of the poet. The vocation of the poet is to receive the call hailing the holy,[53] the reception of which allows the poet to fulfill his vocation of building the site of historical *Dasein*.[54]

In his *Contributions to Philosophy*, the related term *Zuruf* (call, or demand) is used by Heidegger when discussing of the call of being or the call of the appropriating event (*Ereignis*),[55] a call that ushers forth to the human and to which the human must respond in order to ground its proper *Dasein*.[56] In his "Letter on Humanism," Heidegger speaks of this call of being—or, rather, of the ability to receive and heed the call—as the ability that distinguishes the human from the animal:

> [T]he essence of the human consists in being more than merely human, if this is represented as being a rational living being [*Lebeswesen*][. . . .] The "more" means: more originally and therefore more essentially in terms of his essence. But here something enigmatic manifests itself: the human being is in thrownness. This means that the human being, as the ek-sisting counterthrow of being, is more than *animal rationale* precisely to the extent that he is less bound up with the human conceived in terms of subjectivity.[57] The human being is not the lord of beings. The human being is the shepherd of being [*Hirt des Seins*]. Humans lose nothing in this "less"; rather, they gain in that they attain the truth of being. They gain the essential poverty of the shepherd,

whose dignity consists in being called [*gerufen*] by being itself into the preservation of being's truth. The call [*Ruf*] comes as the throw from which the thrownness of Da-sein derives.[58]

The human is what it is—namely, the shepherd of being[59]—owing to the call of being, a call that throws *Dasein* into its genuine historicality. The proper vocation—the proper *Beruf* of the human—consists in attending to, and responding to, this call (*Ruf*).[60]

It is this call of being that is ushering forth from the birdsong within the Heraclitus lectures. As it sings (of) the tidings of being, the bird calls forth the open of being, the opening of the world into which its essence disperses: the bird's singing heralds the call of the opening of being. (In this register, we recall the call of Zarathustra's eagle from chapter 3.) There is a passage within *The Event* (GA 71) that perhaps helps clarify exactly how this occurs. Heidegger there writes that being "is groundless and therefore does not know any 'why.' Beyng *is*, in that it is pure appropriating event. As the abyssal ground, however, beyng is the beginning of all consignment of beings to their essence. For here prevails the deep mystery that everything, resting in itself, harbors incontestable strangeness and becomes the call [*Ruf*] which inceptually calls forth [*hervorruft*] the rarity of self-belonging."[61] In other words, if one looks at beings in the right way—for example, if one looks at them, as Heidegger suggests in the Heraclitus lectures, as the inceptual Greeks did, or with the kind of poetic listening mentioned by Heidegger in his Nietzsche lectures (as discussed in chapter 3)—then one sees the "incontestable strangeness" of beings and is called toward the mystery of being itself. If one attends properly to the manner in which beings call forth (or point to) being itself, one can be reminded of what one, owing to one's entanglement in the contemporary forgetfulness of being, had forgotten: namely, the mysterious fact that there are beings at all rather than nothing.

It is important to note the temporal and structural sequence at work within Heidegger's logic of the call. The human is called by being, a call that requires a response: the call thus comes *prior* to the human's response and is structurally constitutive of it. In other words, the call comes *before* the vocation and determines its essential content. Such a sequence is evident in Heidegger's language of thrownness (*Gerworfenheit*) and implicit in his imagery of the shepherd (*Hirt*).[62] The human being is not the master (*Herr*) of beings: it does not have a princely priority over them. Rather, the human *follows after* and *attends to* beings, in the same way that shepherd follows after and attends to his animals. One notes in passing that, precisely at that moment within "Letter on Humanism" that Heidegger brings the essence of the human into its proper distinction, he does so by way of an image that casts the human as essentially *following after the animals*.

Having now grasped the significance of *Kunde* and *Ruf*, we turn finally to *Zauber*, "enchantment." Heidegger has said that the birdsong lets "the enchantment" unfold. *Zauber* is an extraordinarily rare word within Heidegger's corpus, occurring only occasionally and never becoming part of his technical vocabulary.[63] Despite this, it occupies what one might call an "experimental" role in Heidegger's attempt to articulate the unfolding of being itself.

This can be seen in one of Heidegger's dialogues, *Zur Erörterung der Gelassenheit: Aus einem Feldweggespräch über das Denken* (in *Aus der Erfahrung des Denkens*), where a Teacher, a Scholar, and a Scientist discuss *Zauber* briefly while describing the openness that surrounds all beings.[64] This openness, according to the Teacher, is "like a region through whose enchantment [*Zauber*] everything that belongs to it returns to that wherein it rests," a region that serves as "the region of all regions" (*die Gegend aller Gegenden*).[65] Regarding this region of all regions, the Scientist suggests that "the enchantment [*Zauber*] of this region might well be the reign of its nature, its regioning, if I may call it that."[66] Such enchantment—such regioning of this region in which all beings find their abode—is the gathering of being itself to which the human must attune itself. *Zauber* is thus a word for the carrying out of being's gathering, that is, the manner in which being unfolds as the region for all beings and gathers those beings into its opening. As von Herrmann suggests, the "region" can be understood as the truth, or the clearing, of being:[67] one can thus understand *Zauber* as the unfolding or essencing of the clearing (or the truth) of being.[68]

As Davis has rightly observed, such regioning of the region can be thought of as functionally similar to the worlding of the world;[69] one sees this clearly in GA 102 when Heidegger writes that he wants "to think, more preliminarily and with more fore-sight, the '*region*' as 'world' and 'four-fold.' "[70] Enchantment can thus be understood as the fourfold opening of the world, that is, the way in which the world opens itself up into (or as) the four dimensions of the fourfold.[71] (We will return to the fourfold at length in chapter 6.) This, in turn, is understood by Heidegger as the way in which *Ereignis* occurs: "*Ereignis* itself: Appropriating event and thanking are favor, enchantment. They place the enchantment, the enchanting, into the 'between' that opens; the 'between' possesses, altogether inceptually, this basic character."[72] Ultimately, then, *Zauber* is a way that Heidegger thinks the unfolding of world,[73] that is, the unfolding of being itself as *Ereignis*, as the mysterious opening of the fourfold.[74]

Remarkably, then, it is through its singing that the bird, when understood inceptually, allows the worlding of the world to show itself as the discharging of *Ereignis* into (or as) the fourfold of being.

~

Having now analyzed *Kunde* (tidings), *Ruf* (the call), and *Zauber* (the enchantment), one can see that the bird in GA 55, in its singing, allows the call of being, as the opening of world, to unfold: it sings the call of being in such a way as to let its enchanting mystery show itself and remain a mystery. As Weigelt has noted, such enchanting mystery exceeds rational intelligibility.[75] This is precisely what is shown within the passage from GA 55, where such enchantment only becomes visible when one turns away from the modern scientific understanding of the bird toward the inceptual Greek experience. The tidings, the call, and the enchantment of being come to the human not in the form of discursive assertions or syllogisms, but rather as *song*—and an *animal* song at that.

Yet, what is the precise character of this song? As in *almost* all of Heidegger's engagements with animals (see chapter 3), the bird to which Heidegger refers here is speechless: it is ἄλογον, without λόγος, without the word, unable to express itself (*es sich nicht ausspricht*) by means of language.[76] However, although the bird does not express itself, and therefore certainly does not *speak* of the open, it nonetheless *indicates* it: "The bird, flying, singing, connects to and points to the open [*bindet und weist ins Offene*]."[77] The bird *weist* the open: it intimates, gestures toward, refers to, or points to the open.[78] If one takes some steps away from modernity and experiences the bird in the way the Greeks did—not the *word* "bird" so much as the *being*, the living animal itself in its appearing—one lets the bird gather together a certain range or dimension of significations; or, rather, one lets it gather together *the* range or dimension of signification, namely, the open region in which (or as which) beings appear and have meaning. Thus, although the bird does not *articulate* being as the open through discursive speech, it nonetheless *points* to it, through its very being, and also through its song.

Heidegger thus understands the bird as *gathering together* the open. That is, the animal here *calls forth* the open, evinces it, calls it to mind, and specifically to a modern mind that had otherwise forgotten it. But the bird, who is ἄλογον, calls forth the open without saying it, points toward the open without seeing it *as such*.[79] The bird, then, would be a kind of blind sign or mute archive, holding within itself (without knowing it) remembrances of the open. That is, the animal would hold *for us* such a memory of the open, singing the memory of it to us so as to remind us of it. And it would do this without itself knowing the open, without itself being able to *see* or *grasp* or *understand* being. To say this even more strongly: although the bird in the Heraclitus lectures is ἄλογον, without λόγος as the originary gathering of beings, it nonetheless serves a function *identical to λόγος* as it unfolds the tidings, call, and enchantment of the gathering of being. The birdsong gathers the human toward the world in a manner functionally identical to λόγος.

It is crucial to emphasize that it is not the case that the human can simply and willfully take steps away from the modern forgetfulness of being and saunter into a recollection of being: that is, the overcoming of the errancy of modernity, as the lecture course makes quite clear, is decidedly not to be carried out by way of an operation of the human *will*. This is owing to the fact that the movement away from modernity is precisely a movement away from the will and the Hegelian, Nietzschean, and above all Christian metaphysics in which the will plays such a foundational role.[80] Indeed, the catastrophe decried by Heidegger and mentioned at the outset of this chapter is a catastrophe that follows upon the modern human's attitude toward (and entanglement in) the will, as the closing lines of the lecture course make clear: "The danger in which the 'holy heart of the people' of the Occident stands is not that of decline: rather, it is that we, bewildered, shall yield to the will of modernity and race into it."[81] Thus, the human cannot *will* to step away from the modern forgetfulness of being without reinforcing that very forgetfulness; rather, the human must be *called away* from modernity, *called back* from its forgetfulness: and it is for this reason that Heidegger mentions the Sirens at the end of the passage. Immediately after marking the bird's entanglement (*verstricken*) in the open, Heidegger writes, somewhat desultorily: "In Greek, σειρά means tether. The Sirens are, 'in Greek,' the captivating ones [*die Bestrickenden*] in a manifold sense of the word."[82] The bird—entangled, enmeshed, immersed in the open of the clearing of being—calls the human to that open like a Siren, reminding the human of it through its wordless song: indeed, it is precisely *because* of its proximal, immediate entanglement in being that the animal is capable of calling the human in this manner. The human thus does not move itself toward the clearing by way of an operation of the will, but is *pulled* toward it, *compelled* toward it, by the animal. The human cannot overcome the perils of the will on its own: it *needs* the animal to call it, to beckon it, to *sing* to it as the Sirens sang to Odysseus as he undertook his long and perilous journey *homeward*.

To better understand the precise character of this singing, a brief turn to Heidegger's engagement with Rainer Maria Rilke in "What Are Poets For?," delivered in 1946 (three years after the Heraclitus course), is instructive. As Heidegger there writes, singing (*singen*) is a kind of thoughtful saying that proceeds without reflection, without, therefore, a subjectivized, willful, assertoric attitude toward language: "To sing, truly to say worldly existence, to say out of the haleness of the whole pure draft and to say only this, means: to belong to the precinct of beings themselves. This precinct, as the very nature of language, is Being itself. To sing the song means to be present in what is present itself. It means: Dasein."[83] The singer—that is, the poet—does not make assertions, which always refer to particular beings, but rather sings the song of being: the poet sings the open.[84] Heidegger also writes of such singing in his *Elucidations of Hölderlin's Poetry*. Here, too, it is the poet who sings, only now such singing is expressly said to be a singing of the open of *nature*: "The poets are those future ones whose being will be measured by their adaptation to the essence of 'nature.' "[85] He then goes on to say, using quite nearly the same language he employs in the Heraclitus lectures, that "nature" is to be understood in terms of the early Greek understanding of φύσις:

> Φύσις is an arising and an emerging [*das Hervorgehen und Auf-gehen*], a self-opening, which, while rising, at the same time turns back into what has emerged, and so shrouds within itself that which on each occasion gives presence to what is present. Thought as a fundamental word, φύσις signifies a rising into the open: the lighting of that clearing [*das Lichten*] into which anything may enter appearing, present itself in its outline, show itself in its "appearance" (εἶδος, ἰδέα) and be present as this or that. Φύσις is that rising-up which goes-back-into-itself [*das auf-gehende In-sich-zurück-Gehen*]; it names the coming to presence of that which dwells in the rising-up and thus comes to presence as open. [. . .] Φύσις is the emergence of the clearing [*der Aufgang der Lichten*], and thus it is the hearth and the place of light.[86]

The poets, Heidegger goes on to say, are those who belong (*gehören*) to this φύσις and correspond (*entsprechen*) "to the wonderfully all-present, to the powerful, divinely beautiful":[87] in other words, the poets are those who correspond, in their singing, to the clearing of the open of being, the ones whose vocation consists of attending to the call of being. These poets are those future ones who align themselves with φύσις and whose singing shelters being by bringing it into "saving nearness" (*sparenden Nähe*), thereby preserving and protecting it. This singing is later associated by Heidegger with the enunciation of the four-fold:[88] "The calling out of the singers is a looking out for immortality, for the divinity that is sheltered in the holy. The calls are like a looking out from the earth into the width of heaven."[89] The poets, the futural ones, sing forth the fourfold of the clearing of being and preserve it, drawing it into their protection: or, one might suggest, drawing it into the protection of *Artemis*, goddess of φύσις and of the animals within it.

Likewise, the bird from the Heraclitus lectures, in singing forth the tidings, call, and enchantment of being, lets the fourfold of being's clearing come to light. Although Heidegger does not use the language of the fourfold anywhere within the Heraclitus lectures, one can see its logic operative within the passage dealing with the birdsong. Heidegger "takes a few steps [*nur wenige Schritte*]" away from the modern, and toward the Greek, understanding of the bird (and of the animal more broadly). Yet, can one conceive of steps, even conceptual steps, in any way except as being oriented toward the *ground*, as taking place on the *earth*? Heidegger, his feet on the earth, steps away from the modern, zoological understanding of the bird, and sees the bird instead as "the animal through whose swaying and hovering the free dimension of the open unfolds." In other words, after taking his steps and looking up from the earth toward the sky, Heidegger lets the flight of the bird disclose the open region of the sky in its distinction from, and thus connection to, the earth.

In opening this open region—that is, in calling or singing it to us and in *signing* it to us in this way—the bird also indicates, refers, or points to closure and concealment—as, for example, Heidegger says, "in mourning." This opaque comment—an opaque comment that has to do precisely with the opaque, that is, the dark, the lightless, the concealed—is the closest Heidegger comes to naming the bird he has in mind: for with the mention of mourning, one cannot but think of the mourning dove or, perhaps even more immediately, of the swan, the bird associated with Artemis's brother Apollo. In any case, regardless of the specific bird Heidegger has in mind, the language of mourning calls to mind the operations of loss, of absence, and, specifically, of the losses and absences related to *death*. In other words, when one thinks of mourning, one thinks of *mortality*.[90]

In his *Elucidations of Hölderlin's Poetry*, Heidegger describes this act of mourning in relation to the poets, all within the compass of an analysis of Hölderlin's thinking of *nature*:

> Nature seems to be sleeping; yet she is not sleeping. She is awake, but awake in the manner of mourning. Mourning withdraws from everything into the memory of one thing only. The remembrance of mourning remains near to what has been taken from it and seems to be distant. Mourning is not merely pulled back by a current to something that was lost. It lets what is absent come again and again. And the mourning poets, too, for their part, only seem to be confined to their isolation and imprisoned in it. They are not "alone." In truth, "they are always divining." Their divination thinks forward into the distant, which does not withdraw, but rather is, as what is coming. But because what is coming itself still rests in its primordiality and remains there, the divining of what is coming is both a fore-thinking and a thinking-back. In this way, the poets persist in their belonging to "nature."[91]

As a thinking of what is to come, mourning (so understood) would be a thinking of concealment, and specifically a thinking of the concealment of what has yet to be unconcealed, namely, the nature of unconcealment itself, of φύσις itself, the very nature of nature, the very being of being. And this would be, perhaps above all, a thinking of *death* as the counterpart to life, of submergence as the intimate obverse of emergence. To relate this now back to the animal: the song of the bird, in intimating the concealment that belongs essentially to the clearing of being, sings—as do the Sirens—of death.

And yet, as we saw in the previous chapter dealing with Heidegger's lectures on Hölderlin's "Germania," animals, according to Heidegger, cannot mourn. Although animals are capable of experiencing pain and suffering, such suffering remains otherwise than sorrow or mourning, both of which are reserved only for that being who stands in an open relation to being (i.e., the human).[92] Because the animal is outside of language, and (therefore) outside of being, it does not stand in a knowing relation to the nothingness of death and is therefore incapable of mourning. Nevertheless, in the Heraclitus lectures, *even without knowing that it is doing* so, the animal points to or intimates death, "as in mourning." Just as in the lectures on Hölderlin's "Germania," then, the bird in the Heraclitus lectures, itself incapable of mourning, nevertheless *brings* mourning to the human, pointing to it and drawing the human toward it. In this way, the bird heralds the fundamental attunement of holy mourning so essential for Heidegger in preparing the ground for the other inception.

We see, then, that Heidegger takes steps along the earth, looks up at the bird in the sky, and thinks about mortality. What, then, of the gods? In the sentences immediately prior to the engagement with the bird, Heidegger twice emphasizes the intimate connection between animals and gods for the Greeks, an intimacy owed to the Greek understanding of *life* as the "self-unlocking and self-opening in the open."[93] Through thinking of life in terms of this self-emerging and self-appearing, the Greeks brought the animal "into an appropriate relation to the essence of the gods."[94] In other words, the gods, though not named here, are in the background, their essence being essentially the same as that of the animal, in the sense that both serve as a site of a pure emergence into the open. (All of this is implicit, as discussed above, in the association of Heraclitus's thought with the goddess Artemis.) Additionally, Heidegger's mention of the Sirens gestures toward the gods: for the Sirens were, while not gods, certainly divine, and had a kind of limited immortality. In comparing the bird to the Sirens, Heidegger intimates the divine, or rather suggests that the bird itself, in its singing, makes such intimations. (Moreover, one might perhaps again think of the swan here, whose intimate relation to Apollo, one of the two gods crucially important to Heidegger's Heraclitus lectures, is well attested.)

Simply put, the bird sings the play-space of φύσις which, for Heidegger, is to be understood as nothing other than the unfolding of the fourfold: "φύσις names that prior emerging within which earth and sky, sea and mountain, tree and animal, human and god emerge and thereby show themselves as what emerge, so that they, in light of this emerging, are known as 'beings.'"[95] The skyward bird, entangled in being but not aware of it, calls to the modern human on the earth below, who for its part is entangled (*verstrickt*) in a subjectivized understanding of *beings* and utterly awash in a forgetfulness of being without even being aware of it.[96] In this way, the bird is that without which the modern human could not remember the open: it is that which reminds the modern human of being. The bird, in letting the fourfold unfold, is a supplement without which the modern human could not recall the clearing of being.[97]

This commemorative function of the bird indicates that there is a certain *temporal priority* given to the animal here. Although the modern human stands in the open no less than the Greeks did (since such a standing is constitutive of the human and cannot be entirely abandoned or left behind), the modern human does not stand in it in the same way: rather, the modern human has become unaware of the open, captivated instead by the particular beings that appear within it. By *taking a few steps away* from this modern understanding—that is, by walking away from our modern captivation in beings *backward* toward the Greeks (i.e., those earlier humans)—the modern human can remember something of the open itself, of *being* itself, of the open clearing of being's unfolding. In other words, *prior* to us moderns having forgotten the open, the bird was always already entangled in the open in such a way as to indicate it and thus function as a sign of remembrance—as a commemorative symbol of the open. *Prior* to our having forgotten the open, the bird was always already a sign of it, a text pointing to it, an archive of it. The modern human—the human who comes *later*, after the bird as the Greek's understood it—must learn to read this text and access this archive so as to open itself (again) to the open.

But one sees, here, an *ontological* priority as well. The animal is the being who, not in speech, *but in its very being*, opens the open that we—also owing to our very being—have forgotten. The human, precisely as that (catastrophic) being who can see and say the open, can also forget the open; and the animal, precisely as the being who cannot see or say the open, is that being who *never* forgets it, who *cannot* forget it, whose very *life* forever calls forth the open. In this way, the animal remains nearer to being than the human, who, though it can never entirely conceal itself from being, can nonetheless wander away from it.[98] It is precisely the animal's entanglement in being that always allows it to serve as a sign of it. It is through reading this sign and recalling the inceptual meaning of being that the human will bring about its transformation into its proper *Dasein* and save itself and the earth from the catastrophe of the forgetfulness of being—save it, that is, from itself. The human is in *need*, Heidegger writes, of such "a prolonged transformation so that it may enter into its inception and learn to recognize that a consideration on 'the essence of truth' is the essential thinking within the inception of being itself, and only this."[99] The lecture course as a whole is concerned with preparing the modern human for exposure to this inception, an exposure that would lead to a transformation of the essence of the human.[100] Such preparation occurs, as we have seen, by stepping away from the modern scientific view of animality toward an inceptual experience of it, an experience that allows the human to hear the call of being that sounds forth through the wor(l)dless animal.

At the very end of the 1944 lecture course, which focuses on Heraclitus's understanding of λόγος, the forgetfulness of being has reached its apex and has configured itself into the modern human's unrestrained will to will. Unable to will itself out of such forgetfulness, the human needs being *to call* to it in order to transform itself into its proper essence: "In stillness, beyng turns toward the sheltering of the clearing into which it, as what is still preserved as what was always already there in advance, once gifted its grace in a manner that commences, in order to give the essence of the human a sole dignity: namely, to become the safe-keeper [*das Wahrende*] of the truth of beyng."[101] Through receiving the gift of being—a gift, as we have seen, that calls forth from the animal as enchanted tidings—the human will be transformed into the safe-keeper, *das Wahrende*, of the truth of being: someone who, we might say, follows after and attends upon being's unfolding in the way that a shepherd follows after the animals under his care.[102]

∼

The preceding interpretation of Heidegger's birdsong from GA 55 draws Heidegger into proximity to a position that he expressly rejects, both within that text and in other various places: namely, the position of Rainer Maria Rilke.[103] The parameters of this position are captured for Heidegger in the following lines from the *Eighth Duino Elegy*, lines that Heidegger calls "profoundly errant":[104]

> With full gaze, the animal sees
> the open. Only our eyes are,
> as if reversed, entirely like snares
> set around it, blocking the freedom of its out-going.
> What is outside, we know only from the animal's face.[105]

Heidegger then interpolates Rilke's lines thusly: "[T]he animal [. . .] alone sees the open. The human, however, gathers [*entnimmt*] knowledge of the open from the animal."[106]

The understanding of things represented by the *Elegy*, but visible (according to Heidegger) throughout Rilke's poetry, commits a number of errors representative of Rilke's place in the unfolding of Occidental metaphysics. The error immediately germane to the present inquiry is the manner in which Rilke, in suggesting that the animal sees the open, commits an "uncanny hominization" (i.e., anthropomorphizing) of the animal,[107] inverting the positions of human and animal being.[108] For Heidegger, as we all know perhaps too well, "the human, and only the human, constantly sees the open."[109] One finds an elaboration of this point in the *Ister* lectures from 1942: "[B]eing in general has opened itself to the human and is this very open[. . . .] To 'see' the open [. . .] is the distinction of human beings. The animal is animal precisely on account of its not seeing the open, as understood in this way, which is also why it is unable to say the 'is' of being, that is, is altogether unable to say. The animal is ἄλογον—without the word."[110] Given the animal's lack of an open relationship to the open,[111] Rilke's position that it is the animal who brings knowledge of the open to the human is, for Heidegger, errant to the extreme. And yet, we have seen that Heidegger's own engagement with the bird in GA 55 adds important nuance to his position. At the very least, the bird-scene suggests that the *modern* human—that is, the human who lives at the time of Heidegger's inquiry—can gather its knowledge of the open in this way, remembering its essential and distinctive relationship to being through its encounter with the bird. Heidegger's thinking of animality within this passage fundamentally agrees with Rilke's claim that the human "gathers knowledge of the open from the animal," suggesting a certain priority afforded to the animal. The animal is that from which the forgetful human remembers the open, although it is crucial to keep in mind that what Heidegger means by "the open" differs drastically, in his mind, from Rilke's understanding.[112]

To be sure, Heidegger affirms, later on in the lecture course, the difference between the animal and the human, and along the same lines he so often follows. Marking the essential openness of the human to being, Heidegger writes: "Everyone who *is*, as someone, does not merely occur as a being within the clearing (of being). Such a one not only stands 'in' the clearing, as does a rock or a tree or a mountain animal: rather, such a one looks [*blickt*] into the clearing, and this looking [*Blicken*] is one's ζωή—'life,' as 'we' say."[113] Here, it is only the human, and not the animal, who *looks* (*blickt*) into the clearing of being. In his lectures on Parmenides, offered at the University of Freiburg in 1942 (immediately before the lecture course on Heraclitus), Heidegger meditates extensively upon the animal's inability to look into the clearing of being in the manner of the human. In a passage that showcases all of the supposed humanism that contaminates his thinking, Heidegger writes:

> Animals are said to watch us. But animals do not look [*blicken*]. The "peering" [*Spähen*], or "glaring" [*Lauern*], or "gawking" [*Glotzen*] and "gaping" [*Stieren*] of an animal is never a self-disclosure

> of being, and, in its so-called looking [*sogenannten Blicken*], the animal never produces a self-emergence in a being that is disclosed to it. We [i.e., humans] are always the ones who first take up [*aufnehmen*] into the unconcealed such "looking" and who, on our own, interpret [*einlegen*] the way animals "watch" us as a looking. On the other hand, where the human only experiences Being and the unconcealed sketchily, the animal's "look" can concentrate in itself a special power of encounter.[114]

Thus, even though an animal may seem to look at the human, such "looking" fails to enter into being's emergence, and thus fails to relate to beings *as* beings.

Although there can be no doubt that Heidegger sets the human apart from the animal here, and along the same lines that one so often finds repeated throughout his work, what has been overlooked is the way in which even here, where Heidegger notes an abyssal difference between the human and the animal, the latter maintains a certain decisive priority. As Heidegger notes, the human is the one who first *takes up* (*aufnehmen*) the look of the animal into the open of the clearing of being. *Aufnehmen* means "to take up," "to receive," "to pick up," even "to record." In all instances, it is a term whose sense depends upon the priority of what is taken or picked up, of what is received or recorded. The human *encounters* something that was already there—in this case, an animal looking at it—and gathers it up into the open of its experience.

The priority of the Other in such an encounter is emphasized later by Heidegger during a discussion of the human capacity for "looking" (*Erblicken*). As Heidegger argues, such looking depends upon, and occurs subsequently to, a prior showing forth: "[W]hat shines is what shows itself to a looking [*das Erblicken*]. What appears to the looking is the aspect that solicits the human and addresses him [*der an den Menschen ergehende und ihn ansprechende Anblick*], the look [*der Blick*]. The looking performed by the human in relation to the appearing look is already a response [*Antwort*] to the original look, which first elevates human looking into its essence."[115] This original look—which is nothing other than the shining forth of being itself—reaches out to (*ergehende*) and addresses (*ansprechende*) the human, who *then* is able to offer a response (*Antwort*) to it. The looking in which the human engages thus follows upon the originary "look" of being that calls to the human and awaits the human's response. Simply put, the human is "looked upon" by being, a looking that is the very basis of human perception.[116]

Crucially, this originary look of being that makes human looking possible manifests itself in and through particular *beings*; or, at least, this would be the case for the understanding that has sufficiently turned away from the modern understanding of being back toward the inceptual understanding held by the Greeks, thereby recognizing that "for the Greeks, disclosure and emergence prevail in the essence of every inceptually emergent being."[117] It is only because "disclosure and emergence" shine through the unfolding of beings that the human can look at those beings *as beings* and therefore stand in relation to being. In other words, the original *look*—the inceptual unfolding of being—shines through beings, provided we sufficiently turn ourselves away from the forgetfulness of being characteristic of the modern era. A passage from the Heraclitus lectures from 1943 is instructive in this regard:

> We may make efforts to take φύσις in the appropriately Greek sense of the pure emerging: however, even when we do so, we treat it like a gigantic, all-encompassing container into which we stuff those things that we currently conceive of as beings. When we do this, we thereby fail to grasp what is decisive: for φύσις, as the perpetually emerging, is not an inert receptacle, a so-called "container" in the manner that a lampshade spreads over the lamp in such a way that the lamp remains what it is whether the shade "contains" and "covers" it or not. The pure emerging prevails throughout the mountain and the sea, the trees *and the birds*: their being itself is determined through and as φύσις and is only experienced in that way. Neither mountain nor sea nor any being needs the "container," for each being, insofar as it is, "is" in the manner of emerging.[118]

Φύσις—that is, being itself—unfolds through, and as, the emergence of beings. Mountain, sea, trees, birds: these *are* the emergings of φύσις, the unfolding of being: and it is *this* prior unfolding that, in each case, the human *then* takes up and interprets, a showing-forth that is therefore always already there prior to such a taking-up.

Heidegger points unambiguously to this priority when, back in the Parmenides lectures, he speaks of the "primordial consent [*anfängliche Einvernehmen*] given to being" by the human that precedes any act of human perception. Prior to any apprehension on the part of the human, there is the self-showing of being itself to which the human must consent; or, rather, to which the human, by its very nature, simply *does* consent.[119] Such consent on the part of the human points to the apriority of being's shining, a shining that is carried out by and through beings as they emerge into, and as, the opening of being.[120]

Thus, while, for Heidegger, the animal is unable to look into the clearing of being, the human is only able to do so through its encounter with beings: beings such as "mountain and the sea, the trees and the birds." To tie this more explicitly to the birdsong from the Heraclitus lectures, the human cannot look into the clearing of being without the animal always already having opened the clearing for it. Only the human can look into the clearing, but it cannot do so without the animal having *first* reminded the human of what to look for. The animal is that *through which* the human looks into the inceptual clearing of being.

The modern human, living in the destitute time to which both Heidegger and Rilke refer, has lost the "is": it has lost the ability to relate to being and therefore to its own essential nature.[121] In this way, the human has become *like* the animal, unable to see or to say being: and the catastrophe to which Heidegger refers is precisely the situation in which the human has come to understand itself as an animal, as the *animal rationale*.[122] Indeed, this situation is made clear through the fact that Heidegger uses the same language—the language of *entanglement* (*Verstricken*)—to refer both to the animal's embeddedness in its environment *and* the modern human's entanglement in beings. It is because the animal is entangled in being, lacking requisite *distance* to it, that it is unable *to think* being: and it is because the modern human is entangled in its subjectivity that it is unable to think the inceptual; it is owing to its entanglement in *beings*, rather than being, that "it is very difficult for us to put our own opinions aside and think the inceptual of inceptual thinking like beginners, like 'inceptors': that is, it is very difficult for us simply to think, and to think simply."[123] The modern human is so entangled in its preoccupation with beings that it has forgotten being; and through such forgetting, the human has become *like an animal*.

The birdsong from the Heraclitus lectures suggests that what is needed to remember that we are *not* animals is an encounter with the animal itself: the animal, in this way, reminds the modern human of the difference between our being and animal being. But it also, of course, reminds the modern human of being in distinction to beings: the animal announces, wordlessly, the ontological difference. The animal, as the living archive of the open, reminds the modern human not only of inceptual thinking, but of the inceptual itself: the animal-archive is the inception of our knowledge of being, and thus of beings as such.

Given all of this, it seems only fitting to end with Rilke, whose words we could now imagine as having been uttered by Heidegger himself, in his own name, in 1943, as he sought to bring his destitute Germany into a remembrance of the saving power of being:

> With full gaze, the animal sees
> the open. Only our eyes are,
> as if reversed, entirely like snares
> set around it, blocking the freedom of its out-going.
> What is outside, we know only from the animal's face.[124]

Chapter Six

The Animal-Thing

It could be the case, not only that the determination of the human essence does not originate in a question about the human, but that it does not originate from a question at all, precisely for the reason that this determination cannot be obtained from the human.

—the Guide, in *Country Path Conversations* (GA 77:103/66)

We have now seen the manner in which the animal, for Heidegger, sings the fourfold of being's unfolding. In this way, the animal, when thought inceptually, is capable of reawakening the human to the henceforth forgotten meaning of being and of initiating a concomitant transformation of the human into its role as the site of being's clearing.

In order to understand the mechanics of this transformation in greater detail, we turn to Heidegger's 1949 Bremen lectures "The Thing" and "Positionality" (in GA 79), which represent Heidegger's first sustained inquiry into the structure of the fourfold. On the surface, a turn to these lectures seems out of place, for in them Heidegger has very little to say about animality. Additionally, these lectures are among those texts in which Heidegger *seemingly* betrays a certain human exceptionalism by carrying out a rigid ontological segregation between the animal and the human, and least insofar as—like *Being and Time* twenty-two years earlier—he differentiates the animal's "perishing" from human dying:[1]

The mortals are human beings. They are called mortals because they can die. To die means to be capable of death as death.

> Only the human dies. The animal perishes. It has death neither ahead of itself nor behind it. Death is the shrine of Nothing, that is, of that which in every respect is never something that merely exists, but which nevertheless presences, even as the mystery of Being itself. As the shrine of Nothing, death harbors within itself the presencing of Being. As the shrine of Nothing, death is the shelter of Being. We now call mortals mortals—not because their earthly life comes to an end, but because they are capable of death as death. Mortals are who they are, as mortals, present in the shelter of Being. They are the presencing relation to Being as Being.[2]

According to this passage—which Derrida calls "unnuanced"—the animal does not "have" (its) death before itself: it does not relate to death *as* death.[3] Owing to the fact that, for Heidegger, death is the concealed (abyssal) ground of being—the "shrine of the Nothing," as he calls it—the animal, unable to relate to the Nothing, is also unable to stand in relation to being: that is, it is unable to grasp being *as such*. Much later in the Bremen lectures, Heidegger suggests that the inability of the animal to die is connected to its inability *to think*, thereby seemingly betraying the tried-and-true metaphysical prejudice that animals, unlike the human, are incapable of thinking in any robust sense.[4]

Little is expressly said about animality within the lectures beyond this; in this way, the lectures seem merely to reinforce the dominant scholarly view that Heidegger's engagement with the animal remains entrenched within a human exceptionalism rife with metaphysical biases regarding the inferiority of the animal. Indeed, one of the few additional comments Heidegger does make about "the animal" within this text is that authentic thinking must *free* the human from its designation as an animal (or living being) in order to bring about its transformation into the *mortal* properly understood.[5] On the surface, then, it seems as though Heidegger wants to get the human as far away from the animal as possible.

Despite all of this, there are three issues to note regarding Heidegger's posture toward the animal within the Bremen lectures. First, one sees at play within the above passage, and in exactly the form that has been encountered again and again throughout the present volume, a certain methodological priority allotted to the animal. Precisely at that moment that Heidegger wishes to delineate the character of the human, he turns toward the animal as that against which, and in terms of which, the human is to be set in relief. In this way, Heidegger—just at that moment he attempts to set the human apart—indicates the intimate connection between the human and the animal Other: the animal is the ground, the *sine qua non*, on the basis of which the human will (come to) clarify its own nature.

Second, as we will see, the transformation of the human into the *mortal*—a transition that, in a very real sense, is the very purpose of the Bremen lectures—*follows upon* an encounter with the animal. Although the text has little to say about "the animal" in general, an encounter with *particular animals* takes place within it that bears crucially upon Heidegger's understanding of the fourfold (and, therefore, of being). At the very end of "The Thing," Heidegger designates four animals—heron, deer, horse, and bull—as qualifying as *things* properly understood.[6] As such *things*, these four animals are capable of drawing the human into a mindful consideration of the fourfold unfolding of being, thereby bringing about the human's transformation into the shepherd of being. In this way, the animal is seen to have an ontological priority over the human to the extent that the encounter with the animal is structurally constitutive of the human's understanding (and *enactment*) of its own being. Moreover, to the extent that the encounter with the animal casts the human into a consideration of its own essence as the shepherd of being—a position that, for Heidegger, constitutes an "original ethics," as he puts it in "Letter on Humanism"—the animal can be said to have an ethical priority over the human as well: for the encounter with the animal is needed in order for the human to live ethically (in a Heideggerian sense). Thus, despite finding scant mention within the Bremen lectures, the animal nonetheless plays a foundational role therein in initiating a transformation of the human into its ownmost essence by situating the human into its proper abode, its proper *ethos*.

In order to grasp this role in greater detail, it is first necessary to consider the role of *things* within Heidegger's thinking of the fourfold; and in order to do this, it is necessary to appreciate Heidegger's understanding of the historical context from out of which his analysis of *things* takes place. The Bremen lectures, given in 1949, were Heidegger's first public lectures after the war; and, as was the case in his 1943 lectures on Heraclitus (analyzed in the previous chapter), these lectures betray a certain anxiety on Heidegger's part about the contemporary state of the world. By the time the war ended, Heidegger's concerns about the devastation of which modern technologies were capable was at its fever pitch.[7] GA 79 begins with Heidegger marking the way in which modern technologies (such as the airplane, radio, film, and television) have resulted in a widespread contracting of *distance*: indeed, the very function of such technologies seems to be an absolute diminution or eradication of distance itself. However, although these technologies bring events that would otherwise remain remote *near*, they in no way bring about actual *nearness*: for, precisely through bringing beings spatially and temporally near, such apparatuses have in fact occluded access to *nearness* itself. Above all, the reduction of distances brought about by modern technology has resulted in an obliviousness to that which is most near, namely, being itself.

As Heidegger will develop at length in "Positionality," such a drive toward absolute proximity, where "everything actual converges in the uniformly distanceless,"[8] has brought about a situation in which the things of the world show themselves as standing around waiting to be put to use by the human: that is, things show themselves as standing-reserve,[9] where this term denotes the absolute availability of all things to be on call to be put to ordered use by the human. Such absolute availability, characteristic of the era of "enframing" (*Gestell*), presents things as *reserves* or *stores* set within the nexus of human machinations. The result is a comportment toward things on the part of the human that radically differs from that which dominated prior to the prevalence of modern technology. In a particularly infamous passage, Heidegger describes this situation in the following terms:

> Through such requisitioning the land becomes a coal reserve, the soil an ore depository. This requisitioning is already of a different sort from that whereby the peasant had previously tended his field. Peasant activity does not challenge the farmland; rather it leaves the crops to the discretion of the growing forces; it protects them in their thriving. In the meantime, however, even the tending of the fields has gone over to the same requisitioning that imposes upon the air for nitrogen, the soil for coal and ore, the ore for uranium, the uranium for atomic energy, and the latter for orderable destruction. Agriculture [*Ackerbau*] is now a mechanized food industry, in essence the same as the production of corpses in the gas chambers and extermination camps, the same as the blockading and starving of countries, the same as the production of hydrogen bombs.[10]

The human's relationship to nature in its various forms has transformed from a situation of waiting-upon to one of *demanding*, of *challenging* from nature that it supply an endless yield. It has also resulted in a worldview that sees all entities, big or small—for example, plants, humans, corpses, countries, and atoms—as functionally equivalent. Everything *means* the same in the age of enframing: namely, standing-reserve. Although Heidegger does not directly mention animals in the above passage, *Ackerbau*, as the cultivation of land, at least entails animal labor; moreover, as the following passage from "What Are Poets For?" makes clear, animals are also implicated within the ruthless logic of standing-reserve: "Not only are living things [*Lebendige*] technically objectivated in stock-breeding [*Züchtung*] and exploitation; the attack of atomic physics on living matter as such is in full swing. At bottom, the essence of life is supposed to yield itself to technical production."[11] In other words, *all* living things—plant, animal, human, and even the microscopic cells that comprise these—have been collapsed into the single category of *product*, whose sole function is to serve the human's actualization of its will to power.

Such a challenging of nature—a challenging into which the human, for its part, is drawn by being itself[12]—amounts, for Heidegger, to an *attack* (*befallen*) against the earth.[13] The actual assault against the earth through technological and economical exploitation is more than a metaphor for the human's forgetfulness of the concealed ground of being—it is the logical outgrowth of it: and the wholesale destruction of the earth through an atomic apocalypse, very much on Heidegger's mind following the devastating attacks on Hiroshima and Nagasaki, would only be the final culmination of the forgetting of being implicit in Platonic metaphysics and the technological/ scientific worldview to which it, according to Heidegger, gave rise:

> The human is transfixed by what could come about with the explosion of the atomic bomb. The human does not see what for a long time now has already arrived and even is occurring, and for which the atomic bomb and its explosion are merely the latest emission, not to speak of the hydrogen bomb, whose detonation, thought in its broadest possibility, could be enough to wipe out all life on earth. What is this clueless anxiety waiting for, if the horrible has already occurred?
>
> The horrifying is what transposes all that is out of its previous essence. What is so horrifying? It reveals and conceals itself in the way that everything presences, namely that despite all overcoming of distance, the nearness of that which is remains outstanding.[14]

Thus, as was the case in GA 55 six years earlier, Heidegger's Bremen lectures take place from out of a situation of global duress in which the greatest catastrophe imaginable—namely, the eradication of the "is"[15]—is slowly but surely coming to fruition; and it is in an effort to resist this collapsing of the world into absolute distancelessness—to resist, therefore, the forgetfulness of being prevailing in the modern era—that Heidegger turns to his consideration of *things*. Through an attentive meditation on the way in which *things* show themselves (i.e., what Heidegger will call "the thinging of the thing"), Heidegger attempts to reawaken the human to the nearing of the near, namely, to the emerging of being itself; and, as we will see, this reawakening entails an encounter with *animals*, among other things.

Heidegger begins his inquiry by noting that, although the human has long been surrounded by things, it has never properly grasped those things as *things*: that is, the human has never yet experienced the *thing* in its proper aspect. Taking a jug (*Krug*) as a paradigmatic thing, Heidegger attempts to bring about—for the first time—an authentic showing-forth of a thing *as* a thing. Such an endeavor necessarily involves a destructuring of the representation of *things* as objects (i.e., over against a Cartesian subject); indeed, it involves a destructuring of the suitability of the very paradigm of re-presentation as a viable model for exposing the genuine thingness of things (i.e., the being of beings). As Heidegger observes, the jug is primarily characterized by a certain independence from the human, a "self-standing" over against the human that precedes any representation of it as an object: "The jug remains a vessel whether we represent it in our minds or not."[16] The very first step of Heidegger's inquiry thus reveals a certain *priority* that belongs to things, that is, the manner in which their standing-forth precedes any operation of human representation. In what follows, we will see this priority emphasized and, eventually, intensified almost without limit.

In his next step, Heidegger questions the suitability of understanding things in terms of the framework of *production*. Although one might think that the jug, as an *artifact*, is the result of a productive process, such a view fails to attend to the underlying essence of the jug. (In Heideggerian parlance, one could say that while it is *correct* that the jug was produced, it is not *true*: that is, such a conception does not bring the full essence of the jug to light.) Above all, such a view (mis)understands the jug as having come about as a result of an operation of human (re)presentation; the productive paradigm thus merely reinscribes (or, rather, serves as the metaphysical ground of) the objectification of the thing. (In other words, the artisan first envisions the form or εἶδος of the jug, and then re-presents that form in formed matter.) The understanding of the thing as an artifact thus misses the apriority of the thing by attempting to displace it and insert the human's representational capacities as the ground of the thing's thinghood.

Heidegger then takes what is perhaps the most decisive step of his examination. Turning away from the jug as either an object or, in what amounts to the same, as the result of a process of production, Heidegger suggests that "the thinghood of the jug lies in that it is as a vessel [*Gefäß*]."[17] As Heidegger argues, it is the emptiness (*Leere*) of the jug—that is, "this nothing in the jug" (*dieses Nichts am Krug*)—that constitutes the thing-hood (*Dinghafte*) of the jug properly understood. It is only by virtue of this emptiness, this *nothingness*, that the jug can be a vessel and hold the wine it is meant to outpour.[18] (As Heidegger puts it even more strongly in *Country Path Conversations*, "[T]he nothingness of the jug is really what the jug is" [*dieses Nichts am Krug ist eigentlich das, was der Krug ist*].)[19] What makes this turn so radical is that, in turning toward *nothingness* as the essential characteristic of the jug, Heidegger definitively silences metaphys-ics' ability to grasp the thingness of the thing: for metaphysics, grounded as it is within a representational framework, cannot represent *nothing*.[20] By focusing on the *nothingness* of the jug as the ground of its ability to hold and store wine, Heidegger breaks with such a metaphysical framework and undertakes a fresh path toward the thinghood of the thing. Science, for its part, would find such a path misguided, and would say that the jug is not empty at all but is filled with air, air that is then displaced when wine is poured into the jug.[21] But such an explanation, thoroughly steeped within representational metaphysics, sidesteps the thingness of the jug rather than showing it in its proper aspect. Even worse, such a view *destroys* the thing, indeed, destroys *all* things insofar as it utterly fails to allow things to show themselves independently of human representation. As Heidegger puts it, "[S]cience has already annihilated [*vernichtet*] the thing as thing long before the atom bomb exploded."[22]

It is important to observe that, in annihilating the thing, science (and representational metaphysics more broadly) has cut the human off from an experience of the emptiness of the jug: that is, it has obscured the human's view of the *Nothing*. But *nothingness* serves as the concealed (abyssal) ground from out of which being, as emergence, unfolds: thus, in occluding access to the Nothing of the jug, science is contributing to the forgetfulness of being that dominates in the contemporary era.[23] ("Modern science" and "meta-physics" just are, for Heidegger, functional synonyms for the forgetfulness of being.)[24] To phrase this somewhat paradoxically, science, in annihilating the thingly character of the thing, annihilates the *Nothing* of the thing: it annihilates the alethic character of being.[25] As Heidegger had previously averred, this annihilation is *worse* than that brought about by the atomic bomb, if only because the former serves as the latter's ground of possibility. In breaking with representational metaphysics, Heidegger has brought the human back into an awareness of the Nothing at the heart of being.

Such a break is necessary, Heidegger claims, in order to *first* access things in their proper unfolding: for "the thing remains obstructed as thing [. . .]; things have not yet ever [*noch nie*] been able to appear as things at all."[26] However, the fact that things have yet to be grasped in their being is not (simply) owing to neglect on the part of the human to attend to the thingness of things. Rather, the human has not yet grasped the essence of things because those things have *yet* to show themselves as such. This crucial point gestures further toward the *priority* of things operative within the human's relation to them. As Heidegger goes on to say, "[T]he human can only neglect what has already been allotted him. The human can represent, regardless of the manner, only that which has first lit itself up from itself and shown itself to him in the light that it brings with it."[27] This light—this shining forth—precedes the human's grasp of it; the thingness of the thing is thus *prior* to the human's apprehension of it. Such priority is further emphasized by Heidegger later when he discusses the word "thing" (*Ding*). There, Heidegger claims that the word "thing" and its German counterpart name "what concernfully approaches [*angeht*] the human in some way."[28] It is thus not the human, through its mental machinations, who brings about the thing: rather, the *thing* "comes of its own accord to the human in a concernful approach."[29] As we will soon see, such an approach on the part of the thing will ultimately bring about a radical transformation of the human's self-understanding.

Returning to the analysis of the jug, Heidegger now indicates the way in which the capacity of the jug to hold and retain wine is oriented toward the out-pouring, or the *giving*, of the wine. This out-pouring, understood as *gift* (*Geschenk*), ultimately accounts for the essence of the jug;[30] and it is here, with mention of the gift, that Heidegger begins to articulate the four poles of the fourfold. The wine in the jug depends upon water drawn from a spring. The spring, in turn, depends upon the "dark slumber of the earth"; and this, for its part, depends upon the sky as the source of rain. Both earth and sky "abide in the wine" in a unified way, insofar as rain and sun, vine and soil, all contribute to the being of the wine.[31]

Although the gift of wine is typically intended for mortals, in consecration or sacrifice it can also be meant for "immortal gods," and it is indeed only here that the gift of the out-pouring finds its proper essence.[32] Only by *offering* the wine as a gift to the immortals *in sacrifice* does the wine show itself in its fullest essence: for it is through pouring out wine (or water) as sacrificial libation that the four poles of the fourfold come together in their proper alignment. As Heidegger writes:

> In the gift of the pour that is a libation, the mortals abide in their way. In the gift of the pour that is an oblation, the divinities abide in their way, divinities who receive back the gift of the giving as the gift of a donation. In the gift of the pour, the mortals and divinities each abide differently. In the gift of the pour, the earth and sky abide. In the gift of the pour there abides at the same time earth and sky, divinities and mortals. These four, united of themselves, belong together. Obligingly coming before all that presences, they are folded into a single fourfold.
>
> In the gift of the pour abides the single fold [*Einfalt*] of the four.
>
> The gift of the pour is a gift insofar as it lets the earth and sky, the divinities and mortals abide.[33]

The pouring of wine from the jug in sacrifice lets the fourfold unfolding of being come to presence: that is, it lets the very presencing of being open up in its full dimensionality.[34] (Indeed, the very word "thing," for Heidegger, refers to this unfolding).[35] The thing *announces*, *points to*, or *articulates* the fourfold unfolding of being.

As a bit of a detour, one can ask: Does the animal haunt this discourse of Heidegger's on *sacrifice*?[36] To be sure, Heidegger does not mention animals by name here (although Mitchell has convincingly argued that, properly understood, the appellation "mortals," within the context of Heidegger's thinking of the fourfold, must include animals alongside humans).[37] But can one think of *sacrifice*, of the offering operative in *Opfer*, without thinking also of the animal? In his brief meditation on sacrifice, Heidegger relates the German word *Guß* to the Greek χέειν, "to pour."[38] Certainly, such ancient devotional offerings of wine occurred often enough on their own without an attending animal sacrifice; and yet, such out-pouring of wine was an established part of animal sacrifices in ancient Greece, as is well attested in Homer and the tragedies.[39] (Moreover, such wine was often stored and transported in wineskins, i.e., vessels made of dead animals.)[40] So, one can ask: Which was sacrificed *first*—the animal, or the wine? And even if the latter, does not the widespread practice of animal sacrifice add an inescapable nuance to the word "sacrifice," such that one cannot think the procedure without also thinking of the animal—and, indeed, in very same way that one is bound to think of the goats and bulls sacrificed at the Dionysia when one thinks or utters the word "tragedy"?[41]

If any of this were so, would it mean that this discourse on the jug in "The Thing" is foregrounded upon the animal, and that the animal is submerged within the background of Heidegger's thinking of the jug? Would it also mean that the scene of the sacrificial chalice (*Opfergerätes* and *Opferschale*) described in *The Question concerning Technology* is, *a fortiori*, a scene of animal sacrifice?[42] Is the animal hidden somewhere behind Heidegger's talk of the "four modes of occasioning" responsible for bringing the sacrificial chalice into being, barely visible but nonetheless operative in the background? And what of the *festival* and the *feast* mentioned during the analysis of the jug in *Country Path Conversations*? Can the *feast* be thought without reference to the *meat* of the animal, so ubiquitous to festivals and feasts, be they Greek or German?[43] And regarding Heidegger's vast employment of the language of "sacrifice" when thinking the role of the poet in founding the new inception, or the role of the thinker in thinking that inception, or the role of the German youth in the face of National Socialism:[44] Would such a metaphorics of sacrifice be grounded in the archaic offering of the animal to the gods? In short, can one employ the language of *sacrifice*, with its *tragic* origins, without also ineluctably conjuring the ghost of the animal Other? Would there ever have been, or could there ever be, a sacrifice *without* the animal?

Turning back now from this detour, it is important to note the *priority* of the *thing* as it eventuates the fourfold unfolding of being. The *thing* is that without which, and that on account of which, being is able to open up into its full expanse: it is how being, as fourfold, presences to the human, the *way*, the *how*, of the world's unfolding. In other words, without the *thing* approaching and addressing the human, being's unfolding would remain inconspicuous: the *thing*, in thinging, makes the human attentive to the otherwise overlooked (or occluded) nearness of being. This means that the thing *precedes* and occasions the opening of being's unfolding: "The thing lets the fourfold abide. The thing things the world. Every thing lets the fourfold abide in something that each time abides from the single fold of the world."[45] This priority of the thing is verified in Heidegger's so-called "Black Notebook" where he writes that "the simple onefold of the thing in the event lies before [*liegt vor*] any differentiation of ontological difference and indifference."[46] Thus, things *are*, and are prior to the opening of world as the fourfold, prior to the discharging of the foundational differing of beings from being. The human is only made aware of the worlding of the world, the regioning of the region, the appropriating event *through* the encounter with things, things that are therefore always already there prior to the human's grasp of the world in its full dimensionality.

Nevertheless, despite this priority of the thing, the encounter requires a certain comportment on the part of the human that *lets* the thing unfold as the opening of world: "When and how do the things come as things? They do not come through the machinations of humans. But they also do not come without the vigilance [*Wachsamkeit*] of the mortals. The first step to such vigilance is the step back [*der Schritt zurück*] from merely representational, i.e., explanatory thinking into commemorative thinking."[47] The human thus needs *to let* things show themselves in their proper priority, a letting that is achieved to the extent that the human can move away from understanding itself as the (representational) ground of beings. Such a vigilant "stepping back" away from the fetters of representational thinking should remind us of the step back toward the inceptual understanding of the bird that Heidegger undertook in his lectures on Heraclitus (as analyzed in the previous chapter).[48] It can also perhaps be understood as equivalent to the movement toward "releasement" (*Gelassenheit*) that Heidegger develops, among other places, in his *Country Path Conversations*, where the steps taken along the country path symbolize a movement away from representational thinking and toward a preparation for the (true) showing-forth of things.[49] Finally, one might also understand this "stepping back" in terms of Heidegger's overall destructuring of Western ontology, the very point of which is to open up thinking for a new inceptual showing-forth of being(s).

Crucially, as "The Thing" makes clear, this stepping back further gestures toward the *priority* of things: "The step back, on the contrary, departs altogether from the domain of merely personal attitudes. Addressed [*angesprochen*] by the world's essence from within it, the step back takes up its residence in a correspondence [*Entsprechen*] that answers [*antwortet*] this."[50] The step back toward the thing is thus carried out as an *answer* that *responds* to the world's essencing, a response that therefore follows upon, and is subsequent to, an address that calls to the human. The human comportment comes *after* the essencing of world occasioned by the *thing* and seeks to correspond to this. Simply put: *letting* always and only follows upon a call from that which is *to be let*.

As Heidegger has said, this response is carried out as commemorative thinking (*andenken*), a thinking that thoughtfully remembers by thinking toward (*an*) the *thing*. However, what is remembered is *not* the thing itself, which, as Heidegger has already said, has never yet shown itself to the human. Rather, what is remembered through such commemorative thinking is *being* itself, that is, the nearest of the near (or nearness itself). The *thing* is that through which the human is able to remember that which the contemporary era has led it to forget: namely, being itself in its utmost nearness. As Heidegger goes on to argue, it is through such commemorative thinking of being that the human is *conditioned* (or "be-thinged": *Be-dingten*) by the thing: "When we let the thing in its thinging essence from out of the worlding world, then we commemorate the thing as thing. Thoughtfully remembering in this way, we allow the worlding essence of the thing to concernfully approach us. Thinking in this way we are met by the thing as thing. We are, in the strict sense of the word, conditioned [*Be-dingten*]. We have left the arrogance of everything unconditional behind us."[51] With this, Heidegger inverts the relationship between the human and things characteristic of Cartesian (and ultimately, for Heidegger, Platonic) metaphysics. The human is no longer the measure of that which is: it is no longer the ground of being. Rather, *things* are the ground of being's unfolding and thus serve as the measure of the human's reception of being(s). No longer the subjective ground of the being of beings, the human is *conditioned* by things insofar as things awaken the human to the inceptual meaning of being. Such conditioning is the strongest possible confirmation of the absolute apriority of the thing. Things, in conditioning the human, displace the human as the center of beings, serving instead as the center around and from out of which the fourfold opens: the human follows after, and is dependent upon, the thinging of the thing.

It is through such *thinging*, such conditioning, that the essence of the human is transformed into its proper essence, for it is through remembering being in the face of the *thing* that the human enters into its proper essence as the protector, or the watcher, of being(s): "When we think the thing as thing, then we protect [*schonen*] the essence of the thing in the region from where it essences. Thinging is the nearing of world. Nearing is the essence of nearness. Insofar as we protect the thing as thing, we dwell in nearness."[52] Such protection amounts to a kind of *sheltering* of those beings through which the fourfold of the world opens. Through such sheltering, the human itself "dwells in nearness"—that is, it abides in the open clear-ing of being. Through protecting the opening of the fourfold that ushers forth through *things*, the human comes to relate to itself as the *there* of being's unfolding: in a word, it becomes the steward of being.[53] It is thus the encounter with the thing—the thing that is always already there, prior to the human's grasping of its own proper identity—that transforms the human *from* "the human" into its role as *Da-sein*.

It is at the very end of "The Thing" that Heidegger indicates that animals, alongside other things, are capable of awakening the human to being in this way, thus initiating a transformation of the human's essence: "The thing is nimble: jug and bench, footbridge and plow. But a thing is also, after its manner, tree and pond, stream and mountain. Things are, each abiding [*je weilig*] thing-like in its way, heron and deer, horse and bull.[54] Things are, each abiding thing-like after their manner, mirror and clasp, book and picture, crown and cross."[55] Heron and bull, horse and deer, are thus just as capable as the jug of pulling the human out of its immersion in representational thinking and opening it to the manifold unfolding of being, inceptually understood.[56] Through encountering such animals—and, one presumes, other animals as well, such as dogs, cows, pigs, and, of course, *cats*—the human becomes aware of the world and of its own role within it. Moreover, this encounter with the animal *conditions* the human by alerting it to its own proper essence as the steward, the protector, of being(s). Following after the animal—who, as unconditional thing, always already occupies a place of absolute (i.e., unconditioned) apriority—the human enters into its proper role as the *shepherd* of being.

As argued above, part of what makes the encounter with the thing so transformative is its ability to reawaken the human to the *Nothingness*, that is, the concealment, at the core of being's unfolding: indeed, a proper attentiveness to such concealment is characteristic of the inceptual under-standing of being.[57] Such nothingness was shown by Heidegger to reside within the emptiness of the jug: the jug, as thing, conceals concealment (within) itself. Does the animal, understood as thing, also carry with it a *nothingness* to which the human can be reawakened? By revisiting a passage discussed at the outset of this chapter, one can see that this is indeed the case. As mentioned above, Heidegger differentiates the human from the animal within "The Thing" along the lines of the latter's inability *to die*:

The mortals are human beings. They are called mortals because they can die. To die means to be capable of death as death.

> Only the human dies. The animal perishes. It has death neither ahead of itself nor behind it. Death is the shrine of Nothing, that is, of that which in every respect is never something that merely exists, but which nevertheless presences, even as the mystery of Being itself. As the shrine of Nothing, death harbors within itself the presencing of Being. As the shrine of Nothing, death is the shelter of Being. We now call mortals mortals—not because their earthly life comes to an end, but because they are capable of death as death. Mortals are who they are, as mortals, present in the shelter of Being. They are the presencing relation to Being as Being.[58]

So understood, it is only the human who, in its unique ability to relate to death *as* death, comes face to face with "the shrine of the Nothing"—becomes, that is, a *mortal*.[59] However, as also mentioned earlier, it is precisely by turning toward the animal Other and distinguishing itself from it that the human becomes aware of this unique capacity. In other words, although the animal cannot relate to the Nothing of death, it is among those things (like artworks and jugs) that *lets* the human so relate. In light of the entirety of the analysis presented here, one can say that the animal, understood as *thing*, awakens the human to the concealed ground of being's unfolding, thereby conditioning the human into its proper role as the shepherd of being. In this way, the animal-thing—as the site of the *difference* between being and beings—carries the Nothing within itself and serves as a site of the human's exposure to (the Nothingness) of being. Through such exposure, the human transforms into the *mortal*; the animal-thing is thus that without which such a transformation cannot take place.[60] The human *needs* the animal Other to cast it into the propriety of its ownmost essence; in this way, the encounter with the animal-thing brings about the "original ethics" described by Heidegger in "Letter on Humanism."[61] Insofar as the encounter with the animal serves as the entry way into a consideration of the human's proper abode (or *ethos*) within the clearing of being, the animal-thing is that which provokes, and renders possible, an original ethics in the Heideggerian sense.

But there is a greater ethical promise to Heidegger's thinking here that is worth considering. As mentioned at the outset of this chapter, Heidegger's analysis of *things* takes place within a historical context wherein all distances have begun to collapse and "everything that presences is equally near and far."[62] This is the historical moment of enframing where all things have become standing-reserve waiting around for the human to exploit in the service of its own unrestrained will toward absolute will.[63] Within such a framework, an erasure of difference has resulted whereby all things, regardless of their unique character, have been reduced to their role as equipment. Ultimately, this framework results in the effacing of difference itself, namely, the ontological difference: for the era of modern technology is, above all else, the era when being has been forgotten and has been thoroughly mistaken for *a* being.[64] It is also the era in which the prioritizing of the human as the ground of all beings—that is, the positing of the human as being itself—reaches its highest apogee.[65]

Within this historical moment of distancelessness, where the nearness of being has been eschewed in favor of the nearness of *beings*, all beings have become equivalent and the *meaning* of being has been forgotten. In such a situation, as previously quoted, "[a]griculture is now a mechanized food industry, in essence the same as the production of corpses in the gas chambers and extermination camps, the same as the blockading and starving of countries, the same as the production of hydrogen bombs."[66] The human's comportment toward beings is dominated by a will to penetrate and exploit, and every being has become merely an instrument by which the human can realize its will for absolute *autonomy*, unlimited *sovereignty*. Driven by such a will, the human, far from being a shepherd of being, becomes its most dangerous threat: "By not letting things be in their restful repose, but rather—infatuated by his progress—stepping over and away from them, the human becomes the pacesetter [*Schrittmacher*] of the devastation, which has for a long time now become the tumultuous confusion of the world."[67] In the age of enframing, the human, in addition to being the victim of being's withdrawal, has also become its most ardent, unrestrained agent.

As the preceding analysis has revealed, the animal-thing is capable of reawakening the human to the distance appropriate to things, and this by way of a recollection of the nearest of the near, that is, being itself. In this way—namely, by (re)introducing the distance/difference appropriate to being(s)—the animal-thing resists the pernicious effects of enframing.[68] It is only because of the all-encompassing reach of enframing that the human perceives the land as a resource to be reaped without limit, or a country as something to be systematically starved for political purposes, or the atom as something to be split in order to generate enormous energy or widespread death, or—what amounts to the same—the human as something to be produced (*Fabrikation*) into a corpse within a concentration camp. By casting the human out of this framework, the encounter with the animal-thing resists the reduction of all things to units of calculable and manipulatable *stock*. Such an encounter would generate a new sensitivity to the patient growing of plants that film, with its manipulation of *time*, has occluded; it would also disrupt the transformation, already well-underway, of the human into standing-reserve—not just as a corpse but also as a faceless resource within an economy of means and ends directed toward the unrestrained production of more material resources.[69] The animal-thing thus promises a transformation not only of the human's ethical stance toward the earth, but also of that toward the human, insofar as a proper assaying of the animal-thing would bring about a situation wherein the differences between things—between, for example, the cultivation of land and the widespread eradication of human populations—would again become visible.[70]

Moreover, the promise of Heidegger's thinking of the animal-thing for questions of animal ethics should not be overlooked, nor has it been by certain attentive scholars.[71] Once grasped in its proper role as *thing*, the animal, in conditioning the human, would disrupt the attitude toward the animal that has prevailed within the age of enframing: namely, the view that the animal is nothing more than live*stock* to be used by the human in the carrying out of its own unrestrained machinations.[72] By stepping away from a representational framework that has presented the animal as contingent upon and subservient to the human, the latter would come to know the animal as that which occasions its own essential involvement in the unfolding of being.[73] This would entail recognizing the *priority* of the animal Other in making possible an attentive, transformative experience of being in its full unfolding.

Such a recognition would dissolve the hegemony of the scientific approach over the question of the animal, an approach that, to be clear, has resulted in millennia of mistreatment and suffering for animal Others. The posture that views the human and the animal as biologically/genetically proximal has, in the service of obtaining evidence for such proximity, brought untold suffering to billions upon billions of animals by way of experimentation, captivity, transport and relocation, and murder.[74] In the name of *sameness*—in the name, that is, of bringing the animal and the human near to one another in a biological continuum (where all "animals," including the human, are just variations of the *same* basic genetical material)—science has again and again demonstrated the fundamentally anthropocentric ground of its comportment toward the animal by reducing its role to standing-reserve for the edification and material improvement of humankind. Through such a reduction, the animal Other is never allowed to show itself as it is, to the extent that it serves as the locus of any number of biological, zoological, chemical, or physical projections imposed externally upon it. Even when such projections have been made with the purported goal of improving the living conditions of animals—for example, by discovering something within them enough like human consciousness or intelligence to warrant human ethical consideration—the sciences reinforce and further calcify the problematic posture they seek to overcome: one does not do justice to the autonomy of the Other by looking for evidence of such autonomy with a scalpel and microscope. Science, like the metaphysics that serves as its core, has decidedly proved itself to be the conceptual and literal abattoir to which the animal Other has been lead as a matter of course.

By encountering the animal-thing in its otherness, Heidegger reintroduces an unsurpassable, abyssal distance between the human and the animal, thereby creating a space wherein the fetters of the metaphysical/scientific approach to animality can be overcome. This encounter (first) makes possible a reconsideration of how the human ought to *dwell* on the earth, beneath the sky, *alongside the animal-things* in the midst of which it finds itself. Said more strongly: in order for the human to become ethical in the robust sense, it must *first* encounter the animal-thing. Such an encounter would not be wholly different from that described by Derrida in his *The Animal That Therefore I Am*, where the ipseity of the human is conditioned by, and dependent upon, a denuding exposure to the gaze of the animal Other, nor would it differ wildly from the encounter described by Derrida in his *The Politics of Friendship* where he speaks of the responsibility toward the Other that precedes and makes possible all ethics:

> We are already caught up, we are caught out, in a certain responsibility, and the most ineluctable responsibility. [. . .] We are invested with an undeniable responsibility at the moment we begin to signify something. But where does this begin? Does it ever begin? The responsibility that assigns freedom to us *without leaving it with us*, as it were—we see it coming from the other. It is assigned to us by the other, from the place of the Other, well before any hope of reappropriation permits us the assumption of this responsibility—allowing us, as we say, to assume responsibility, *in the name, in one's own name*, in the space of *autonomy*.[75]

The ethical possibility of overcoming the age of enframing is pro-scribed to the human by the animal-thing, a pro-scription that reveals the absolute priority of the animal Other. The human can only come home to the House of Being—it can only become the shepherd of being—by *following after* the animal: its proper dwelling, its ownmost *ethos*, and the future of the West depend upon it.

Conclusion

Final Word

The animal looks at us, and we are naked before it. Thinking perhaps begins there.

—Derrida, *The Animal That Therefore I Am* (2008, 50)

Regarding the question of the animal—could there ever be a final word?

The preceding study, if nothing else, must incline us toward answering this question in the negative, and for two essentially related reasons. To begin with, regarding the question of the animal, there will always be more to say. This is owing both to the enduring *strangeness* or *foreignness* of the animal Other (i.e., the ultimately inaccessible *mystery* of its interior life) and to the fact that the process of ontological comparison—the "to and fro" described by Heidegger in his "Black Notebook"—is endless, and exactly to the extent that the identity of human *Dasein* forever remains indeterminate.[1] The transformative capacity of the human—that is, the extent to which it must make a decision about its own being in the face of its thrownness[2]—is finally limited only by the final finality itself, namely, *death*. So long as the human is living, it is engaged in the project of self-determination, a project that, as we have seen at length, continually entails a (re)turn to the animal Other as that against and in terms of which the human's being will come into its proper relief. So long as this process continues, the human is continually engaged in the process of differentiating itself from the Others with whom it finds itself, Others who are (therefore) always already there. In this way, there will always be more to say about the animal, the human, and their relation, a saying that will therefore remain forever incapable of bringing the full nature of the animal, or *Dasein*, into articulation.

The second reason that there can be no final word regarding the animal is significantly more complicated and has to do with the manner in which, as we have seen, the animal serves as an entryway for the human into a consideration of being itself. As such an entryway, the animal is the necessary detour through which the human must travel in order to grasp its own role as *Da-sein*—as, that is, the shepherd of being. As it enters into this detour, the human journeys away from itself and gets (back) on track toward an inceptual experience of being, an experience through which it finds clarity regarding its own essence as the *there* of being's clearing. The detour through the animal is, in this way, a detour through being itself.

Such a journey is reminiscent of the journey of the poet described by Heidegger in his various works on Hölderlin, a journey that has everything to do with reminiscence. As discussed in chapter 4, the poet must leave the familiar of his home and enter into the foreign in order to (re)turn back into his own proper essence and bring about a commemorative thinking of being. For Hölderlin, that foreign is the heavenly fire of Greece, a fire to which the poet must expose himself in order to found his—and, indeed, *our*—proper *Dasein*. For Heidegger, such fire names the region of the *holy*, and it is to the radiant fire of the holy that the poet must expose himself in order to find himself, risking annihilation in the process.[3]

In his lectures on Heraclitus from 1943 and 1944, which serve as one of Heidegger's own journeys into the foreign of inceptual Greece, Heidegger speaks of the Greek experience of fire (πῦρ). Through an encounter with various of Heraclitus's fragments, Heidegger argues that, for Heraclitus, "fire flames and is, in enflaming, the excising separation between the light and the dark: enflaming joins the light and the dark against, and into, one another."[4] This fire, also given the name "lightning" by Heraclitus, "'steers,' surveys, and shines over the whole of beings in advance and permeates this whole pre-luminously in such a way that, in the blink of an eye, the whole joins itself, kindles itself, and excises itself each time into its conjoinedness."[5] So understood, fire (πῦρ) is the same as φύσις:[6] that is, it names being itself as "the clearing of all that is cleared" (*die Lichtung alles Gelichteten*).[7] Fire names the clearing emergence of being, inceptually understood.

One wonders, in passing, whether this fire to which the poet exposes himself is the same fire that lights the torches of Artemis, the Light-Bringer, the tracker and huntress who chases after the animal through the mountains, clearing the path in front of her from out of the darkness and rendering unto the animals the concealment into which they, as living, must eventually pass. Is it the fire of the clearing of being that lights the torches of Artemis, goddess of φύσις and overseer of Heraclitus's—and, indeed, Heidegger's—thinking?

Regardless, it is this fire to which the poet—or the one who listens poetically—must journey in order to bring about a transformation from the "human" into *Dasein*, that is, to come to see himself *as Da-sein*, as the *there* of being's emergent unfolding.[8] It is this fire, this *lightening lightning* of being, to which the poet exposes himself in *nakedness*, standing stripped and bare before the emergent clearing of being.[9] In his lectures on Hölderlin's "Der Ister," Heidegger describes the experience of the poet—that is, that one sufficiently attuned to being's unfolding—as he encounters the foreign fire:

> The poet, as poet, is the one who points, thus something that shows, and is thereby a "sign"[. . . .] The showing is of such a kind as to first let appear that which is to be shown. Yet such a sign can, in saying, let appear that which is to be said only because it has before this already been shone upon by that which thus appears as what is to be poetized. This sign must therefore be struck and blinded in the face of the "fire." This is why it is initially unable to find the word, so that it seems as though this showing had lost its tongue.[10]

The poet is thus a sign meant to point to, and intimate, the holy: meant, that is, to point to the fiery radiance of the clearing of being. And yet, it is precisely his naked exposure to this fire that nearly scorches him and robs him of his ability to speak: "[T]he poets, are 'a sign'—they are those who 'have almost lost our tongue in foreign parts.' "[11] The fire of being brings the poet to the brink of *silence*, to a situation where he has nearly lost his language (*Sprache*), the "distinctive sign" not just of the poet but of the human traditionally understood.[12] The poet's silence is itself a souvenir, a commemorative keepsake, of his journey into the radiance of being: "The shaking of the holy is preserved and made quiet by a single poet in the stillness of his silence."[13] It is thus not through speech but rather through reticent silence that the poet points to, and intimates, being.[14]

One recalls that, within the contours of Heidegger's reading of Hölderlin, it is an *eagle* who brings the holy to the poet, who "soars over the Alps and brings Germania tidings of the highest [*die Botschaft des Höchsten*],"[15] who serves as "the messenger of the god" and who thus mediates between the poet and the holy.[16] It is an eagle, then, who makes possible the poet's exposure to the holy fire, to the being of beings, to the very event of being's clearing. Said more generally, it is an animal who mediates between the human and the heavenly fire of being, who makes possible an exposure to such fire and brings the human to the brink of holy silence.[17] One also recalls the bird in Heidegger's lectures on Heraclitus, who sings of the enchantment of being's tidings, pointing to and intimating the emergence of being. In both cases, it is an animal who exposes the poet, in his *nakedness*, to the clearing of being.

It is in light of all of this that we can understand the second sense in which there can be no final word regarding the animal Other. As the preceding chapters have shown, the encounter with the animal is one way by which the human may enter into the unfolding of being itself. By coming face-to-face with the animal Other, the human experiences itself in its difference, thereby coming to know itself as the *there* of being. Such an experience entails an experience of difference itself, of *the* difference, namely, of the ontological difference between beings and being; for, although the animal is certainly not being itself, it intimates the tidings of being, thereby serving as an opening to it: the animal is the herald of being. To come to know oneself as the *there* of being thus comes about through the denuding encounter with the animal. Through its encounter with the living being, the human encounters the fire of what is most foreign: being itself in its concealed emergence.

But such exposure brings the human to the point of speechlessness: that is, it brings the human to a place where the words readily available to describe such an encounter—words like "animal," "human," or even "being"—prove inadequate. The metaphysically determined concepts of "human" and "animal" both falter in the face of the exposure to the animal itself and the being to which it owes its emergence, elevating the human beyond the conceptual understanding to which it is accustomed (i.e., into which it was *thrown*). In this way, the animal renders the human silent, robbing it of speech, of λόγος—robbing it, therefore, of the ability that, from at least Aristotle onward, has differentiated the human from all (other?) animals. In the face of the animal Other—that is, in the face of the intimate foreignness discernible in the life of the living being—the human becomes speechless, ἄλογον, without the word, relinquishing its status as the ζῷον λόγον ἔχον. (We will return to this point below.) The fire, the πῦρ, announced by an animal—say, a *cat*—is the foreign that robs the human of speech: the cat's πῦρ catches the human's tongue.

In this way, then, there can be no final word regarding the question of the animal: for the animal is precisely that which robs the human of the word. Or, perhaps it is better to say that the encounter with the animal precisely brings about the final word, initiating the collapse of the metaphysical configuration of the human/animal relation and the vocabulary it undergirds. The animal, as that which opens the human up to a mindful consideration of being, is that which provokes our silence, in this way making the human *almost* like an animal, *almost* like that which is without λόγος.

To be sure, for Heidegger, animals cannot properly be said to be silent:[18] for, in order to keep silent, one must already be in the word.[19] Although animals do not speak—"because they have nothing to say"[20]—such lack of speech is not to be understood as genuine silence, which, for Heidegger, is nothing other the mindful listening to being itself that constitutes the proper essence of *Dasein*. Nevertheless, the encounter with the animal—like the encounter with a work of art or a *thing*—can move the human into the hesitant silence befitting the naked exposure to being. Without the word, yet not properly silent, the animal brings the human to a place of reticent silence in the face of the holy opening of being itself.

But such silence, far from marking the end of a possible encounter with the animal, in fact marks its first genuine possibility, as it also marks the possibility of an inceptual transformation of the human. In his *Contributions to Philosophy*, Heidegger writes at length of an other inception that would move beyond the conceptual strictures of the metaphysical tradition, an inception that is to be carried out in a "bearing silence."[21] This other inception—one that only becomes possible through an engagement with the first inception[22]—will bring about a transition from the "human," understood as the *animal rationale*, to *Dasein* by preparing for the latter a leap into the clearing of being, a leap that, as Vallega-Neu puts it, "is attuned by awe, by a silent hesitating reservedness in which thinking abides in the opening of be-ing's withdrawal."[23] The thinking of the new inception will prepare a humanity that, "as what grounds and acts as steward [*Wächterschaft*],"[24] must first be cast into an ontological indeterminacy, a grey area of uncertainty where the human no longer knows who—*or even what*—it is:

> In the progression away from the inception, the human became the *animal rationale.* In the transition out of the first end of Western thinking into its other inception, there has to be questioned, in a *still higher* necessity, with the carrying out of the question of truth, the question of who we are. This question will point in the direction of the possibility of whether the human is not only the preserver of unconcealed beings but is precisely

> the *steward of the openness* of being. Only if we know that we do not yet know who we are do we ground *the one and only* ground which may release the future of a simple, essential Dasein of the historical human from itself.[25]

Only by leaping into a radical questioning of its self-understanding as *animal rationale*—that is, only by looking into the face of the animal Other and experiencing that Other in its essential difference—can the human move beyond the first inception and enter into its proper role as the steward—or the *shepherd*—of being.[26]

Stewardship is understood by Heidegger as the way in which the human—or, at least, a properly attuned human—can *shelter* (*Bergung*) the eruption of being through particular beings. As Polt writes, "[S]heltering enables beings to emerge as the beings that they are, and enables be-ing as appropriation to take place."[27] This sheltering occurs through the human's encounter with particular beings, such as artworks.[28] By exposing us to the interplay of earth and world, concealment and unconcealment, the artwork allows the human entry into the conflictual nature of being itself, and specifically into the concealment that serves as its ground. As the previous chapter showed, *things*, too, enable such sheltering, insofar as they make visible the unified fourfold of being's opening.

As has now been shown at length, animals also enable this sheltering, serving as one way through which the human can recollect and enter into the opening of being itself. Although "the sheltering itself is carried out in and as Dasein," animals are one of the beings capable of calling the human to the concealed ground of being's unfolding. As Heidegger writes in his *Contributions to Philosophy*, "The sheltering abides not only in modes of production [i.e., such as artworks and things] but just as originally in the mode of reception in encountering the lifeless and the living: stone, plant, animal, human. The being-taken-back into the self-secluding earth happens here."[29] The animal, then, is among those entities capable of awakening the human to the concealment from out of which the inceptual unfolding of being eventuates, thereby transforming the human into the shepherd of being. Heidegger goes on to say that the very purpose of philosophy is "to find and make appear the simple sights and native forms in which the essential occurrence of being is sheltered and taken to heart."[30] Said otherwise, it is the job of the philosopher to watch over and attend to the beings in which being shows itself, the way a shepherd watches over the flock.

It is crucial to understand the sequence at play in this operation of sheltering. It is not so much that *Dasein* shelters the truth of being in the beings it encounters: rather, it is precisely through carrying out this sheltering that the human first *becomes Dasein*: "Da-sein happens in the modes in which truth is sheltered out of the securing of the cleared-concealed event."[31] In other words, it is only by becoming attentive to the being within beings that the human becomes aware of its role as the *there* of being, the *Da* of *Sein*. Through its sheltering encounter with beings, the human is *cast* into its destined role as the place of being's unfolding. Said otherwise: *Dasein follows after* the beings it shelters, the beings that (therefore) come before. The movement into *Dasein* is subsequent to, and contingent upon, the exposure to the being of the beings that occurs through a mindful encounter with those very beings.

The sheltering encounter with beings, which is the very purpose of philosophy, thus brings about a transformation of the human into (its proper) *Dasein*. Regarding this transformative role of philosophy, Heidegger, in GA 94, writes the following:

> To philosophize: to be under no superior.
> The new, not inceptual, end-like beginning.
> Philosophy! Finally its essence is up for discussion: it is to bring:
> Dasein into silence (positively)
> being into words (language—truth)
> and the pretense about humanity into silence—thus it is to hazard humanity (positively).[32]

The task of philosophy is thus to bring about a transformation of humanity by exposing the human to the beings in which being is sheltered: it is to engender within the human a proper comportment toward (the being within) beings.[33] Such exposure "hazards" a new humanity, one freed from the conceptual limitations of the "human," the "animal," and their metaphysically determined relation. In other words, the sheltering encounter with beings such as artworks, *things*, and animals opens the possibility of a new way of configuring the human, namely, as the *there* of being's unfolding.

In *On Inception* (GA 70), Heidegger offers the following regarding this new configuration: "'The human' must no longer in the first place be animal, not even ζῷον λόγον ἔχον—rather, the human must immediately sacrifice its belonging to this to the inception in its suddenness. But whence this must? From the singularity of being."[34] In the suddenness of the inception—in, that is, the Moment of being's clearing—the human must relinquish its characterization as an animal, even as that animal who has language as its defining characteristic. But, as the scare-quotes around "the human" indicate, such a Moment will also entail a relinquishing of the concept of "humanity" as it has been traditionally determined. In the face of its encounter with being, "the human" is no longer to be understood as *either* human *or* animal, but is rather to be thought of in terms of *Da-sein*.

And yet, in a footnote after the Greek phrase ζῷον λόγον ἔχον, Heidegger gives the following caveat: "Unless we think ζῷον alethically." This means to say that the human is no longer to be thought of as an animal, even as the animal with λόγος, *unless* such animality is thought of in terms of ἀλήθεια. In other words, so long as the "animal" is rethought within the context of a thorough understanding of ἀλήθεια as the open clearing of being—as long as ζωή ("life") is thought in terms of φύσις as the clearing of being—then the human could rightly be called an "animal," where this word would now be freed from its metaphysical, biological, and theological determinations.[35] Thus, along with the transformation of the human (as *animal rationale*) into *Dasein* comes a transformation of the understanding of animality itself, of *life* itself, which is now to be conceived of in relation to the intimate conflict of concealment and unconcealment that characterizes being.[36]

To the extent that the aim of philosophy is to bring about this foundational transformation of the human essence, one could say that the aim of inceptual thinking is to prepare the human's transformation *into an animal*, alethically understood. In order to overcome its characterization as *animal rationale*, the human must become a ζῷον, an animal, now thought in relation to the clearing of being: and this transformation begins through the encounter with the animal as that being in whom the unfolding of being from out of concealment is sheltered.

The encounter with the animal Other is thus one track, among others, to the other inception and the transformation of the human that this entails. And yet, the animal is an *exemplary* track owing to the unique mystery that the animal, as *living*, poses to *Dasein*: for in the animal, with whom we share (a) *life*, we see an abyssal kinship, a remote intimacy. As Heidegger writes in "Letter on Humanism," "of all the beings that are, presumably the most difficult to think about are living creatures, because on the one hand they are in a certain way most closely akin to us, and on the other are at the same time separated from our ek-sistent essence by an abyss."[37] The animal is the most difficult to think: of all beings, its essence remains most concealed, most *mysterious*. As the most mysterious, the animal is most able to awaken us to the Mystery itself: namely, the concealment at the abyssal ground of unconcealment, of openness, of world, of the clearing of being. In the face of the animal Other, the human sees the Nothing that serves as the abyssal ground of its very own *Dasein*. In this way, the encounter with the animal *denudes* the human of its metaphysical attire, leaving it naked and without determinacy. In this manner, the human stands naked before the animal, naked *owing to* the animal, naked and finally able to see itself—and the animal Other—in their fullest virginity.

If there were ever to be a final word regarding the animal, then, it would need to be followed by a *question mark*: a sign of the unfathomable mystery of the animal, the detour through which acquaints the human with its own limitless mystery and with the Mystery itself.[38] Or it would need to be the word of a *poet* whose thoughtful reflections evade the domineering hubris of the assertoric and hover instead in the humility proper to thinking. Such poetic thinking would attend to beings, follow after them and shelter within them the being to which they, wordlessly and worldlessly, give voice. Through such attending, such *shepherding*, the poet would prepare a new site for human *Dasein*:

> Shepherd of departure,
> shepherd, dispossessed,
> but bearer of the expropriation
> into the demarcation
> of the Secret.
> Shepherd of the departure
> of the arrival
> of inceptual poems.
> Herding, he gives heed,
> therein giving himself
> into the selfsame;
> self-giving, self-driven
> in the richness
> of high hardship in silence,
> cheered by nearness in its distance.
> Herding, he settles

streams and fields,
rocks and trees,
bridges and springs,
in their flight
into things.[39]

~

Herding the animals forward, and thus following behind them, the poet philosopher founds his new home in the truth of beyng.[40]

Notes

Introduction

1. On this passage, see Trawny 2018, 230–31.
2. GA 46:23/19; Heidegger's emphasis.
3. GA 46:23/19.
4. GA 46:23/19.
5. GA 46:23/19.
6. GA 46:23/19.
7. See Turner 2009, 144.
8. GA 9:326/248; GA 89:306/244.
9. GA 33:124/107.
10. GA 39:82/75.
11. GA 55:95/72.
12. GA 2:320/224.
13. GA 55:25/21.
14. See also Rae 2015, 31ff.; Sternad 2017, 108; Tonner 2011, 204–5.
15. See Derrida 1989, 11–12. See also Cykowski 2021, 19.
16. See Haraway 2008, 20–21, who finds Derrida's approach incomplete.
17. Derrida 2008, 5–6.
18. Derrida 2008, 18.
19. GA 9:354/256; trans. modified.
20. GA 9:357/258.
21. For an early example, see GA 38 (from 1934), 135, where existence (i.e., *Dasein*) is said to belong solely to humans. For an example from the middle period, see GA 5:60 (spanning the years 1935–1946): "Where there is no language, such as in the being of stones, plants, and animals there is also no openness of beings and, consequently, no openness of non-beings or of emptiness" (my translation). For a late example, see GA 89:16 and 244 (from 1959–1969). See also Elden 2006, 274.
22. See GA 29/30:372/255. On this, see Agamben 2004, 60.
23. See Derrida 2008, 388.

24. See GA 34:236. See also Elden 2006, 282.

25. On the manner in which a detour (*Umweg*) and a roundabout investigative approach (*Umwegverstehen*) are sometimes precisely what is needed to access beings in their genuine being, see GA 9:7/9 and GA 52:73/60. See also Ruin 1994, 69.

26. GA 54:118/80.

27. Derrida 1989, 11–12.

28. GA 54:125/85.

29. Krell 2015, 51.

30. GA 8:18/16; trans. modified.

31. Krell 2015, 49. See also Krell 1992, 255–56.

32. Krell 2015, 50.

33. Derrida 1987, 173. Krell suggests that Heidegger's discourse on the hand is a kind of *revenge* against animals on Heidegger's part born out of jealousy of the superior ability that apes display in swinging from tree to tree (Krell 2015, 52).

34. Both Derrida and Krell give insufficient attention to the various modes of *receiving* at play in Heidegger's analysis of the hand, focusing entirely on the hand's operations of *signing*, which both interpret as indicating the dominance of *giving* in Heidegger's analysis. See Derrida 1987, 173. See also Krell 2015, 50.

35. See GA 81:227, for example, for Heidegger's play between *fangen* and *an-fangen*. See also GA 78: 335.

36. GA 23:17.

37. See Naas 2014, 5, who says it was "clearly not just another Heidegger seminar for Derrida," and that Derrida had a "powerful fascination" with it. See also Cykowski 2021, 20.

Chapter One

1. See, for example, Di Cesare 2018. See also Mitchell 2017, xvii; Faye 2009.

2. The passage occurs on unnumbered pages in both the German and English volumes. Although the passage was written by Heidegger, it was inserted at the outset of GA 94 not by Heidegger but by the editor of the volume, Peter Trawny.

3. GA 94:5/1. See also GA 91:182, where Heidegger asks quite nearly the same questions, now expressly within the context of the animal/human relation: "Human and animal. What is the human? Who is the human? Who are we? Where is the play of the human in the whole of beings?"

4. GA 94:5/1; trans. modified.

5. GA 94:426/309.

6. GA 94:149/109. Much more so than Judaism, Christianity is implicated within the notebooks as being the source of the modern forgetfulness of being and the destitution to which it has led. (Christianity is mentioned dozens of times within the notebook and *always* within a critical light.) To the extent that Judaism

is historically and essentially related to Christianity, one could argue that an implicit critique of Judaism is no less present throughout the entirety of the notebook. Indeed, at one point, Heidegger indicates the essential connection between Judaism and Christianity in the following way: "The Christian is descended from Judaism. Within the timeframe of the Christian West, i.e., of metaphysics, this [i.e., Judaism] is the principle of destruction. What is destructive in the reversal of the consummation of metaphysics—i.e., the reversal of Hegel's metaphysics by Marx. Spirit and culture become the superstructure of 'life'—i.e., of economics, i.e., of organization—i.e., of the biological—i.e., of the 'people'" (GA 97:20, my translation). For Heidegger, Christianity (and thus Judaism) is also the source—or, at least, *a* source alongside others—of the understanding of the human as the rational animal (GA 96:11/10).

7. GA 94:45/34, 48/36.

8. See GA 94:170/124, 425/308, 504/366–67.

9. GA 94:77/58; trans. modified.

10. GA 94:45/34.

11. GA 94:358/261.

12. GA 94:79/60; emphasis is Heidegger's own.

13. GA 94:366/267, 445/323.

14. GA 94:81/62.

15. GA 94:218/160.

16. GA 94:5/1.

17. GA 94:83/63.

18. GA 94:83/63.

19. See GA 27:3, where it is said that the animal cannot philosophize.

20. Cf. Heidegger's lectures on Parmenides from 1942, where Heidegger states that "All cats are false. The feline is the false" (GA 54:43/29).

21. See, for example, GA 5:45/33; GA 21:164; GA 22:207/169; GA 65:295/233.

22. See, for example, GA 29/30:292/198.

23. GA 94:367/267.

24. See GA 38:161/133.

25. GA 94:84/63. See also GA 35:86/65.

26. GA 94:84/63.

27. GA 94:84/63.

28. GA 94:84/63.

29. See GA 41:223/151–52, where Heidegger claims we can only ever have *mediate* knowledge of "what is going on in the animal" (*was im Tier vorgeht*).

30. GA 94:84/64; trans. modified.

31. GA 18:14/12.

32. GA 39:141/125.

33. GA 94:84/64; trans. modified.

34. GA 94:84/64.

35. Cf. GA 24:270/191.

36. GA 94:84/64; trans. modified.

37. See GA 66:138/118, 140/120.

38. GA 94:84/64; trans. modified.

39. GA 94:84/64.

40. Jaran 2018, 794.

41. GA 94:45, 48, 87, 101, 172, and esp. 375.

42. GA 94:97/73.

43. See GA 94:79/60, 446/324.

44. GA 94:80/60.

45. GA 94:85/64–65.

46. GA 94:77–78/59.

47. See GA 25:20/14–15. See also GA 85:16/14.

48. GA 38:138; trans. modified.

49. On such immediacy, see Sforza 2022, 77.

50. Jaran is thus correct in arguing that, for Heidegger, "we become human beings when we *cast ourselves off* from innerworldly beings and thus distinguish ourselves from the rest of beings" (Jaran 2018, 796). However, he does not duly emphasize the role that animals play in the initiating of this casting-off.

51. GA 94:411/299. See also Jaran 2018, 796.

52. GA 94:84/64.

53. GA 94:425/309.

54. GA 94:43/33.

55. GA 94:239/175.

56. GA 94:57/44.

57. GA 94:367/268.

Chapter Two

1. See GA 88:285.

2. See GA 29/30:263/177. See also Cykowski 2021, 1.

3. See, for example, Derrida 1989, 49. See also Krell 1992, 130; MacIntyre 1999, 45; Calarco 2008, 222.

4. See especially Cykowski 2021.

5. Cf. Lindberg 2004, 57.

6. See the introduction.

7. Cykowski 2021, 6.

8. Cykowski 2021, 6.

9. GA 29/30:383/264. See also GA 9:326/230; GA 66:113/94.

10. GA 18:30/22.

11. See Rubio and Fernández 2010, 66.

12. GA 2:75/71.

13. As Cerbone puts it, to be *Vorhanden* is "just being there and no more" (Cerbone 2021, 538).

14. See also GA 21:1/1.

15. GA 18:34/25.

16. Derrida, in *Of Spirit*, writes: "The animal, as Heidegger recognizes elsewhere, is certainly not a *Vorhandene*" (Derrida 1989, 21; see also Sforza 2022, 47.) It is not clear exactly where the "elsewhere" to which Derrida refers is; however, regardless of the textual location, Derrida is incorrect. Heidegger argues variously that the animal is not *merely* or *simply* "at-hand": but, as being-there, as being *present*, the animal, like all extant entities, is indeed a *Vorhandene* in the broad, fundamental sense.

17. See GA 35:57/45.

18. See GA 20:261/193.

19. See GA 19:270/186.

20. GA 18:18/14; Heidegger's emphasis.

21. See Hayes 2007, 272ff.

22. GA 22: 207/169.

23. See also Heidegger's 1925 lecture course on Dilthey: "Life is the kind of reality which is in a world and in fact in such a way that it has a world. Every living being has its environing world not as something present and on hand next to it, but as something which is *there* [*da ist*] for it as disclosed, uncovered. This world can be very simple for a primitive animal. But life and its world are never two things side by side, like two chairs. Rather, life 'has' its world. Even in biology this form of awareness is gradually coming to the fore. Here, one now ponders the basic structure and sense of the animal. But we overlook the essential thing here if we do not see that the animal has a world" (Kisiel and Sheehan 2010, 259). See also Turner 2009, 146.

24. GA 18:40/57.

25. GA 18:21/16.

26. On the importance on *Befindlichkeit* in Heidegger's consideration of the animal, see Krell 2013, 89. Also, see Slaby 2021, 242, who relates "disposition" with phenomenological intentionality.

27. GA 18:54/38.

28. See Hayes 2007, 291.

29. See Fritsche 1999, 66. See also Kearney 1980, 176–95; Held 1993, 93.

30. GA 18:50/36.

31. GA 18:52/37.

32. GA 18:99/68; trans. modified.

33. See also GA 84:592.

34. Krell 2013, 89.

35. See Sforza 2022, 7.

36. GA 18:325/220.

37. See GA 18:44/31.

38. See Derrida 2008, 22, 144.

39. GA 2:314/219.

40. GA 2:316/221. On this, see Strauss 2000, 102.

41. *Eindringlich* can have all of these senses.

42. GA 2:318/222.

43. See Sforza 2022, 205.

44. On this, see Schmidt 1997, 195–96. See also Peach 2008, 13.

45. On this, see Dastur 2012, 38–39.

46. GA 2:317/221; my emphasis.

47. GA 2:316/221.

48. GA 2:318/222.

49. GA 2:328/229. See also GA 88:62.

50. See Derrida 1993, 76.

51. GA 2:320/224; my emphasis.

52. GA 2:324/226.

53. GA 2:94/66.

54. GA 2:328/229.

55. GA 2:317/222.

56. GA 2:318/222.

57. Cykowski 2021, 3, 13, 185.

58. Cykowski 2021, 14.

59. See GA 29/30:62/93, 82/123, 292/422, 296/428, and especially 352/512. See also Bejinariu 2018, 236.

60. Derrida calls the analysis of the animal therein "patient, laborious, awkward, sometimes aporetical" (Derrida 1989, 47). On the reserve with which Heidegger carries out his analysis, see Mitchell 2015, 98n22.

61. GA 29/30:6/4; my emphasis. See also Cykowski 2021, 45–46.

62. GA 29/30:5.

63. Cykowski 2021, 62. Cykowski helpfully refers to this homesickness as "a kind of *Ur*-attunement."

64. GA 29/30:5.

65. GA 29/30:261/176.

66. On the inability of the human to engage in purely animalistic φωνή, see Sforza 2022, 181.

67. GA 29/30:263/178; my emphasis.

68. On the ontological character of the "comparative examination," see Sforza 2022, 36.

69. See GA 29/30:389/268.

70. Cf. Derrida 1989, 49; also, cf. Végső 2020, 221.

71. GA 29/30:408/282; my emphasis.

72. GA 29/30:263/177.

73. Cf. Derrida 1989, 11, 57.

74. GA 29/30:263/177.

75. GA 29/30:265/178; my emphasis.

76. See GA 3:227/159.

77. GA 29/30:153/102; my emphasis.

78. GA 29/30:399/275; trans. modified.

79. GA 29/30:399/275.

80. See GA 9:31/27, 109/86.

81. See GA 29/30:400/276.

82. GA 29/30:265/179.

83. GA 29/30:266–67/180.

84. GA 29/30:433/299.

85. GA 29/30:433/299.

86. GA 29/30:385/265.

87. As Heidegger writes in the Bremen lectures: "Death is the shrine of the Nothing" (GA 79: 17/17). We will return to this important passage in chapter 6.

88. On "the middle," see Krell 1992.

89. GA 29/30:274/185–86; my emphasis.

90. See Jaran 2018, 794.

91. GA 29/30:287/194.

92. GA 29/30:153/102.

93. GA 29/30:295/201.

94. For a discussion of transposition in *The Fundamental Concepts of Metaphysics*, see Winkler 2007, 528ff. See also Turner 2009, 149–50.

95. GA 29/30:296/201; trans. modified; my emphasis.

96. GA 29/30:296/202; my emphasis.

97. GA 29/30:297/202; trans. modified.

98. GA 29/30:303/206.

99. GA 29/30:307/210.

100. See Bejinariu 2018, 247.

101. GA 9:189/126.

102. GA 89: 306–7/244; Heidegger's emphasis.

103. On such originary openness, see GA 3:262/184.

104. See also GA 83:326, where Heidegger writes that the world of the animal—if indeed it is a world—remains closed off (*verschlossen*) to the human.

105. GA 29/30:308/210. On this passage, see Lindberg 2004, 75ff.

106. GA 18:29/22.

107. Derrida 2008, 157.

108. See Derrida 2008, 159.

109. Cykowski notes how Derrida skips large sections of *The Fundamental Concepts of Metaphysics* (Cykowski 2021, 39). See also Naas 2014, 6, who notes

that Derrida, in "Geschlect II," defers a treatment of *The Fundamental Concepts of Metaphysics*, a deferment that he then made good on in *Of Spirit*.

110. See also Derrida 1989, 50–51.

111. GA 29/30:308/210.

112. GA 29/30:308/210; trans. modified.

113. See Krell 1992, 116: "Heidegger tries to enter into the animal's world."

114. See Derrida 2008, 7.

115. Derrida 2008, 17. Derrida returns to Heidegger's understanding of animality in both volumes of *The Beast and the Sovereign* and deals with *The Fundamental Concepts of Metaphysics* at length in the second volume. However, he does not mention the passage regarding domesticated animals.

116. GA 29/30:309/211.

117. See GA 82:346.

118. See Agamben 2004, 62.

119. GA 29/30:392/270; my emphasis.

120. GA 29/30:394/272.

121. GA 29/30:366/531; Heidegger's emphasis.

122. Löwith 1945, 279.

Chapter Three

1. See GA 6.2:294/218, and see also 307/229.

2. GA 46:23/19.

3. GA 6.1:52/54.

4. GA 6.1:246/26.

5. See Krell 1992, 267.

6. See Hemming 1998, 268.

7. GA 29/30:8/6.

8. GA 6.1:264/45.

9. GA 6.1:265/45.

10. On the connection between *hören* and *Gehören*, see GA 99:11.

11. See, for example, *Also sprach Zarathustra*, sec. 3ff.

12. See, for example, GA 29/30:442. See also GA 89:19/16.

13. GA 6.1:265/45.

14. GA 6.1:266/46.

15. GA 6.1:266/46.

16. GA 6.1:266/46; trans. modified.

17. GA 6.1:267/47.

18. GA 6.1:267/47.

19. See GA 94:5.

20. See Derrida 2008, 142.

21. See GA 29/30:448/310ff.

22. See GA 6.1:274/54.

23. On solitude, see GA 29/30:8–10/5–7.

24. GA 6.1:267/47.

25. On the eagle as solitary, see GA 81:245/433: "Solitary doesn't mean: isolated and abandoned, but rather; belonging to the one released [*gelassen*] to its own in the releasing [*lassenden*] listening of remembrance. Has anyone ever seen a flock of eagles?"

26. GA 6.1:269/49.

27. See also GA 8:73ff.

28. GA 6.1:267/47; trans. modified.

29. GA 6.1:279/59.

30. Polt 2021, 498.

31. See also GA 89:230/184.

32. GA 6.1:267/47; trans. modified.

33. GA 6.1:279/59.

34. GA 6.1:280/59.

35. GA 6.1:280/59.

36. GA 6.1:281/60; trans. modified.

37. GA 6.1:269/49; trans. modified.

38. GA 6.1:270/50.

39. GA 6.1:270/50.

40. GA 6.1:270/51.

41. GA 6.1:271–72/51–52.

42. GA 6.1:272/52.

43. GA 6.1:272/52.

44. GA 52:163/138.

45. GA 6.1:274/54.

46. GA 6.1:274/54.

47. GA 6.1:275/54.

48. GA 6.1:276/56.

49. GA 6.1:276/56.

50. GA 6.1:277/56.

51. On the difference of animal time and human temporality, see GA 49:48–49.

52. GA 6.1:277/56; trans. modified.

53. GA 6.1:277/57.

54. GA 6.1:244/24.

55. GA 6.1: /24.

56. GA 6.1:278/57.

57. GA 6.1:278/58.

58. GA 6.1:279/58.

59. GA 6.1:279/58–59.

60. GA 6.1:280/60.

61. GA 6.1:281/60.

62. GA 6.1:281/60.

63. GA 6.1:282/61.

64. GA 6.1:251/32.

65. GA 6.1:251/32.

66. GA 6.1:251/32.

67. GA 6.1:278/58.

68. On the affinity of poet and animal, see Mitchell 2015, 114.

69. GA 6.1:268/48.

70. See GA 65:28/24.

71. On the idea that the contemporary human being is not *yet Dasein*, GA 6.1:246 /26. See also GA 65:296ff./233ff.

72. GA 38:160/133.

73. GA 38:89ff./73ff. See also GA 40:6/6; GA 69:96. In his 1926 lecture course on Aristotle, Heidegger is a little more hesitant on this issue: "[I]t is difficult to determine whether animals have the capacity to perceive time" (GA 22:311/229).

74. GA 38:133/110.

75. GA 38:138–39/115–16.

76. See GA 16:239.

77. See GA 16:335, where Heidegger writes of the manner in which authentic historicity can only come about in tension with the *unessence* of history.

78. GA 54:238/160; my emphasis.

79. GA 94:77/58.

Chapter Four

1. On the meaning of this phrase, see McNeill 2013, 227.

2. Mitchell 2015, 107.

3. Mitchell 2015, 88–89.

4. To a certain extent, Heidegger's thinking of the fourfold, at least with respect to the notion of "world," agrees with the understanding of animality showcased in *The Basic Concepts of Aristotelian Philosophy*, analyzed at length in chapter 2.

5. Mitchell 2015, 107.

6. In "An Den Knaben Elis," Elis, in turn, is associated *vis-à-vis* the *down-going* with Nietzsche's Zarathustra.

7. Mitchell 2015, 108.

8. Mitchell 2015, 108.

9. Mitchell 2015, 108.

10. Mitchell 2015, 109.

11. GA 12:41/166.

12. Mitchell 2015, 110.

13. GA 12:41/166.

14. GA 12:42/167.

15. Mitchell 2015, 113.

16. Mitchell 2015, 114.

17. GA 12:76–77/197.

18. Trakl 1969, 26; my translation and emphasis.

19. GA 2:364ff./353ff.

20. Derrida 2008, 3–4.

21. Derrida 2008, 11.

22. GA 12:57/180.

23. GA 39:79/73; trans. modified.

24. GA 39:79/73.

25. GA 39:137/121. On mourning, see McNeill 2013, 227.

26. GA 39:81/75.

27. GA 39:82/75.

28. GA 39:62/58.

29. GA 39:75/68.

30. See GA 98:245, where Heidegger writes that the animal's manner of expression is "incomparably different from language [*Sprache*]."

31. GA 39:174/159.

32. GA 39:289/262.

33. GA 39:289/262.

34. GA 39:43–44/43.

35. GA 39:45/44.

36. On the difference between human and animal listening, see GA 85:110/94.

37. GA 75:8. See also Bambach 2022, 275.

38. As Bambach has convincingly argued, "The Western Conversation" must be understood within the context of Heidegger's own experience of the desolation to which the war had led and his enduring hope for a transformation of German existence. See Bambach 2022, 278.

39. GA 75:85.

40. GA 75:83.

41. *Schwingen* can mean both "soaring" and "wings."

42. The dialogue begins: "Als schwinge das Wort . . ." (As the word soars . . . ; GA 75:59).

43. See Bambach 2022, 282.

44. Bambach 2022, 275.

45. GA 75:85.

46. GA 75:87; my emphasis.

47. GA 75:87.

48. Bambach 2022, 75.

49. See Bambach 2022, 283.

50. GA 75:128.

51. See Warnek 2006, 58: "As an awakening to the absence of gods, Hölderlin's poetry is thus also an awakening to the lack of the home, to *the lack of proper being for mortal human life,* an insistence upon a tragic estrangement or alienation at the heart of that life."

52. See Gosetti-Ferencei 2004, 181.

53. GA 53:5/4.

54. GA 53:23/21.

55. GA 53:183–84/147.

56. See Denker 2022, 83.

57. Cf. GA 75:75–76.

58. GA 53:113/91.

59. GA 53:113/91.

60. GA 53:67/54.

61. GA 53:69/55.

62. Young 2002, 97.

63. Young 2002, 97.

64. GA 53:76/63.

65. GA 53:72/59.

66. GA 53:72/59.

67. GA 53:127/103.

68. See GA 53:94/76, where Heidegger states that *only* the human is capable of homelessness and, thus, of coming to be at home.

69. GA 53:80/66.

70. See GA 53:154–55/124.

71. GA 53:83/68.

72. GA 53:84/69.

73. GA 53:89/73; my emphasis.

74. GA 53:76/94.

75. GA 53:76/94.

76. See GA 29/30:309/211.

77. As Warminski puts it: "That is, man goes out and seeks his home in beings (*Seiendes*), masters it through his technology, but is always called back to the same nothing by his essential finitude, his death, and this nothing is the nothing *of* Being—the only place he can *be* at home" (Warminski 2013, 163).

78. GA 4:23–24/42, 121/143.

79. GA 4:87/112.

80. GA 4:95/118, 133/155, 165/188–89.

81. GA 4:10/27.

82. GA 4:85/110.

83. See GA 52:31–32.

84. GA 4:154/177; my emphasis.

85. GA 4:165–66/190.

86. GA 4:168/193.

87. GA 4:56.

88. Mitchell 2015, 193.

89. On the connection between "the holy" and φύσις, see Magrini 2022, 179. See also Capobianco 2014, 5.

90. GA 4:166/190.

91. GA 4:166/191–92.

92. GA 4:168/193.

93. GA 4:170/194.

94. See GA 4:105/128.

Chapter Five

1. GA 55:83/63.

2. GA 54:113/91.

3. GA 55:83/63.

4. GA 55:83/63.

5. GA 55:123/91.

6. GA 53:94/77.

7. GA 55:102/76.

8. GA 55:142/107.

9. GA 55:101/76.

10. GA 55:25/20.

11. GA 55:141/106.

12. To a great extent, Heidegger's turn to Heraclitus remains within the arch of his preoccupation with Hölderlin. Within the Heraclitus lectures, Heidegger marks Hölderlin's "nearness" to Heraclitus (GA 55:30–31/25), and the lectures are peppered with references to him and invocations of his poetry. See GA 55:15/14, 30–31/25, 189/145, 211–12/160–61, 221/167, 230/175, 273/207.

13. See GA 55:176/132, 272/206, 278/211.

14. GA 55:14/13.

15. GA 55:19/16.

16. See GA 54:9/5. It is perhaps worth mentioning, given Heidegger's encounter with Trakl's blue deer discussed in chapter 4, that deer were sacred to Artemis. On Artemis, see Sallis 2016, 6–12.

17. GA 55:14/13.

18. GA 55:15/13.

19. See also GA 54:7/5. One wonders if the sort of hunting of the essence of *Dasein* described by Heidegger in GA 94 (43/33), and analyzed in chapter 1, would remain under the aegis of Artemis, goddess of the hunt.

20. GA 55:16/14.

21. GA 55:17/15.

22. GA 55:17/15.

23. GA 55:17/15.

24. GA 55:18/15.

25. GA 55:26/21.

26. GA 55:17/15.

27. GA 55:25–26/21.

28. GA 55:25/20.

29. At one point, Heidegger seems to allow the possibility that living beings *die* (*sterben*): "Unfailingly, we believe we know in an immediate way the 'living' as such, even without an expressed essential determination of life. We distinguish, for example, the living from the dead [*Totem*]. However, we do not group the dead [*das Tote*] together with the lifeless which, like a stone, has no life at all and therefore cannot die [*nicht sterben*] and can never be dead [*tot*]. We distinguish life and death and yet do not know what 'life' and death are" (GA 55:92/70). The implication here is that the living (i.e., animals broadly conceived) can die (*sterben*) and be dead (*tot*).

30. GA 55:135/102.

31. This is also true to the extent that φύσις and ζωή, "emergence" and "life," mean the same within inceptual thinking. Any discourse on φύσις would thus also be a discourse on the living, that is, on the animal broadly conceived.

32. GA 55:108/81.

33. GA 55:96/72.

34. GA 55:104/76. Cf. Lindberg 2004, 60, who does not take GA 55 into consideration within her inquiry.

35. See GA 55:172/130.

36. GA 55:108/81; trans. modified.

37. GA 55:95/72.

38. See GA 55:159/120. See also GA 55:170/128.

39. GA 55:108/81.

40. GA 12:115–19/28–32.

41. GA 38:159/131.

42. GA 38:168/140.

43. GA 33:103/122.

44. See GA 12:255–57/135–36.

45. See GA 81:240.

46. See GA 39:221/202, 294/226.

47. GA 38:87/73–74.

48. See GA 36/37:100/80. See also GA 89:114/87; GA 102:157. On the animal's lack of history, see also GA 33:133.

49. See GA 66:182/160.

50. For a similar claim made about Heidegger's analysis in *The Fundamental Concepts of Metaphysics*, see Winkler 2007, 523.

51. See GA 99:11.

52. In *What Is Called Thinking*, Heidegger carefully distinguishes between a call and a mere cry or utterance: "But calling is something else than merely making a sound. Something else, again essentially different from mere sound and noise, is the cry. The cry need not be a call, but may be: the cry of distress. In reality, the calling stems from the place to which the call goes out. The calling is informed by an original outreach toward. . . . This alone is why the call can make a demand. The mere cry dies away and collapses. It can offer no lasting abode to either pain or joy. The call, by contrast, is a reaching, even if it is neither heard nor answered. Calling offers an abode. Sound and cry and call must be clearly distinguished" (GA 8:129/124). (See also GA 74:142/110.) In saying, in the Heraclitus lectures, that the birdsong lets the call unfold (*anwesen*), Heidegger is thus suggesting that the bird is making a demand on those who hear it and offering them an abode.

53. GA 4:28/46.

54. GA 4:28/47. See also GA 4:151/172; Vallega-Neu 2018, 10.

55. GA 65:383/303.

56. GA 65:82/66, 384/304, 407/323, 492/387, 233/184.

57. See also GA 10:210/129.

58. GA 9:342/245; trans. modified.

59. For a helpful elucidation of what Heidegger means by this phrase, see GA 89:223/178.

60. See GA 12:29/206.

61. GA 71:121/103.

62. At one point, Heidegger associates *Verzauberung*—"enchantment," the root of which is *Zauber*, to which we will soon turn—with thrownness (*Geworfenheit*): "Enchantment as the enveloping thrownness into the concealed 'there' (truth of beyng)" (GA 76:297).

63. See Weigelt 2021, 276.

64. GA 13:45–46/65.

65. GA 13:45/65.

66. GA 13:45/65.

67. Herrmann 1994, 381.

68. See GA 102:220.

69. Davis 2014, 377, 386.

70. GA 102:205. Heidegger also marks here the connection between region, ἀλήθεια, and *Ereignis*.

71. See Lüders 2001, 42.

72. GA 71:314/273. On world and *Ereignis,* see Polt 2006, 50.

73. Weigelt 2021, 277.

74. On the relationship between *Ereignis* and the fourfold, see GA 65:310. See also Mitchell 2015, 319.

75. Weigelt 2021, 276.

76. See GA 55:217/164. On the extent to which the question of λόγος and the animal must remain open, see GA 33:124/107.

77. See Krell 1987, 47.

78. The verb *weisen* plays an important role in Heidegger's *Feldweg-Gespräche* (GA 77) from 1944–1945. It is etymologically related to the name for the character *Der Weise* (the Guide), who likely represents Heidegger himself, and who works to bring an inceptual understanding of things to the attention of the Scholar and the Scientist. The Guide is the one who does not say, but rather points, gestures, indicates, or hints toward an adequate understanding of being. Regarding the operations of *weisen,* the Guide says the following: "This does not preclude the sense that one may be a *Weiser* in the sense of a guide, where by this word I do not mean one who knows [*Wissenden*], but rather one who is capable of pointing [*weisen*] into that wherefrom hints come to humans. Such a guide [*Weiser*] is also able to show [*weisen*] the manner [*Weise*], the way, in which these hints are to be followed" (GA 77:84/54).

79. See Krell 1987, 35, 38.

80. See GA 55:26, 66/52, 105ff./78ff.

81. GA 55:181/135.

82. GA 55:72/96.

83. GA 5:316/135.

84. GA 5:316/135.

85. GA 4:55/78.

86. GA 4:56/79.

87. GA 4:55/78.

88. Heidegger expressly notes that the purpose of the lecture is to bring about a thinking of the fourfold (GA 4:153/176).

89. GA 4:168/193.

90. On the intimate relation of death and mourning, see Dastur 2012, 3.

91. GA 4:55/77.

92. GA 39:82/75.

93. GA 55:95/72.

94. GA 55:95/72.

95. GA 55:88/67.

96. GA 54:151/225.

97. In his "On the Question of Being," Heidegger writes the following about the human: "The human is, in its essence [*Wesen*], the commemoration [*Gedächtnis*]

of being" (GA 9:411). As he goes on to say, the human is the commemoration (or remembrance) of *being* crossed out, *being* with an X over it, where the X marks both the inadequacy of the modern metaphysical understanding of being and the fourfold as which being (properly understood) opens itself (411). Keeping the verbal sense of *Wesen* (which Heidegger often emphasizes) in mind, one might say that the human is, in its *unfolding*, the commemoration of the fourfold of being's clearing. This is precisely the function the bird plays within GA 55.

98. See GA 55:323/242. See also GA 55:386/287.

99. GA 55:176/132.

100. See GA 55:278/210.

101. GA 55:387/288.

102. On the connection between *Hirt* and *Wahrende*, see GA 5:348; GA 11:118; GA 78:335; GA 79:71.

103. See Lindberg 2004, 74.

104. GA 55:220/166.

105. GA 55:220/166.

106. See also GA 54:230/155.

107. GA 54:152/226.

108. See Krell 1987, 39.

109. GA 54:151/224.

110. GA 53:91/113.

111. See GA 70:77.

112. GA 5: 284/104.

113. GA 55:172/130.

114. GA 54:158–59/107.

115. GA 54:158–59/107: trans. modified.

116. GA 54:160/108.

117. GA 54:157/106, 100/67.

118. GA 55:102/77; my emphasis. See also GA 54:221–22/149.

119. GA 54:160/108. See also Levin 1999, 210.

120. See GA 54:237/159, where Heidegger writes that "the human gets a glimpse of [the] open while comporting himself, as he always does, to beings." See also GA 54:242/163: "Truth [i.e., being as ἀλήθεια] dwells in everything that comes to presence."

121. See GA 54:239.

122. GA 55:169/223. See also GA 45, where Heidegger suggests that the understanding of the human as *animal rationale* came about as a result of "an inability to sustain that great inception in which the human had to bring himself before beings as such and had to be a being in the midst of beings" (GA 45:148/123; trans. modified).

123. GA 55:93/70.

124. GA 55:220/166.

Chapter Six

1. On this, see Derrida 2011, 120.

2. GA 79:17–18/17. See also GA 88:62.

3. Derrida 2011, 122.

4. GA 79:114/107.

5. GA 79:114/107.

6. Derrida, in volume 2 of his *The Beast and the Sovereign*, mentions this remarkable passage only in passing. See Derrida 2011, 125.

7. On all of this, see Mitchell 2015, 33ff.

8. GA 79:44/42.

9. GA 79:25/25.

10. GA 79:27/26–27. On this passage, see especially Babich 2007, 46ff.

11. GA 5:290/109.

12. GA 79:30/29.

13. GA 79:27/26.

14. GA 79:4/4.

15. GA 55:83/63.

16. GA 79:5–6.

17. GA 79:8/7.

18. GA 79:8/8.

19. GA 77:130/85.

20. See GA 9:106/95. See also GA 77:130/84.

21. GA 79:8/8 See also GA 77:131/85.

22. GA 79:9/8.

23. One should note the connection here between Heidegger's discussion in the Bremen lectures of the role of emptiness/nothingness as disclosive of being and his analysis of *tools* in *Being and Time* two decades earlier. In section 16 of *Being and Time*, Heidegger describes the phenomenon of finding a sought-for object *missing*. As he writes, "[C]ircumspection comes up with emptiness [*Leere*] and now sees for the first time [*erst jetzt*] what the missing thing was at hand *for* and at hand *with*. Again, the surrounding world [*Umwelt*] makes itself known" (GA 2:100–101/70). Thus, both *Being and Time* and the Bremen lectures describe an encounter with *emptiness*—that is, with *nothingness*—that brings the human face-to-face with the open of being itself.

24. See GA 55:84/63.

25. See GA 9:106/96.

26. GA 79:9/9.

27. GA 79:9/9.

28. GA 79:13/12.

29. GA 79:15/13.

30. GA 79:11/10.

31. Strictly speaking, earth is already present in the jug even before it is filled, insofar as it is made *of* earth and stands independently *on* the earth. Water, and by extension the sky, would also already be present, insofar as earth is pliable only when wet. See GA 77:126/82.

32. GA 79:12/11.

33. GA 79:12/11.

34. See GA 77:135/88, where this unfolding of being is called "the abiding expanse" or "the open region."

35. GA 79:14/13.

36. On Heidegger and sacrifice, see Vedder 2008.

37. Mitchell 2015, 114.

38. He also relates it to the Indo-European "ghu," from which the English word "gut" (i.e., intestine) is ultimately derived.

39. See Parker 2011, 145.

40. See Immerwahr 1992.

41. See Schmidt 1994, 4.

42. GA 7:10–12.

43. GA 77:136/88.

44. On sacrifice and the poet, see GA 52:134/114; on sacrifice and the thinker, see GA 94:372/272; on sacrifice in National Socialism, see GA 39:72/66; GA 96: 262. See Ott 1988, 218.

45. GA 79:20/19.

46. GA 102:187.

47. GA 79:21/19.

48. See GA 55:95/72.

49. See Davies 2024.

50. GA 79:20/19.

51. GA 79:20/19.

52. GA 79:20/19.

53. GA 79:72/67.

54. It is perhaps worth noting that these are the two land-based animals mentioned in Sophocles's first choral ode.

55. GA 79:21/21.

56. One recalls the deer from Heidegger's reading of Trakl discussed in chapter 4. See Mitchell 2015, 109–15.

57. See, for example, GA 65:101/80, 245/193.

58. GA 79:17–18/17.

59. On "the shrine of the Nothing," see Mitchell 2015, 234.

60. Cf. Derrida 2011, 122: "Such a power or potency [i.e., of relating to the nothing of death *as such*] defines the mortal, man as mortal." What Derrida

misses is that the human is enabled *by the animal-thing* to possess and exercise this power: the power to relate to death as death follows upon an encounter with the animal Other. On this, see chapter 2 of the present volume.

61. GA 9:356/271.

62. GA 79:16/16.

63. See Mitchell 2015, 34. See also GA 55:192/147.

64. See GA 15:370.

65. See GA 5:94. On this, see Ewegen 2021, 416–18.

66. GA 79:27/26–27. On this, see Harman 2010, 22.

67. GA 77:229/149.

68. See GA 100:259, where Heidegger indicates that enframing (*Gestell*), which is (as the culmination of the will to power) the very essence of metaphysics, is nothing other than "the complete forgottenness of the fourfold."

69. GA 7:18–19. See also GA 5:290/109.

70. See Cave 1982. See also Blok 2014.

71. See especially Schalow 2000. See also Benso 1994, 162–63; Kennedy 2016; Turner 2009.

72. See Turner 2009, 160.

73. See Kennedy 2016, 463.

74. See Derrida 2008, 25.

75. Derrida 1997, 231–32.

Conclusion

1. On the animal's strangeness (*Befremdlichkeit*), see GA 89:307/244.

2. On this decision, see GA 66:113/95.

3. GA 53:168/134–35, 174/139. On this exposure, see McNeill 2013, 226.

4. GA 55:161/122.

5. GA 55:162/123.

6. GA 55:161/122.

7. GA 55:168/127.

8. On the connection between the holy and fire, see Magrini 2022, 143.

9. See GA 39:31/30. See also Michell 2015, 130.

10. GA 53:189/151–52.

11. GA 53:189/151–52.

12. GA 53:189/151.

13. GA 4:67/89.

14. One recalls that the call of conscience, assessed by Heidegger in *Being and Time*, occurs *silently* (GA 2:363/252).

15. GA 53:41/35.

16. GA 39:288/262.

17. See GA 39:114/104, where Heidegger says that Germania receives the eagle's tidings in silence. See also Richardson 1963, 428.

18. GA 36/37:108/85–86. See also GA 51:64/54; GA 98:244.

19. GA 36/37:106ff./84ff.

20. GA 89:114/87. See also GA 36/37:100/80.

21. GA 65:77/62. For a rich and compelling account of Heidegger's "sigetic" logic, see Gonzalez 2008. See also Vallega-Neu 2018, 28ff.

22. See Polt 2006, 67.

23. Vallega-Neu 2003, 73. On this leap, see GA 79:122/144. See also GA 66:85/71; Polt 2006, 107.

24. GA 65:430/340.

25. GA 45:190/163.

26. On the shepherd as watcher, see GA 7:97–98.

27. Polt 2006, 193–94. See also GA 70:10.

28. Polt 2006, 198.

29. GA 65:72/57. For a similar passage—though one where animals are not mentioned—see GA 94:382/278.

30. GA 65:72/57.

31. GA 65:30/26.

32. GA 94:20/15.

33. See GA 65:6/5. See also GA 89:280/222–23.

34. GA 70:127. See also Polt 2006, 239.

35. See Agamben 2004, 80.

36. We have already seen, in Heidegger's birdsong discussed in chapter 5, what such an inceptual understanding of the animal might look like.

37. GA 9:326/230.

38. On the relation of *questioning* to silence in the face of being, see GA 95:276/216.

39. GA 81:84/141; trans modified.

40. Herding, for Heidegger, consists of "both a driving forward and also a leading" (*Das Hüten ist sowohl ein Treiben als auch ein Leiten*; GA 15:87/51).

Works Cited

Heidegger's Texts

All editions from the *Gesamtausgabe* were published by Vittorio Klostermann.

GA 2. *Sein und Zeit.* Edited by Friedrich Wilhelm von Herrmann. 1977. Translated by Joan Stambaugh as *Being and Time* (State University of New York Press, 1996).

GA 3. *Kant und das Problem der Metaphysik.* Edited by Friedrich-Wilhelm von Herrmann. 1991. Translated by Richard Taft as *Kant and the Problem of Metaphysics* (Indiana University Press, 1997).

GA 4. *Erläuterungen zu Hölderlins Dichtung.* Edited by Friedrich-Wilhelm von Herrmann. 1981. Translated by Keith Hoeller as *Elucidations of Hölderlin's Poetry* (Humanity Books, 2000).

GA 5. *Holzwege.* Edited by Friedrich-Wilhelm von Hermann. 1977. Translated by Albert Hofstadter as "What Are Poets For?," in *Poetry, Language, Thought,* by Martin Heidegger (Harper and Row, 1971).

GA 6.1/6.2. *Nietzsche* I and II. Edited by Brigitte Schillbach. 1996. Translated and edited by David Krell as *Nietzsche* (4 vols.; Harper and Row, 1979–1987).

GA 7. *Vorträge und Aufsätze.* Edited by Friedrich-Wilhelm von Herrmann. 2000.

GA 8. *Was heißt Denken?* Edited by Paola-Ludovika Coriando. 2002. Translated by J. Glenn Gray as *What Is Called Thinking?* (Harper and Row, 1968).

GA 9. *Wegmarken.* Edited by Friedrich-Wilhelm von Herrmann. 1976. Translation edited by William McNeill as *Pathmarks* (Cambridge University Press, 1998).

GA 10. *Der Satz vom Grund.* Edited by Petra Jaeger. 1997. Translated by Reginald Lilly as *The Principle of Reason* (Indiana University Press, 1991).

GA 11. *Identität und Differenz.* Edited by Friedrich-Wilhelm von Herrmann. 2006.

GA 12. *Unterwegs zur Sprache.* Edited by Friedrich-Wilhelm von Herrmann. 1985. Translated by Peter D. Hertz and Joan Stambaugh as *On the Way to Language* (Harper and Row, 1971).

GA 13. *Aus der Erfahrung des Denkens.* Edited by Hermann Heidegger. 1983. Translated by John M. Anderson and E. Hans Freund as *Discourse on Thinking* (Harper and Row, 1966).

GA 15. *Seminare.* Edited by Curd Ochwadt. 1986. Translated by Charles H. Seibert as *Heraclitus Seminar, 1966/67, with Eugen Fink* (University of Alabama Press, 1979).

GA 16. *Reden und andere Zeugnisse eines Lebensweges.* Edited by Hermann Heidegger. 2000.

GA 18. *Grundbegriffe der aristotelischen Philosophie.* Edited by Mark Michalski. 2002. Translated by Robert Metcalf and Mark Tanzer as *The Basic Concepts of Aristotelian Philosophy* (Indiana University Press, 2009).

GA 19. *Platon: Sophistes.* Edited by Ingeborg Schüßler. 1992. Translated by Richard Rojcewicz and André Schuwer as *Plato's "Sophist"* (Indiana University Press, 1997).

GA 20. *Prolegomena zur Geschichte des Zeitbegriffs.* Edited by Petra Jaeger. 1979. Translated by Theodore Kisiel as *History of the Concept of Time: Prolegomena* (Indiana University Press, 1985).

GA 21. *Logik. Die Frage nach der Wahrheit.* Edited by Walter Biemel. 1976. Translated by Thomas Sheehan as *Logic: The Question of Truth* (Indiana University Press, 2010).

GA 22. *Die Grundbegriffe der antiken Philosophie.* Edited by Franz-Karl Blust. 1993. Translated by Richard Rojcewicz as *Basic Concepts of Ancient Philosophy* (Indiana University Press, 2008).

GA 23. *Geschichte der Philosophie von Thomas von Aquin bis Kant.* Edited by Helmuth Vetter. 2006.

GA 24. *Die Grundprobleme der Phänomenologie.* Edited by Friedrich-Wilhelm von Herrmann. 1975. Translated by Albert Hofstadter as *Basic Problems of Phenomenology* (Indiana University Press, 1982).

GA 25. *Phänomenologische Interpretation von Kants Kritik der reinen Vernunft.* Edited by Ingtraud Görland. 1977. Translated by Parvis Emad and Kenneth Maly as *Phenomenological Interpretation of Kant's Critique of Pure Reason* (Indiana University Press, 1997).

GA 26. *Metaphysische Anfangsgründe der Logik im Ausgang von Leibniz.* Edited by Klaus Held. 1978. Translated by Michael Heim as *The Metaphysical Foundations of Logic* (Indiana University Press, 1984).

GA 27. *Einleitung in die Philosophie.* 1996. Edited by Otto Saame and Ina Saame-Speidel.

GA 29/30. *Die Grundbegriffe der Metaphysik. Welt—Endlichkeit—Einsamkeit.* Edited by Friedrich-Wilhelm von Herrmann. 1983. Translated by William McNeill and Nicholas Walker as *The Fundamental Concepts of Metaphysics: World, Finitude, Solitude* (Indiana University Press, 1995).

GA 33. *Aristoteles, Metaphysik Θ 1–3: Von Wesen und Wirklichkeit der Kraft.* Edited by Heinrich Hüni. 1981. Translated by Walter Brogan and Peter Warnek as

Aristotle's "Metaphysics" Θ 1–3: On the Essence and Actuality of Force (Indiana University Press, 1995).

GA 34. *Vom Wesen der Wahrheit. Zu Platons Höhlengleichnis und Theätet.* Edited by Hermann Mörchen. 1988. Translated by Ted Sadler as *The Essence of Truth: On Plato's Cave Allegory and Theaetetus* (Continuum, 2002).

GA 35. *Der Anfang der abendländischen Philosophie: Auslegung des Anaximander und Parmenides.* Edited by Peter Trawny. 2011. Translated by Richard Rojcewicz as *The Beginnings of Western Philosophy: Interpretation of Anaximander and Parmenides* (Indiana University Press, 2015).

GA 36/37. *Sein und Wahrheit.* Edited by Hartmut Tietjen. 2001. Translated by Gregory Fried and Richard Polt as *Being and Truth* (Indiana University Press, 2010).

GA 38. *Logik als die Frage nach dem Wesen der Sprache.* Edited by Günter Seubold. 1998. Translated by Wanda Torres Gregory and Yvonne Unna as *Logic as the Question concerning the Essence of Language* (State University of New York Press, 2009).

GA 39. *Hölderlins Hymnen "Germanien" und "Der Rhein."* Edited by Susanne Ziegler. 1980. Translated by William McNeill and Julia Ireland as *Hölderlin's Hymns "Germania" and "The Rhine"* (Indiana University Press, 2014).

GA 40. *Einführung in die Metaphysik.* Edited by Petra Jaeger. 1983. Translated by Gregory Fried and Richard Polt as *Introduction to Metaphysics* (Yale University Press, 2000).

GA 41. *Die Frage nach dem Ding. Zu Kants Lehre von den transzendentalen Grundsätzen.* Edited by Petra Jaeger. 1984. Translated by James Reid and Benjamin Crowe as *The Question concerning the Thing* (Rowman and Littlefield, 2018).

GA 45. *Grundfragen der Philosophie. Ausgewählte "Probleme" der "Logik."* Edited by Friedrich-Wilhelm von Herrmann. 1984. Translated by Richard Rojcewicz and Andre Schuwer as *Basic Questions of Philosophy: Selected "Problems" of "Logic"* (Indiana University Press, 1994).

GA 46. *Zur Auslegung von Nietzsches II. Unzeitgemäßer Betrachtung "Vom Nutzen und Nachteil der Historie für das Leben."* Edited by Hans-Joachim Friedrich. 2003. Translated by Ullrich Haase and Mark Sinclair as *Interpretation of Nietzsche's Second Untimely Meditation* (Indiana University Press, 2016).

GA 49. *Die Metaphysik des deutschen Idealismus: Zur erneuten Auslegung von Schelling: "Philosophische Untersuchungen über das Wesen der menschlichen Freiheit und die damit zusammenhängenden Gegenstände."* Edited by Günter Seubold. 1991.

GA 51. *Grundbegriffe.* Edited by Petra Jaeger. 1981. Translated by Gary E. Aylesworth as *Basic Concepts* (Indiana University Press, 1993).

GA 52. *Hölderlins Hymne "Andenken."* Edited by Curd Ochwadt. 1982. Translated by William McNeill and Julia Ireland as *Hölderlin's Hymn "Remembrance"* (Indiana University Press, 2018).

GA 53. *Hölderlins Hymne "Der Ister."* Edited by Walter Biemel. 1984. Translated by William McNeill and Julia Davis as *Hölderlin's Hymn "The Ister"* (Indiana University Press, 1996).

GA 54. *Parmenides*. Edited by Manfred S. Frings. 1982. Translated by André Schuwer and Richard Rojcewicz as *Parmenides* (Indiana University Press, 1992).

GA 55. *Heraklit: Der Anfang des abendländischen Denkens. Logik: Heraklits Lehre vom Logos*. Edited by Manfred S. Frings. 1979. Translated by J. Goesser Assaiante and S. Montgomery Ewegen as *Heraclitus: The Inception of Occidental Thinking and Logic: Heraclitus' Doctrine of the Logos* (Bloomsbury, 2018).

GA 65. *Beiträge zur Philosophie (vom Ereignis)*. Edited by Friedrich-Wilhelm von Herrmann. 1989. Translated by Richard Rojcewicz and Daniela Vallega-Neu as *Contributions to Philosophy (of the Event)* (Indiana University Press, 2012).

GA 66. *Besinnung*. Edited by Friedrich-Wilhelm von Herrmann. 1997. Translated by Parvis Emad and Thomas Kalary as *Mindfulness* (Continuum, 2006).

GA 69. *Die Geschichte des Seyns*. Edited by Peter Trawny. 1998. Translated by William McNeill and Jeffrey Powell as *The History of Beyng* (Indiana University Press, 2015).

GA 70. *Über den Anfang*. Edited by Paola-Ludovika Coriando. 2005.

GA 71. *Das Ereignis*. Edited by Friedrich-Wilhelm von Herrmann. 2009. Translated by Richard Rojcewicz as *The Event* (Indiana University Press, 2013).

GA 74. *Zum Wesen der Sprache und Zur Frage nach der Kunst*. Edited by Thomas Regehly. 2010. Translated by Adam Knowles as *On the Essence of Language and the Question of Art* (Polity, 2023).

GA 75. *Zu Hölderlin: Griechenlandreisen*. Edited by Curd Ochwadt. 2000.

GA 76. *Leitgedanken zur Entstehung der Metaphysik, der neuzeitlichen Wissenschaft und der modernen Technik*. Edited by Claudius Strube. 2009.

GA 77. *Feldweg-Gespräche*. Edited by Ingrid Schüßler. 1995. Translated by Bret W. Davis as *Country Path Conversations* (Indiana University Press, 2010).

GA 78. *Der Spruch des Anaximander*. Edited by Ingeborg Schüßler. 2010.

GA 79. *Bremer und Freiburger Vorträge*. Edited by Petra Jaeger. 1994. Translated by Andrew J. Mitchell as *Bremen and Freiburg Lectures: "Insight into That Which Is" and "Basic Principles of Thinking"* (Indiana University Press, 2012).

GA 81. *Gedachtes*. Edited by Paola-Ludovika Coriando. 2007. Translated by Eoghan Walls as *Thought Poems* (Rowman and Littlefield, 2012).

GA 82. *Zu eigenen Veröffentlichungen*. Edited by Friedrich-Wilhelm von Herrmann. 2018.

GA 83. *Seminare: Platon—Aristoteles—Augustinus*. Edited by Mark Michalski. 2012.

GA 84. *Seminare: Kant—Leibniz—Schiller*. Edited by Günther Neumann. 2013.

GA 85. *Vom Wesen der Sprache. Die Metaphysik der Sprache und die Wesung des Wortes. Zu Herders Abhandlung "Über den Ursprung der Sprache."* Edited by Ingrid Schüßler. 1999. Translated by Wanda Torres Gregory and Yvonne Unna as *On the Essence of Language: The Metaphysics of Language and the Essencing of the Word* (State University of New York Press, 2004).

GA 88. *Seminare (Übungen) 1937/38 und 1941/42*. Edited by Alfred Denker. 2008.

GA 89. *Zollikoner Seminare*. Edited by Peter Trawny. 2017. Translated by Franz Mayr and Richard Aksay as *Zollikon Seminars* (Northwestern University Press, 2001).

GA 91. *Ergänzungen und Denksplitter.* Edited by Mark Michalski. 2022.

GA 94. *Überlegungen II–VI.* Edited by Peter Trawny. 2014. Translated by Richard Rojcewicz as *Ponderings II–VI: Black Notebooks, 1931–1938* (Indiana University Press, 2016).

GA 95. *Überlegungen VII–XI.* Edited by Peter Trawny. 2014. Translated by Richard Rojcewicz as *Ponderings VII–XI: Black Notebooks, 1938–1939* (Indiana University Press, 2017).

GA 96. *Überlegungen XII–XV.* Edited by Peter Trawny. 2014. Translated by Richard Rojcewicz as *Ponderings XII–XV: Black Notebooks, 1939–1941* (Indiana University Press, 2017).

GA 97. *Anmerkungen II–V.* Edited by Peter Trawny. 2015.

GA 98. *Anmerkungen VI–IX.* Edited by Peter Trawny. 2018.

GA 99. *Vier Hefte I und II.* Edited by Peter Trawny. 2019.

GA 100. *Vigiliae und Notturno (Schwarze Hefte 1952/53 bis 1957).* Edited by Peter Trawny. 2019.

GA 102. *Vorläufiges I–IV (Schwarze Hefte 1963–1970).* Edited by Peter Trawny. 2022.

Other Texts

Agamben, Giorgio. 2004. *The Open: Man and Animal.* Translated by Kevin Attell. Stanford University Press.

Babich, Babette. 2007. "Heidegger's Will to Power." *Journal of the British Society for Phenomenology* 38 (1): 37–60.

Bambach, Charles. 2022. *Of an Alien Homecoming.* State University of New York Press.

Bejinariu, Alexandru. 2018. "Animal Experience: A Formal-Indicative Approach to Martin Heidegger's Account of Animality." *Human Studies* 41 (2): 233–54.

Benso, Silvia. 1994. "On the Way to an Ontological Ethics: Ethical Suggestions in Reading Heidegger." *Research in Phenomenology* 24:159–88.

Blok, Vincent. 2014. "Being-in-the-World as Being-in-Nature: An Ecological Perspective." *Studia Phaenomenologica* 14:215–35.

Calarco, Matthew. 2008. *Zoographies: The Question of the Animal from Heidegger to Derrida.* Columbia University Press.

Capobianco, Richard. 2014. *Heidegger's Way of Being.* University of Toronto Press.

Cave, George. 1982. "Animals, Heidegger, and the Right to Life." *Environmental Ethics* 4 (3): 249–54.

Cerbone, David. 2021. "Occurrentness (*Vorhandenheit*)." In *The Cambridge Heidegger Lexicon*, edited by Mark Wrathal. Cambridge University Press.

Cykowski, Beth. 2021. *Heidegger's Metaphysical Abyss: Between the Human and the Animal.* Oxford University Press.

Dastur, Françoise. 2012. *How Are We to Confront Death?* Fordham University Press.

Davies, Katherine. 2024. *Heidegger's Conversations: Toward a Poetic Pedagogy.* SUNY Press.

Davis, Bret. 2014. "Returning the World to Nature: Heidegger's Turn from a Transcendental-Horizonal Projection of World to an Indwelling Releasement to the Open-Region." *Continental Philosophy Review* 47:373–97.

Denker, Alfred. 2022. "Martin Heidegger und Georg Trakl: Die andere Zwiesprache zwischen Denken und Dichten." *Phainomena* 31 (120/121): 79–92.

Derrida, Jacques. 1987. "*Gesclecht* II: Heidegger's Hand." In *Deconstruction and Philosophy*, edited by John Sallis. University of Chicago Press.

———. 1989. *Of Spirit: Heidegger and the Question*. Translated by Geoffrey Bennington and Rachel Bowlby. University of Chicago Press.

———. 1993. *Aporias*. Stanford University Press.

———. 1997. *The Politics of Friendship*. Translated by George Collins. Verso.

———. 2008. *The Animal That Therefore I Am*. Translated by David Willis; edited by Marie-Louise Mallet. Fordham University Press.

———. 2011. *The Beast and the Sovereign*. Vol. 2. Translated by Geoffrey Bennington. University of Chicago Press.

Di Cesare, Donatella. 2018. *Heidegger and the Jews: The Black Notebooks*. Polity.

Elden, Stuart. 2006. "Heidegger's Animals." *Continental Philosophy Review* 39 (3): 273–91.

Ewegen, S. Montgomery. 2021. "Fighting Fire with Fire: Thinking Φύσις at the Inception." *Research in Phenomenology* 51 (3): 414–25.

Faye, Emmanuel. 2009. *Heidegger: The Introduction of Nazism into Philosophy*. Yale University Press.

Fritsche, Johannes. 1999. *Historical Destiny and National Socialism in Heidegger's Being and Time*. University of California Press.

Gonzalez, Francisco. 2008. "And the Rest Is 'Sigetik': Silencing Logic and Dialectic in Heidegger's 'Beiträge zur Philosophie.'" *Research in Phenomenology* 38 (3): 358–39.

Gosetti-Ferencei, Jennifer. 2004. *Heidegger, Hölderlin, and the Subject of Poetic Language*. Fordham University Press.

Haraway, Donna. 2008. *When Species Meet*. University of Minnesota Press.

Harman, Graham. 2010. "Technology, Objects, and Things in Heidegger." *Cambridge Journal of Economics* 34 (1): 17–25.

Hayes, Josh. 2007. "Deconstructing Dasein: Heidegger's Earliest Interpretations of Aristotle's 'De Anima.'" *The Review of Metaphysics* 61 (2): 263–93.

Held, Klaus. 1993. "Europa und die interkulturelle Verständigung: Ein Entwurf im Anschluß an Heideggers Phänomenologie der Grundstimmungen." In *Heidegger und Europa*, edited by Hans-Helmuth Gander. Vittorio Klostermann.

Hemming, Laurence. 1998. "Who Is Heidegger's Zarathustra?" *Literature and Theology* 12 (3): 268–93.

Herrmann, Friedrich-Wilhelm von. 1994. *Wege ins Ereignis: Zu Heideggers "Beiträgen zur Philosophie."* Vittorio Klostermann.

Immerwahr, Henry. 1992. "New Wine in Ancient Wineskins: The Evidence from Attic Vases." *Hesperia* 61 (1): 121–32.

Jaran, François. 2018. "On the Ontological Origin of Ethics: A Philosophical-Anthropological Approach." *Philosophy Today* 62 (3): 785–801.

Kearney, Richard. 1980. "Heidegger and the Possible." *Philosophical Studies* 27:176–95.

Kennedy, Tara. 2016. "The Ethics of Treating Animals as Resources: A Post-Heideggerian Approach." *Frontiers of Philosophy in China* 11 (3): 463–82.

Kisiel, Theodore, and Thomas Sheehan, eds. 2010. *Becoming Heidegger*. Noesis.

Krell, David. 1987. "Daimon Life, Nearness and Abyss: An Introduction to Zaology." *Research in Phenomenology* 17:23–53.

———. 1992. *Daimon Life: Heidegger and Life Philosophy*. Indiana University Press.

———. 2013. *Derrida and Our Animal Others: Derrida's Final Seminar, "The Beast and the Sovereign."* Indiana University Press.

———. 2015. *Phantoms of the Other: Four Generations of Derrida's Geschlecht*. State University of New York Press.

Levin, David. 1999. *The Philosopher's Gaze: Modernity in the Shadows of Enlightenment*. University of California Press.

Lindberg, Susanna. 2004. "Heidegger's Animal." *Phänomenologische Forschungen* 2004:57–81.

Löwith, Karl. 1945. "Nietzsche's Doctrine of Eternal Recurrence." *Journal of the History of Ideas* 6 (3): 273–84.

Lüders, Detlev. 2001. "Der 'Zauber der Welt' und das heutige 'Chaos': Heidegger und die moderne Dominanz des Dürftigen." *Heidegger Studies* 17:21–43.

MacIntyre, Alasdair. 1999. *Dependent Rational Animals: Why Human Beings Need the Virtues*. Duckworth.

Magrini, James. 2022. "The Holy in Heidegger's Reading of Greek Tragedy: Necessity, Measure, and Law." In *Heidegger and the Holy*, edited by Richard Capobianco. Rowman and Littlefield.

McNeill, William. 2013. "The Hölderlin Lectures." In *The Bloomsbury Companion to Heidegger*, edited by François Raffoul and Eric Nelson. Bloomsbury.

Mitchell, Andrew. 2015. *The Fourfold: Reading the Late Heidegger*. Northwestern University Press.

———, ed. 2017. *Heidegger's Black Notebooks: Responses to Anti-Semitism*. Columbia University Press.

Naas, Michael. 2014. "'World, Solitude, Finitude': Derrida's Final Seminar." *Research in Phenomenology* 44 (1): 1–27.

Ott, Hugo. 1988. *Martin Heidegger: Unterwegs zu seiner Biographie*. Campus Verlag.

Parker, Robert. 2011. *On Greek Religion*. Cornell University Press.

Peach, Filiz. 2008. *Death, "Deathlessness," and Existenz in Karl Jaspers' Philosophy*. Edinburgh University Press.

Polt, Richard. 2006. *The Emergency of Being: On Heidegger's "Contributions to Philosophy."* Cornell University Press.

———. 2021. "Moment (*Augenblick*)." In *The Cambridge Heidegger Lexicon*, edited by Mark Wrathal. Cambridge University Press.

Rae, Gavin. 2015. "Authoritarian and Anthropocentric: Examining Derrida's Critique of Heidegger." *Critical Horizons* 16 (1): 27–51.

Richardson, William. 1963. *Heidegger: Through Phenomenology to Thought*. Fordham University Press.

Rubio, Roberto, and Felipe Fernández. 2010. "Heidegger's Ontology of Life before *Being and Time*: Scope and Limits." *New Centennial Review* 10 (3): 65–78.

Ruin, Hans. 1994. *Enigmatic Origins: Tracing the Theme of Historicity through Heidegger's Works*. Almqvist and Wiksell.

Sallis, John. 2016. *The Figure of Nature: On Greek Origins*. Indiana University Press.

Schalow, Frank. 2000. "Who Speaks for the Animals? Heidegger and the Question of Animal Welfare." *Environment Ethics* 22 (3): 259–71.

Schmidt, Dennis J. 1994. "Why I Am So Happy." *Research in Phenomenology* 24:3–14.

———. 1997. "What We Owe the Dead: Of Mortality, Measure, and Morality." *Research in Phenomenology* 27:190–98.

Sforza, Maria Augustina. 2022. *Sein und Leben: Zur Andersheit des Tieres bei Heidegger*. Vittorio Klostermann.

Slaby, Jan. 2021. "Disposedness (*Befindlichkeit*)." In *The Cambridge Heidegger Lexicon*, edited by Mark Wrathal. Cambridge University Press.

Sternad, Christian. 2017. "Being Capable of Death: Remarks on the Death of the Animal from a Phenomenological Perspective." *Studia Phaenomenologica* 17:101–18.

Strauss, Jonathan. 2000. "Post-mortem: The State of Death as a Modern Construct." *Diacritics* 30 (3): 3–11.

Trakl, Georg. 1969. *Die Dichtungen von Georg Trakl*. Vol. 1. Otto Müller Verlag.

Tonner, Philip. 2011. "Are Animals Poor in the World? A Critique of Heidegger's Anthropocentrism." In *Anthropocentrism. Humans, Animals, Environments*, edited by Rob Boddice. Brill.

Trawny, Peter. 2018. *Heidegger Fragmente: Eine philosophische Biographie*. Fischer.

Turner, Donald. 2009. "Humanity as Shepherd of Being: Heidegger's Philosophy and the Animal Other." In *Heidegger and the Earth: Essays in Environmental Philosophy*, edited by Ladelle McHorter and Gail Stenstad. University of Toronto Press.

Vallega-Neu, Daniela. 2003. *Heidegger's Contributions to Philosophy: An Introduction*. Indiana University Press.

———. 2018. *Heidegger's Poietic Writings: From "Contributions to Philosophy" to "The Event."* Indiana University Press.

Vedder, Ben. 2008. "Giving Oneself Up: Heidegger's Notion of Sacrifice." *Archivo di Filosofiai* 76 (1–2): 369–76.

Végső, Roland. 2020. *Worldlessness after Heidegger: Phenomenology, Psychoanalysis, Deconstruction*. Edinburgh University Press.

Warminski, Andrzej. 2013. *Ideology, Rhetoric, Aesthetics*. Edinburgh University Press.

Warnek, Peter. 2006. "Translating *Innigkeit*: The Belonging Together of the Strange." In *Heidegger and the Greeks: Interpretative Essays*, edited by Drew Hyland and John Manoussakis. Indiana University Press.

Weigelt, Charlotta. 2021. "Enchantment (Zauber)." In *The Cambridge Heidegger Lexicon*, edited by Mark Wrathal. Cambridge University Press.

Winkler, Rafael. 2007. "Heidegger and the Question of Man's Poverty in World." *International Journal of Philosophical Studies* 15 (4): 521–39.

Young, Julian. 2002. "Poets and Rivers: Heidegger on Hölderlin's 'Der Ister.'" In *Heidegger Reexamined: Art, Poetry, and Technology*, edited by Hubert Dreyfus and Mark Wrathal. Routledge.

Index

abandonment of being, 24–27 passim, 108–109
absolute apriority, 6, 7, 15, 37, 71, 170
abyss, 34, 41, 63, 82, 85, 89–90, 93, 160, 165, 184–185
adrift, 24–25, 26, 30, 32, 33, 36, 55, 98, 102
Agamben, Giorgio, 187n22, 194n118, 207n35
alienation, 35, 36
andenken. See commemorative thinking
Anfang. See inception
animal rationale, 24, 25, 26, 27, 31, 49, 95, 101–102, 103–104, 181–182, 184, 203n122
annihilation, 64, 116–117, 166, 178
anthropocentricity, 31
anti-Semitism, 21
Antwort. See response
ape, 13, 90, 188n33
Apollo, 134, 148, 150
appropriation, 91, 96, 118, 126–127
Aristotle, 41–48 passim, 81–82, 180, 196n73
Arnim, Bettina von, 128
Artemis, 133–137, 148, 178–179, 199n16, 200n19. *See also* hunting; *see also* torches
attunement, 108–113, 150, 192n63
Augenblick. See moment

Aufgehen. See emergence
autonomy, 173, 175
ἀλήθεια, 27, 44–45, 119, 138, 184, 201n70. *See also* truth; *see also* unconcealment
ἄλογον, 83, 120, 124, 145, 146, 180

Babich, Babette, 204n10
Bambach, Charles, 113, 115, 197n37, 197n38, 197n43, 197n44, 197n48, 197n49
befuddlement, 55, 56, 57, 59
being-at-hand, 42, 43, 48, 52, 60, 61
being-in-the-world, 45, 47, 52, 53, 65
being-toward-death, 51, 52, 85, 105, 106, 126
being-with, 46, 54, 67, 69, 70, 73
Bejinariu, Alexandru, 192n59, 193n100
Benso, Silvia, 206n71
bird: and song: 92, 94, 105, 115, 127–129, 139, 143–149, 156. *See also* dove; *see also* blackbird; *see also* eagle; *see also* heron; *see also* lark; *see also* swan; *see also* thrush
blackbird, 105–106, 128. *See also* bird
Blok, Vincent, 206n70
Boss, Mernard, 67

Calarco, Matthew, 190n3

call: of being, 142, 143, 145, 151; of
    conscience, 106, 142, 206n14
Capobianco, Richard, 199n89
care, 29, 49, 60, 152
cat, 1, 70–72, 107, 171, 180, 189n20
catastrophe, 131, 132. *See also* downgoing
Cave, George, 206n70
Cerbone, David, 191n13
Christianity, 188n6, 25
clearing, 27, 45, 128, 129, 132, 135,
    139, 148, 150–156 passim, 178,
    179, 184. *See also* open
commemorative thinking, 169, 170, 178
comparative examination, 62, 64, 65,
    74, 75, 96, 192n68
comportment, 95, 97, 98, 169–170;
    toward the animal, 67, 90, 95, 174;
    toward being, 63, 173
concealment, 135, 135–136, 148, 149,
    171, 178, 182, 184, 185
conditioning, 170, 172, 174
conversation, 89, 113, 114; with the
    animal, 89
correspondence, 67–68, 169
Cykowski, Beth, 41, 55, 56, 187n15,
    188n37, 190n2, 190n4, 192n61,
    192n63, 193n109

Dastur, Françoise, 192n45, 202n90
Davis, Bret, 144
death, 49–52, 64, 97, 123, 124
deer, 103, 104, 107, 199n16, 205n56
Denker, Alfred, 198n56
Derrida, Jacques, 40, 51, 70, 72, 107,
    175, 177, 188n33, 191n16, 192n60,
    193n109, 194n115, 204n6, 205n60
destiny, 75, 78, 92, 129, 140
detour: 1, 7–10, 13–14, 17–18,
    24–26, 30–31, 34, 36, 42, 141,
    167, 185; necessary, 9, 14, 18, 51,
    58, 74, 101–102, 107–108, 117,
    123, 126, 133, 178

Di Cesare, Donatella, 188n1
discernment, 83, 87, 93
disposition, 70, 191n26
divine, 150. *See also* holy; *see also*
    mourning
dizziness, 62
dog, 1, 39, 57, 69, 97, 98, 171
domesticated animal, 68, 194n115
dove, 148; *See also* bird
downgoing, 79, 84, 85, 86, 88, 93,
    105–106, 131, 196n6. *See also*
    catastrophe
dwelling, 118, 118–119, 176

eagle, 39, 78–88 passim, 111–115,
    131, 140, 179, 207n17. *See also*
    bird; *see also* messenger
earth, 43, 100, 129, 148, 163, 182,
    205n31
ecstasis, 33
Einsamkeit. See solitude
Elden, Stuart, 187n21, 188n24
emergence, 135, 136, 147, 150, 155,
    178, 180, 200n31
emptiness, 171, 204n23. *See also*
    nothing
enchantment, 139, 144, 145, 146,
    180, 201n62; and *Geworfenheit*,
    201n62
Endlichkeit. See finitude
enframing, 162, 162–163, 172–176
entanglement, 24–36 passim, 95, 104,
    106, 146, 151, 156
environment, 27, 47, 67, 68
Ereignis, 129, 139–140, 140, 142,
    144–145, 201n70, 202n74
essence: of being, 25, 26, 33–34; of
    the human, 25, 30, 57, 116, 141,
    170
ethics: original, 161, 172; ethical
    priority, 161
exceptionalism (human), 78, 159, 160

exposure, 29, 40, 51, 58–68 passim, 87, 107, 120, 126, 133, 151, 172, 179–180, 180, 206n3

face, 24, 63, 64, 71, 81, 85, 93–98, 116–117, 152, 157, 170, 172, 179
facticity, 70. *See also* transposition
fangs, 12, 14
Faye, Emmanuel, 188n1
finitude, 79, 122–123, 123, 198n77
fire, 116, 127, 128, 178, 178–179, 180, 206n8. *See also* πῦρ
fish, 122
foreignness, 35, 123, 180; of the animal, 177
forgetfulness: of being, 24–27, 31, 32, 34, 36, 105, 131–133, 143, 146, 150–155, 164, 165, 188n6
foundational: experience, 29, 30, 31, 34, 59–60, 64, 67, 70, 73; and words, 137–138
fourfold, 43, 99–105, 144, 145, 161, 167, 169, 196n4, 202n74, 202n88, 202n97, 206n68
Fritsche, Johannes, 191n29

gathering, 96, 100, 132–133; of being, 144, 146; of the fourfold, 101
gaze, 152, 157; at the human, 30, 31; of the animal, 88, 92, 107; of the cat, 107
Gespräch. See conversation
Gestell. See enframing
gift; 152, 166, 167
gods, 100, 108–115 passim, 124, 134, 150, 167, 198n51
going-along-with, 66, 68, 71, 71–72. *See also* transposition
Gonzalez, Francisco, 207n21
Gosetti-Ferencei, Jennifer, 198n52
Greece, 116, 127, 132, 167–168, 178;

Greek understanding, 55, 139, 147, 150
ground: of being, 160, 163, 169, 170, 172, 182; of history, 141

hand, 10–16
happening, 96, 140, 141. See also *Kunde*
Haraway, Donna, 187n16
Harman, Graham, 202n66
Hayes, Josh, 191n21, 191n28
Hegel, G. W. F., 121, 146, 188n6
Held, Klaus, 191n29
Hemming, Laurence, 194n6
Heraclitus, 55, 131–137, 140–156 passim, 161, 169, 178, 178–179, 180, 199n12
Herrmann, Friedrich-Wilhelm von, 144, 201n67
herding, 185, 186, 207n40. *See also* shepherd
heroism, 93
heron, 161, 171. *See also* bird
hierarchy, 27, 33, 73, 99–100, 101
Hiroshima, 163
history, 74, 78, 96, 131, 132, 134, 141, 196n77, 201n48
historicity, 96, 97, 196n77
holy, 103, 108–110, 112, 127, 128, 129, 142, 150, 178, 199n89, 206n8. *See also* divine; *see also* mourning
home, 56, 58, 61, 83, 98, 99, 104, 115, 118, 120, 121, 123, 127, 132, 186, 198n51, 198n77
homecoming, 116, 117, 122, 123, 126
homelessness, 102, 102–103, 105, 116–119
homesickness, 56, 58, 59, 192n63
Homer, 167–168
horse, 122, 161, 171
House of Being, 70, 72, 90, 91, 92–93, 98, 176

hunting, 35, 84, 200n19. *See also*
  Artemis
Hölderlin, 89, 100, 101, 108–122
  passim, 126, 127, 128, 199n12,
  140, 142, 149, 178, 179, 198n51

identity, 23, 63, 65, 74, 85–86, 107,
  113, 171, 177; of the human, 24
images, 82, 87, 94, 95
Immerwahr, Henry, 205n40
inception, 25, 114, 115, 150, 151,
  168, 181, 182, 203n122
individuation, 79, 86, 91
instrument, 125, 173
intimacy, 33, 68, 102, 184

jabbering, 89, 92
Jaran, François, 31, 190n40, 190n50,
  190n51, 193n90
jointure, 132–133
journey, 36, 102, 108, 115, 116, 118,
  119, 126, 127, 178, 179
Judaism, 21, 188n6
jug, 164–168, 171, 205n31. *See also*
  fourfold

Kearney, Richard, 191n29
Kennedy, Tara, 206n71, 206n73
Kisiel, Theodore, 191n23
knowledge, 26, 27, 28, 30, 87, 152,
  153, 157
Krell, David, 47, 77, 80, 91, 188n29,
  188n31, 188n32, 188n33, 188n34,
  191n26, 191n34, 193n88, 194n5,
  194n113, 202n77, 202n79,
  203n108
Kunde, 95, 111, 139–142. *See also*
  happening; *see also* lore

language, 43, 82, 89, 93, 96, 106,
  110–113, 124, 125, 132–133, 140,
  145, 147, 148, 179, 183, 187n21,
  197n30. *See also* λόγος

lark, 15, 98. *See also* bird
leap, 35, 181, 182
Levin, David, 203n119
Lindberg, Susanna, 190n5, 193n105,
  200n34, 203n103
λόγος, 46, 47, 81–84, 96, 106, 124,
  132–133, 146, 152, 180, 184,
  202n76. *See also* language
lore, 95–96, 140, 141. See also *Kunde*
Löwith, Karl, 75
Lüders, Detlev, 202n71

machination, 24, 25–26, 113, 122,
  162, 166, 169, 174
MacIntyre, Alasdair, 190n3
Magrini, James, 199n89
McNeill, William, 196n1, 197n25,
  206n3
meat, 168
messenger, 111, 115, 179. *See also* eagle
metaphysics, 56, 57, 77, 78, 133, 152,
  165, 206n68
methodological priority, 10, 11, 109,
  160
Mitchell, Andrew, 99–105, 113, 128,
  167, 188n1, 192n60, 196n68,
  202n74, 204n7, 205n37, 205n56,
  205n59
modernity, 25, 139, 145, 146
moment: of being, 91, 103, 184; of
  downgoing, 79, 86
mortals, 43, 100, 159–160, 167, 172;
  See also fourfold
mourning, 108, 109, 110, 112, 115,
  148, 149, 150, 197n25, 202n90.
  See also divine; *see also* holy; *see also*
  remembrance
mystery, 140, 143, 145, 177, 184, 185

Naas, Michael, 188n37, 193n109
Nagasaki, 163
National Socialism, 25–26, 168,
  205n44

nature: of the animal, 65, 67, 93, 177;
  of the human, 23, 59, 78
nearness, 79, 81, 84, 88, 148, 162,
  163, 170, 170–171, 173, 185,
  199n12
necessary detour. *See* detour
necessity, 23, 24, 26, 36, 51, 91, 181
Nietzsche, Friedrich, 75, 77–86, 88,
  93, 95, 143, 146, 196n6
nothing, 62–66, 85, 86, 93, 106, 110,
  116, 122, 160; of death, 49, 172; of
  the jug, 165. *See also* emptiness
nudity, 107, 175, 180

Odysseus, 146–147
open; of being, 42, 81, 83, 93, 94,
  95, 120, 121, 139, 143, 147–148.
  See also clearing
ontological priority, 8, 41, 42, 65,
  151, 161
originary lore, 140
otherness, 35, 110, 120–121, 123,
  126–127; of the animal, 111, 125
Ott, Hugo, 205n44
οὐσία, 42, 43, 61, 70

Parker, Robert, 205n39
Peach, Filiz, 192n44
perishing, 50, 50–51, 52, 54, 137,
  159, 160, 172
philosophy, 32, 56, 62, 182, 183, 184
pet. *See* domesticated animal
plant, 42, 43, 50, 53, 67, 98, 101,
  110, 111, 119, 163, 182
Plato, 36, 77, 163, 170
poets, 93, 94, 100, 102, 105, 111–
  120 passim, 127, 128, 129, 148,
  178–180, 186, 196n68, 205n44
poetic: listening, 18, 143;
  comportment, 95, 97, 98
political, 46, 173
Polt, Richard, 85, 182, 202n72, 207n22
poverty: in/of world, 64, 70, 73

presence, 42, 47, 60, 61, 119, 140,
  142, 167, 168
pride, 73 82, 82–83, 84, 87, 88, 93.
  See also eagle
priority; absolute, 52, 100; ethical,
  161; methodological, 109, 160
πῦρ, 178–189. *See also* fire
φωνή, 46
φύσις, 55, 128, 129, 132–138,
  147–150, 155, 178, 178–179, 184,
  199n89, 200n31

question: of the animal, 39, 54, 59,
  63, 77, 77–78, 137, 177

Rae, Gavin, 187n14
Richardson, William, 207n17
Rilke, Rainer Maria, 147, 152, 153,
  156, 157
reason, 27, 140
reawakening, 159, 164, 173
refusal, 68, 125–126
region, 99, 144, 145, 148, 169, 178,
  201n70, 205n34
remaining, 54, 66, 88
remembrance, 132, 132–133, 146,
  149, 151, 157, 202n97. *See also*
  mourning
response, 85, 88, 112, 134, 143, 154,
  170
rivers, 117–120
Rubio, Roberto and Felipe Fernández,
  190n11
Ruin, Hans, 188n25

sacrifice, 167, 168, 183, 205n36,
  205n44
Sallis, John, 199n16
Schalow, Frank, 206n71
Schmidt, Dennis J., 192n44, 205n41
science, 165, 174
serpent, 78–88 passim, 93, 98
settlement, 8, 75, 116–119

self-determination, 35, 177

self-transposition, 39, 66. *See also* transposition

Sforza, Maria Augustina, 190n49, 191n16, 191n35, 192n43, 192n66, 192n68

sheltering, 135, 152, 170, 170–171, 182, 183

shepherd, 142, 143, 152, 161, 171–173, 176, 178, 185, 207n26; *see also* herding

silence, 179, 180, 181, 183, 207n17, 207n38

singing, 92, 105, 138, 139–143, 145–148, 150

Sirens, 138, 146, 146–147, 149, 150

sky, 43, 100, 122, 148, 150, 166, 167, 175

Slaby, Jan, 191n26

soaring, 114, 115, 128, 197n41

solitude, 79, 80, 81, 82, 83, 86, 87, 88, 93, 105, 195n23

soul, 30, 31, 102, 103, 105, 109

speaking, 72, 77, 80, 81, 89, 92, 112, 113

speaking-together, 68

standing-reserve, 162, 163, 172–173, 174

Sternad, Christian, 187n14

steward, 171, 181, 181–182, 182

stillness, 87, 93, 152, 179

stock, 163, 173–174, 174

strangeness, 63, 143, 206n1; stranger, 102, 104, 105, 107

Strauss, Jonathan, 192n40

strife, 91, 135, 136–137

striving, 78, 87, 136

submergence, 135–136, 138, 149

suffering, 88, 109, 149, 174

swan, 148, 150. *See also* bird

technology, 26, 162, 173, 198n77

things, 100, 101, 102, 152, 161–174 passim, 182, 183, 186

throwing, 25, 30, 32, 33, 55

torches, 135, 178, 178–179. *See also* Artemis

track, 24–27, 32, 34, 36, 57, 82, 137, 184

Trakl, Georg, 99–108, 113, 117, 131, 199n16, 205n56

transference, 66

transformation, 36, 40, 55, 56, 75, 79, 87, 103, 109, 113–115, 151, 159, 160, 161

transposition, 39, 66–70, 72, 73, 116, 193n94. *See also* going-along-with; *see also* self-transposition

Trawny, Peter, 187n1, 188n2

trepidation, 55, 59

trees, 43, 155, 156, 186

truth, 27, 44, 144, 151, 152, 186; of being, 27, 28, 36, 83, 86, 96, 109, 120, 121. *See also* ἀλήθεια

turn, 24; to/toward the animal, 29, 58, 72, 86, 177

thrush, 105, 106. *See also* bird

Turner, Donald, 187n7, 191n23, 193n94, 206n71, 206n72

twilight, 99–105, 107

Umweg. See detour

uncanny, 62, 98, 106, 121–124, 152–153

uncertainty, 36, 63, 75, 181

unconcealment, 27, 119–120, 135, 136, 138, 149, 182, 184, 185. *See also* ἀλήθεια

understanding: of animality, 21, 40, 59, 99, 100, 138, 139, 184

unity, 22, 23, 88, 91, 92, 93, 95

unsettle, 83, 94, 95, 98, 102, 116, 117, 118–119

untamed, 80

Untergang. See downgoing
ὑποκείμενον, 42, 43. *See also*
  being-at-hand
Ur-Kunde. See originary lore

Vallega-Neu, Daniela, 201n54,
  207n21, 207n23
Vedder, Ben, 205n36
Végső, Roland, 192n70
vigilance, 169
voice, 81, 92, 105, 106, 108, 127,
  128, 129, 185
Vorhandenen. See being-at-hand

wandering, 101, 102, 103, 125, 127
Warminski, Andrzej, 198n77
Warnek, Peter, 198n51
Weigelt, Charlotta, 145, 201n63,
  202n73, 202n75
Western, 25, 113, 114, 115, 169,
  181
wilding, 103, 113

will: for absolute autonomy, 173; to
  power, 77, 163, 206n68
Winkler, Rafael, 193n94, 201n50
withdrawal, 99, 133, 173, 181
words, 91, 92, 93, 138, 180
world, 27–33, 40, 44–48, 52–75
  passim, 89, 101, 131, 140, 144,
  169, 170, 191n23, 193n104, 196n4,
  204n23
worlding, 140, 145, 169, 170
world-poor, 44, 55, 73, 101
worm, 88

Young, Julian, 120, 121

Zarathustra, 75–98 passim, 102, 143,
  194n11, 196n6
Zauber. See enchantment
Zuruf. See call
ζῷον λόγον ἔχον, 46, 180, 183, 184
ζωή, 44, 135, 136, 137, 153, 184,
  200n31. *See also* life